PRAISE FOR

TRUTH OVERRULED

"Every leader in America needs to read this book! It's by far the best summary of what's at stake, combining rigorous research, solid documentation, and brilliant analysis of the implications. Ryan Anderson has written a tour de force."

> —Dr. Rick Warren, author of *The Purpose Driven Life* and pastor of Saddleback Church

"Ryan Anderson is our nation's most compelling and courageous defender of marriage as the union of husband and wife, and of the rights of people who share that belief to express and act on it in their civic, professional, religious, and personal lives. In *Truth Overruled: The Future of Marriage and Religious Freedom* he charts the path forward for those of us who refuse to yield to the destruction of marriage and who will not be bullied into acquiescence or silence."

> —Robert P. George, McCormick Professor of Jurisprudence, Princeton University

"Novelist Walker Percy said of the abortion rights movement a generation ago: 'You may get your way. But you're going to be told what you're doing.' And ever since *Roe v. Wade*, pro-lifers have been telling abortionists that abortion stops a beating heart. When it comes to the question of marriage and family, Ryan Anderson is a Walker Percy for a new day. Anderson is the brightest intellectual star in the pro-marriage movement. He seeks to persuade and provoke with reason, logic, and honesty. *Truth Overruled: The Future of Marriage and Religious Freedom* will equip you to bear witness to ancient convictions in a strange new world."

> —Russell D. Moore, Ph.D., Ethics and Religious Liberty Commission, Southern Baptist Convention

"Ryan Anderson's presence among us at a time such as this—as evidenced most recently by this book—is nothing less than profoundly encouraging and inspiring to all of us who know that our dear country has lost its way. If we can find a path out of our current Slough of Despond, it will be in large part due to winsome heroes like him. Read this book."
—Eric Metaxas, *New York Times* bestselling author of *Bonhoeffer: Pastor, Martyr, Prophet, Spy*

"With the social and legal significance of marriage in debate as never before, and with religious freedom at risk of becoming a second-class right, Ryan Anderson's book could not be more timely. His well-documented analysis of the likely implications of redefining a basic social institution plus his sober forecast of coming inroads on freedom of conscience and religion should give pause to all but the most hardened ideologues. At the same time, his roadmap for fortifying the rights of conscience while rebuilding a culture of marriage will provide encouragement to all who are concerned about America's moral ecology."
—Mary Ann Glendon, Learned Hand Professor of Law, Harvard University

"It takes great courage and extraordinary eloquence to effectively defend the truth about marriage in the public square today, and Ryan Anderson has both. All Americans who are rightly concerned about the future of marriage and religious liberty are greatly indebted to him for this important book."
—Rabbi Meir Y. Soloveichik, Ph.D., Director of the Straus Center for Torah and Western Thought at Yeshiva University

"We live at a privileged moment: a time for what Bonhoeffer called costly grace; a time for Christians to bear witness to the truth in the public square. Ryan Anderson has been doing this courageously for several years now. His new book, *Truth Overruled: The Future of Marriage and Religious Freedom*, is vital reading for anyone seeking to defend the goodness that remains in our nation, and our rights to live in accord with the truth."
—Charles J. Chaput, O.F.M. Cap., Archbishop of Philadelphia

TRUTH OVERRULED

TRUTH OVERRULED

THE FUTURE OF MARRIAGE AND RELIGIOUS FREEDOM

RYAN T. ANDERSON

REGNERY
PUBLISHING
A Division of Salem Media Group

Regnery® is a registered trademark of Salem Communications Holding Corporation

Library of Congress Cataloging-in-Publication Data

Anderson, Ryan T., 1981-
  Truth overruled : the future of marriage and religious freedom / Ryan T. Anderson.
    pages cm
  ISBN 978-1-62157-451-4 (paperback)
  1. Marriage. 2. Same-sex marriage. 3. Marriage--Government policy. 4. Marriage--Religious aspects. I. Title.
  HQ519.A53 2015
  306.81--dc23

                                2015027128

Published in the United States by
Regnery Publishing
A Division of Salem Media Group
300 New Jersey Ave NW
Washington, DC 20001
www.Regnery.com

Manufactured in the United States of America

10 9 8 7 6 5 4 3 2 1

Books are available in quantity for promotional or premium use. For information on discounts and terms, please visit our website: www.Regnery.com.

Distributed to the trade by
Perseus Distribution
250 West 57th Street
New York, NY 10107

To my mom and dad,
who taught me always to tell the truth,
and who have been living the truth about marriage
for over fifty years.

CONTENTS

INTRODUCTION

With its decision in *Obergefell v. Hodges*, the Supreme Court of the United States has brought the sexual revolution to its apex—a redefinition of our civilization's primordial institution, cutting its link to procreation and declaring sex differences meaningless. The court has usurped the authority of the people, working through the democratic process, to define marriage. And it has shut down debate just as we were starting to hear new voices—gay people who agree that children need their mother and their father, and children of same-sex couples who wish they knew both their mom and dad.

If the polls are right, there has also been an astonishingly swift change in public opinion. Most Americans now think that justice, equality, or at least good manners requires redesigning marriage to fit couples (and at this point, *just* couples) of the same sex. Or at least they've been intimidated into saying so.

I argue here that we are sleepwalking into an unprecedented cultural and social revolution. A truth acknowledged for millennia has been overruled by five unelected judges. The consequences will extend far beyond those couples newly able to obtain a marriage license.

If the law teaches a falsehood about marriage, it will make it harder for people to live out the truth of marriage. Marital norms make no sense, as a matter of principle, if what makes a marriage is merely intense emotional feeling, an idea captured in the bumper-sticker slogan "Love makes a family." There is no reason that mere consenting adult love has to be permanent or limited to two persons, much less sexually exclusive. And so, as people internalize this new vision of marriage, marriage will be less and less a stabilizing force.

But if fewer people live out the norms of marriage, then fewer people will reap the benefits of the institution of marriage—not only spouses, but also children. Preserving the man-woman definition of marriage is the only way to preserve the benefits of marriage and avoid the enormous societal risks accompanying a genderless marriage regime. How can the law teach that fathers are essential, for instance, when it has officially made them optional?

The essence of marriage as a male-female union, however, has become an unwelcome truth. Indeed, a serious attempt is well under way to define opposition to same-sex marriage as nothing more than irrational bigotry. If that attempt succeeds, it will pose the most serious threat to the rights of conscience and religious freedom in American history.

Bigots or Pro-Lifers?

Will the defenders of marriage be treated like bigots? Will our society and our laws treat Americans who believe that marriage is the union of husband and wife as if they were the moral equivalent of racists?

Perhaps not. Think about the abortion debate. Ever since *Roe v. Wade*, our law has granted a right to abortion. And yet, for the most part, pro-life citizens are not treated as though they are "anti-woman" or "anti-health." Those are just slurs from extremists. Even those who disagree with the pro-life cause respect it and recognize that it has a legitimate place in the debate over public policy. And—this is crucial—it's *because of that respect* that pro-choice leaders generally respect the religious liberty and conscience rights of their pro-life fellow citizens. Until the insurance-coverage mandates imposed under Obamacare, at least, there was wide agreement that pro-life citizens shouldn't be forced by the government to be complicit in what they see as the evil of abortion. Pro-life taxpayers, for example, haven't been forced to fund elective abortions, and pro-life doctors haven't been forced to perform them.

Will the same tolerance be shown to those who believe the truth about marriage? Will the government respect their rights of conscience and religious liberty? It doesn't look good. So far, the trend has been in the opposite direction. We must now work to reverse that trend.

For years, the refrain of the Left has been that people who oppose same-sex marriage are just like people who opposed interracial marriage—and that the law should treat them just as it treats racists. Indeed, the *New York Times* reported that while the amicus curiae briefs filed with the Supreme Court in *Obergefell* were evenly divided between supporters and opponents of state marriage laws, no major law firm had filed a brief in support of marriage as the union of a man and a woman. "In dozens of interviews, lawyers and law professors said the imbalance in legal firepower in the same-sex marriage cases resulted from a conviction among many lawyers that opposition to such unions is bigotry akin to racism."[1]

In the oral arguments for *Obergefell*, Justice Samuel Alito explored the possible consequences of such a view, asking the Obama administration's solicitor general, Donald Verrilli, if religious schools that uphold marriage as the union of man and woman should be treated as Bob Jones University was when it prohibited interracial dating. When pressed, Verrilli acknowledged that such institutions could lose their nonprofit tax status if marriage were redefined: "It's certainly going to be an issue. I don't deny that. I don't deny that, Justice Alito. It is going to be an issue."[2] But this "issue" could spell financial disaster for thousands of faith-based and other private institutions, from Orthodox Jews and Roman Catholics to Evangelical Christians and Latter Day Saints.

As various states, anticipating the court's imposition of same-sex marriage on the entire country, attempted to protect the religious liberty of their citizens, the media declared such measures to be anti-gay bigotry akin to Jim Crow. *USA Today* ran columns under the headlines "Jim Crow Laws for Gays and Lesbians?"[3] and "Arizona Latest to Attack Gay Rights."[4] In Slate it was "Kansas's Anti-Gay Segregation Bill Is an Abomination,"[5] while a *New York Times* editorial decried "A License to Discriminate."[6] CBS News posted the mendacious headline "Bill Would Let Michigan Doctors, EMTs Refuse to Treat Gay Patients."[7] None of these headlines reflects the reality of the laws in question, but all of them reflect how liberal elites view ordinary Americans.

A number of these laws were state versions of the federal Religious Freedom Restoration Act (RFRA)—a law that has served the American people well since 1993. The federal RFRA protects against violations of religious liberty by the federal government, and state RFRAs protect against state violations.

Passed with ninety-seven votes in the Senate and unanimously in the House, the federal RFRA was signed into law by President Bill Clinton. If the government imposes a substantial burden on the exercise of religion, RFRA requires it to show that it is pursuing a compelling governmental interest through the least restrictive means.

Twenty-one states have now implemented their own versions of this commonsense law. Ten other states have religious liberty protections that their courts have interpreted to provide a similar level of protection. And yet in the year leading up to *Obergefell*, efforts to enact such laws in additional states were met with demagoguery, hysteria, and lies.

When Indiana enacted its own version of RFRA in the early spring of 2015, the attacks on religious freedom took on a new and ominous ferocity, reaching a climax during the Christian Holy Week and Jewish Passover. CNN declared that the NCAA, headquartered in Indianapolis, was "'concerned' over Indiana law that allows biz to reject gays."[8] A *New York Times* story began, "A new law in Indiana allowing businesses to refuse service to same-sex couples in the name of religious freedom has put sports officials under pressure to evaluate whether to hold major events in Indianapolis."[9] The CEOs of Salesforce and Apple threatened to boycott the state, as did the governor of Connecticut and the mayor of Chicago. Senator Charles Schumer and Hillary Clinton (the former one of the cosponsors of the federal RFRA in 1993, the latter the wife of the man who signed it into law) took to Twitter denouncing the "discrimination" that Hoosiers had voted to protect.

The opening sentences of a *USA Today* story captured elite sentiment pretty well: "The reviews are in. From institutions such as the NCAA to major employers such as Eli Lilly and Co. to the city's Republican mayor, Indiana's new 'religious freedom' law is almost universally loathed by Indianapolis' political and economic elite."[10]

Big business, big media, and big government had launched a massive assault on the rights of conscience, and as the *New York Times* reported, big law was at their service:

> Gay rights advocates offer their own reason for why prominent lawyers are lined up on one side of the marriage cases. "It's so clear that there are no good arguments against marriage equality," said Evan Wolfson, the president of Freedom to Marry. "Lawyers can see the truth."[11]

That's right—he said *no good arguments*. This statement is as manifestly self-serving as it is absurd. Reasonable people can acknowledge that there are good arguments on both sides of this debate. Only ideologues think their side has all the arguments and the other side has none. And of course, lawyers can be ideologues too. The ideologues in the elite levels of society want to penalize and coerce ordinary Americans who hold traditional beliefs about marriage.

As if to prove this point, the *New York Times*' Frank Bruni devoted his Easter Sunday column, titled "Bigotry, the Bible and the Lessons of Indiana,"[12] to an attack on orthodox religion, which he sees as "the final holdout and most stubborn refuge for homophobia. It will give license to discrimination. It will cause gay and lesbian teenagers in fundamental-ist households to agonize needlessly." Bruni suggests that Indiana was helpful for launching "a conversation about freeing religions and religious people from prejudices that they needn't cling to"—that is, beliefs rejected by Frank Bruni. He doesn't specify where the "conversation" ends and coercion begins, but he approvingly quotes a gay rights activist and phi-lanthropist who says that "church leaders must be made 'to take homo-sexuality off the sin list.'"

And the day that the Supreme Court redefined marriage everywhere, a newspaper in Harrisburg, Pennsylvania, announced it would no longer run op-eds or letters to the editor in opposition to same-sex marriage: "These unions are now the law of the land. And we will not publish such letters and op-Eds any more than we would publish those that are racist, sexist or anti-Semitic." Facing widespread criticism, the paper eventually backed down, a little, and published an apology.[13] This shows you how elites think—but also how we can be successful in responding.

The False Analogy of Interracial Marriage

So, will we be treated like pro-lifers or like bigots? Same-sex mar-riage advocates insist that the court's *Obergefell* ruling is not like *Roe v. Wade*, which engendered undying controversy, but like *Loving v. Vir-ginia*, the universally accepted decision that struck down bans on inter-racial marriage—a decision now so uncontroversial that most Americans have never heard of it. If that is true, then anyone who opposes *Oberge-fell* is an irrational bigot—the moral and legal equivalent of a racist.

But as I explain in this book, great thinkers throughout human his-tory—and from every political community until about the year 2000—thought it reasonable and right to view marriage as the union of husband and wife. Indeed, this view of marriage has been nearly a human univer-sal. It has been shared by the Jewish, Christian, and Muslim traditions; by ancient Greek and Roman thinkers untouched by the influence of these religions; and by Enlightenment philosophers. It is affirmed by canon law as well as common and civil law.

Bans on interracial marriage, by contrast, were part of an insidious system of racial subordination and exploitation that denied the equality and dignity of all human beings and forcibly segregated citizens based on race. When these interracial marriage bans first arose in the American colonies, they were inconsistent not only with the common law of England but with the customs of every previous culture throughout human history.

As for the Bible, while it doesn't present marriage as having anything to do with race, it insists that marriage has everything to do with sexual complementarity. From the beginning of Genesis to the end of Revelation, the Bible is replete with spousal imagery and the language of husband and wife. One activist Supreme Court ruling cannot overthrow the truth about marriage that is expressed in faith and reason and universal human experience.

We must now bear witness to the truth of marriage with more resolve and skill than ever before. We must now find ways to rebuild a marriage culture. The first step will be protecting our right to live in accordance with the truth. The key question, again, is whether the liberal elites who now have the upper hand will treat their dissenting fellow citizens as they treat racists or as they treat pro-lifers. While the elites disagree with the pro-life position, most understand it. They can see why a pro-life citizen defends unborn life—so for the most part they agree that government shouldn't coerce citizens into performing or subsidizing abortions. The same needs to be true for marriage. And we need to make it true by making the arguments in defense of marriage.

What Do We Do Now?

In January 1973, the U.S. Supreme Court created a constitutional right to abortion throughout all nine months of pregnancy in *Roe v. Wade* and *Doe v. Bolton*. Pro-lifers were told they had lost and the issue was settled. The law taught citizens that they had a new right, and public opinion quickly swung against pro-lifers by as much as a two-to-one margin. One after another, formerly pro-life public figures—Ted

Kennedy, Jesse Jackson, Al Gore, Bill Clinton—"evolved" in their thinking to embrace the new social orthodoxy of abortion on demand. Pundits insisted that all young people were for abortion, and elites ridiculed pro-lifers for being on the "wrong side of history." The pro-lifers were aging, their children increasingly against them. The only people who continued to oppose abortion, its partisans insisted, were a few elderly priests and religious fundamentalists. They would soon die off and abortion would be easily integrated into American life and disappear as a disputed issue.

But courageous pro-lifers put their hand to the plow, and today we reap the fruits. My generation is more pro-life than my parents' generation. A majority of Americans support pro-life policies, more today than at any time since the *Roe* decision. More state laws have been enacted protecting unborn babies in the past decade than in the previous thirty years combined.

What happened?

The pro-life community woke up and responded to a bad court ruling. Academics wrote the books and articles making the scientific and philosophical case for life. Statesmen like Henry Hyde, Edwin Meese, and Ronald Reagan crafted the policy and used the bully pulpit to advance the culture of life. Activists and lawyers got together, formed coalitions, and devised effective strategies. They faithfully bore witness to the truth.

Everything the pro-life movement did needs to be done again, now on this new frontier of marriage. There are three lessons in particular to learn from the pro-life movement:

1. We must call the court's ruling in *Obergefell v. Hodges* what it is: judicial activism.

   Just as the pro-life movement successfully rejected *Roe v. Wade* and exposed its lies about unborn life and about the U.S. Constitution, we must make it clear to our fellow citizens that *Obergefell v. Hodges* does not tell the truth about marriage or about our Constitution.

2. We must protect our freedom to speak and live according to the truth.

    The pro-life movement accomplished this on at least three fronts. First, it ensured that pro-life doctors and nurses and pharmacists and hospitals would never have to perform abortions or dispense abortion-causing drugs. Second, it won the battle—through the Hyde Amendment—to prevent taxpayer money from paying for abortions. And third, it made sure that pro-lifers and pro-life organizations could not be discriminated against by the government. Pro-marriage forces need to do the same: Ensure that we have freedom from government coercion to lead our lives, rear our children, and operate our businesses and our charities in accord with our beliefs—the truth—about marriage. Likewise, we must ensure that the government does not discriminate against citizens or organizations because of their belief that marriage is the union of husband and wife.

3. We must redouble our efforts to make the case in the public square.

    We have to bear witness to the truth in a winsome and compelling way. The pro-life movement accomplished this on different levels. Specialists in science, law, philosophy, and theology laid the foundations of the pro-life case with research and writing in their disciplines, while advocacy groups tirelessly appealed to the hearts of the American people. Pro-lifers did much more than preach, launching a multitude of initiatives to help mothers in crisis pregnancies make the right choice.

Now we must employ reason to make the case for the truth about marriage, communicate this truth to our neighbors, and embody this truth in our families and communities. Just as the pro-life movement discovered the effectiveness of ultrasound and letting women speak for themselves, the pro-marriage movement will, I predict, find the social science on marriage and parenting and voices of the victims of the sexual revolution to be particularly effective. And just as grassroots pregnancy centers exposed the lie that abortion is a compassionate response to unplanned pregnancy, we must show what a truly loving response is to same-sex attraction.

This book explains, in clear and sober terms, the enormous task before us of defending our families, churches, schools, and businesses from opponents who now wield coercive power in government, commerce, and academia. My goal is to equip everyone, not just the experts, to defend what most of us never imagined we'd have to defend: our rights of conscience, our religious liberty, and the basic building block of civilization—the human family, founded on the marital union of a man and a woman.

It's important to point out what I'm *not* doing in this book. I am not making theological arguments. I might point out what various religions teach, simply as a matter of fact, but the arguments I make will all be based on reason: philosophy, jurisprudence, political science, and social science. Nor will I be discussing the morality of same-sex sexual relationships. And finally, I won't be appealing to tradition or history, arguing that because something has been done a certain way, it ought to remain that way. No, I'll be making arguments based on reason about what marriage is, why marriage matters for public policy, and what the consequences are of redefining marriage. I will make reasoned arguments about why religious liberty is a human right, how public policy can best protect it, and why analogies to racism fail. I will suggest pastoral strategies for religious communities to better advance these truths as well.

Some people seem to think that the debate is over. They're wrong. I have visited more than a hundred college campuses in the last few years, and my experience suggests there is hope. At almost every one of these universities, including such elite law schools as Harvard and Yale, students have come up to me after my talk to say that they had never heard a rational case for marriage. Christians would tell me that they always knew marriage was between a man and a woman but never knew how to defend it as a matter of policy and law—that they knew what the Bible revealed and the church taught but lacked a vocabulary for articulating what God had written on the heart. Now they could better explain how faith and reason go together, how theology and philosophy, the Bible and social science all point to the same truth. Reassuring these students is crucially important. Simply preventing them from internalizing doubt, from cowering in shame in the face of aggressive opposition, or from caving in is essential.

It's also crucial to help those who haven't made up their minds to see that this is a matter on which reasonable people of goodwill can be found on both sides. Some people are genuinely on the fence, and we should do what we can to keep them from coming down on the wrong side. Indeed, I have received hundreds of notes over the past year from people who decided to come down on the right side because of some argument I made for marriage.

While we may not be able to convert the committed advocates for same-sex marriage, we should seek to soften their resolve to eliminate us from polite society. Indeed, on campus after campus, students who identify as liberal have admitted that this was the first time they have heard a rational case for marriage. They have told me that they respect the argument—and frequently aren't sure why it's wrong, even if they continue to insist that it is. Winning over these students so that they will respect our right to dissent is essential. We do that, in part, by explaining the reasons for our beliefs about marriage.

At one point in American life, virtually every child received the great gift of being raised to adulthood in the marital bond of the man and the woman—the mom and the dad—whose union gave them life. Today, that number is under 50 percent in some communities, and the consequences are tragic. Same-sex marriage didn't cause this, but it does nothing to help it and will only make things worse. It will reinforce the distorted view that marriage is primarily about adult romantic desires, making the rebuilding of the marriage culture much more difficult.

Whatever the law or culture may say, we must commit now to witness to the truth about marriage: that men and women are equal and equally necessary in the lives of children; that men and women, though different, are complementary; that it takes a man and a woman to bring a child into the world. It is not bigotry but compassion and common sense to insist on laws and public policies that maximize the likelihood that children will grow up with a mom and a dad.

Too many of our neighbors haven't heard our arguments, and they seem unwilling to respect our rights, because they don't understand what we believe. It's up to us to change that perception. We will decide which side of history we are on.

ONE

MEN, WOMEN, AND CHILDREN:
THE TRUTH ABOUT MARRIAGE

Everyone in America is in favor of marriage equality. There, I said it. But it doesn't mean what the Left wishes it meant. Everyone is in favor of marriage equality because everyone wants the law to treat all marriages equally—that is, in the same way. The debate in the United States in the decade and a half before *Obergefell v. Hodges* wasn't about equality. It was about marriage. We disagreed about *what marriage is*.

Of course, "marriage equality" was a great slogan for the Left. It fits on a bumper sticker. You can make a red equals sign your Facebook profile picture. It's a wonderful piece of advertising. And yet it's completely vacuous. It doesn't say a thing about *what marriage is*. Only if you know what marriage is can you then decide whether any given marriage *policy* violates marriage *equality*. Before you can get to considerations of equal protection of the law, you have to know what it is that the law is trying to protect equally.

Sloganeering aside, appeals to "marriage equality" betray sloppy reasoning. Every law makes distinctions. Equality before the law protects citizens from *arbitrary* distinctions, from laws that treat them differently *for no good reason*. To know whether a law makes the right distinctions—whether the lines it draws are justified—one has to know the public purpose of the law and the nature of the good it advances or protects.

After all, even those who want to redefine marriage to include same-sex couples will draw lines defining what sorts of relationships are a marriage and what sorts are not. If we're going to draw lines that are based on principle—if we're going to draw lines that reflect the truth—we have to know what sort of a relationship marriage is. That's why Sherif Girgis, Robert George, and I wrote a book a few years ago titled *What Is Marriage?*[1] You have to answer *that* question before you talk about recognizing marriage equally.

And yet implicit throughout the court's argument in *Obergefell* is the assumption that marriage is a genderless institution. But as Justice Samuel Alito pointed out two years earlier in his dissenting opinion in the federal Defense of Marriage Act case, the U.S. Constitution is silent about what marriage is. Justice Alito framed the debate as a contest between two visions of marriage—what he calls the "conjugal" and "consent-based" views.

Justice Alito cited the book I coauthored as an example of the conjugal view of marriage (also called the "comprehensive" view): a "comprehensive, exclusive, permanent union that is intrinsically ordered to producing new life."[2] On the other side, he cited Jonathan Rauch as a proponent of the consent-based idea that marriage is a commitment marked by emotional union.[3] The Constitution, he explained, is silent on which of these substantive visions of marriage is correct. Justice Alito, of course, was right about the Constitution, as I show in chapter 3. This chapter explores the debate that Justice Alito highlighted—between the two different visions of *what marriage is.*

The "Consent-Based" View of Marriage

The consent-based view of marriage is primarily about an intense emotional union—a romantic, caregiving union of consenting adults. It's what the philosopher John Corvino describes as the relationship that establishes your "number one person."[4] What sets marriage apart from other relationships is the priority of the relationship. It's your most important relationship; the most intense emotional, romantic union; the caregiving relationship that takes priority over all others. Andrew Sullivan says that marriage has become "primarily a way in which two adults affirm their emotional commitment to one another."[5] And as we will see in chapter 3, *this* vision of what marriage is does all of the work in Justice Anthony Kennedy's majority opinion in *Obergefell*.

In *What Is Marriage*, my coauthors and I argue that this view collapses marriage into companionship in general. Rather than understanding marriage correctly as *different in kind* from other relationships, the consent-based view sees in it only a *difference of degree*: marriage has what all other relationships have, but more of it. This, we argue, gets marriage wrong. It cannot explain or justify any of the distinctive commitments that marriage requires—monogamy, exclusivity, and permanence—nor can it explain what interest the government has in it.

If marriage is simply about consenting adult romance and caregiving, why should it be permanent? Emotions come and go; love waxes and wanes. Why would such a bond require a pledge of permanency? Might not someone find that the romance and caregiving of marriage are enhanced by a temporary commitment, in which no one is under a life sentence?

In fact, if marriage is simply about consenting adult romance and caregiving, why should it be a sexually exclusive union? Sure, some people might prefer to sleep only with their spouse, but others might think that agreeing to have extramarital sexual outlets would actually *enhance* their marriage. Why impose the expectation of sexual fidelity?

Lastly, if marriage is simply about consenting adult romance and caregiving, why can't three, four, or more people form a marriage?

There is nothing about intense emotional unions that limits them to two and only two people. Threesomes and foursomes can form an intense emotional, romantic, caregiving relationship as easily as a couple. Nothing in principle requires monogamy. Polyamory (that is, group love) seems perfectly compatible with the consent-based view of marriage.

The consent-based view of *what marriage is* simply fails as a theory of marriage because it can't explain any of the historical marital norms. A couple informed by the consent-based view might live out these norms if temperament or taste so moved them, but there would be no reason of principle for them to do so and no basis for the law to encourage them to do so. Marriage can come in as many different sizes and shapes as consenting adults can dream up. Love equals love, after all. And why, in any case, should the government have any involvement in this kind of marriage? If marriage is just about the love lives of consenting adults, let's get the state out of their bedrooms. And yet those who would redefine marriage want to put the government into more bedrooms.

There is nothing "homosexual" or "gay" or "lesbian," of course, about the consent-based view of marriage. Many heterosexuals have bought into it over the past fifty years. This is the vision of marriage that came out of the sexual revolution. Long before there was a debate about same-sex anything, far too many heterosexuals bought into a liberal ideology about sexuality that makes a mess of marriage: cohabitation, no-fault divorce, extramarital sex, nonmarital childbearing, pornography, and the hook-up culture all contributed to the breakdown of the marriage culture. The push for the legal redefinition of marriage didn't cause any of these problems. It is, rather, their logical conclusion. The problem is that it's the logical conclusion of a bad train of logic.

If the sexual habits of the past fifty years have been good for society, good for women, good for children, then by all means let's enshrine the consent-based view of marriage in law. But if the past fifty years haven't been so good for society, for women, for children—indeed, if they've been, for many people, a disaster—then why would we lock in a view of marriage that will make it more difficult to recover a more humane vision of human sexuality and family life?

The law cannot be neutral between the consent-based and conjugal views of marriage. It will enshrine one view or the other. It will either teach that marriage is about consenting adult love of whatever size or shape the adults choose, or it will teach that marriage is a comprehensive union of sexually complementary spouses who live by the norms of monogamy, exclusivity, and permanency, so that children can be raised by their mom and dad. There is no third option. There is no neutral position. The law will embrace one or the other.

So far I have argued that the consent-based view fails as a theory of marriage. Now I'm going to address what marriage is. Then I'll turn to why marriage matters for public policy and, in the next chapter, to the consequences of redefining marriage.

The Comprehensive View of Marriage

Someone who wants to explain what marriage is has the difficult task of explaining something that every one of our grandparents simply took for granted, that everyone two generations ago thought was common knowledge—that marriage is a permanent, exclusive union of husband and wife. Much of human wisdom is tacit knowledge. Only when it is attacked does it need a formal, explicit defense. Explaining why marriage is the union of a man and a woman is like explaining why wheels are round, but it has to be done. That means going back to first principles, and there's no better guide to first principles than Aristotle.

The philosopher of ancient Greece suggests that we can understand any community by analyzing three factors: the actions that the community engages in, the goods that the community seeks, and the norms of commitment that shape that community's common life. To illustrate how this method of analysis works, let's take an uncontroversial example: the academic community of a university.

An Academic Community

What makes a university an *academic* community rather than a big business or a sports franchise, even though most universities engage in both business and athletics on a large scale? Following the Aristotelian methodology, I argue that a university is an academic community because of the academic actions it engages in, the academic goods it seeks, and the academic norms it lives by.

Members of an academic community engage in academic action. What sorts of things are academic actions? Professors research and write academic articles and books and assign students to read them. They deliver lectures, which students attend and take notes on. Students take exams and write papers, and professors grade and discuss them with students. These are the sorts of activities that constitute an academic community *as* an academic community. Annual giving campaigns and football games are nice additions, but they don't go to the heart of what makes a university a university. These academic activities are the heart of a university (or at least they should be).

Now what are these academic activities ultimately seeking? What are the goods toward which they are oriented? They're oriented toward the goods of the truth and of knowledge. All of the exercises that professors make students perform—the homework, the term papers, the research projects—and all of the work that they themselves do—writing those books and papers and delivering those lectures—are all about eliminating ignorance from our lives and coming to a better appropriation of the truth. Academic actions aren't supposed to be exercises in propaganda or defenses of prejudices. No, they're about discovering the truth so we don't live in ignorance or as slaves to prejudice. Academic actions are oriented toward academic goods, the goods of knowledge and of the truth.

So what norms do such actions in pursuit of such goods require of an academic community? This is where all the commitment to academic integrity, academic freedom, and academic honor codes comes into play. Students shouldn't plagiarize, researchers should cite all of their sources, scientists should assess all of the data, not just those that support their hypothesis. If one researcher finds weaknesses in another's study, the latter shouldn't view it as an attack but as assistance in the common pursuit of truth. When a professor critiques a student's paper, the student shouldn't view it as an insult but as help in his understanding the truth.

Three easy steps: academic actions (research, reading, writing, discussion) are ordered toward academic goods (knowledge of the truth and elimination of ignorance) and thus demand academic norms (academic honesty, academic freedom, academic honor codes) so the community can fulfill its purpose—the discovery of truth.

The Marital Community

We can understand the marital relationship in the same way. What makes marriage different from other forms of community—a football team, say, or a university? In every aspect, marriage is a *comprehensive* relationship. It's comprehensive in the act that uniquely unites the spouses, in the goods that the spouses are ordered toward, and in the norms of commitment that it requires from them.

Marriage unites spouses in a comprehensive act: marital sexual intercourse is a union of hearts, minds, and bodies. Marriage (like the marital act that seals it) is inherently ordered toward a comprehensive good, the creation and rearing of entirely new human organisms, who are to be raised to participate in every kind of human good. And finally, marriage demands comprehensive norms: spouses make the comprehensive commitments of permanency and exclusivity—comprehensive throughout time (permanent) and at every moment in time (exclusive).

If that sounds abstract, let's move in for a closer look. First, the comprehensive act. How can two persons unite comprehensively? To unite comprehensively, they must unite at all levels of their personhood. But what is a person? Human beings are mind-body unities. We are not ghosts in machines or souls that are somehow inhabiting flesh and bones. Rather, we are enfleshed souls or ensouled bodies—a mind-body unity.

Thus, to unite with someone in a comprehensive way, one must unite with him at all levels of his personhood: a union of hearts, minds, and bodies.

Ordinary friendships are unions of hearts and minds. Uniting bodily is not a part of the typical understanding of friendship. But bodily union is part of what it means to be in a spousal relationship. This, of course, raises the question: How can two human beings unite bodily? To answer this, we need to understand what makes any *individual* one body.

What is it that makes each one of us a unified organism? Why aren't we just clumps of cells? The answer is that all of our various bodily systems and parts work together for the common good of our biological lives. Your heart, lungs, kidneys, and muscles and all the other organs and tissues coordinate to keep you alive. Coordination toward a common end explains unity, in this case bodily unity of an individual.

And in most respects you are complete as an individual. With respect to locomotion, you can set this book down, get up, and walk into the kitchen for a bite to eat. With respect to digestion, you can digest that bite all by yourself. With respect to circulation and respiration, you can breathe and pump oxygenated blood throughout your body as an individual. In all of these functions, you're complete.

Yet with respect to one biological function, you are radically incomplete. It takes two to tango, and it takes two to make a baby. In the marital act, a man's body and a woman's body don't just make contact as in a kiss or interlock as when holding hands. The Hebrew Bible reveals something true about our humanity when it says that a man and a woman in the marital act become "one flesh." This isn't merely a figure of speech. The Bible doesn't say the husband and wife are so much in love it's *as if* the two become one. No, the Scriptures rightly suggest that at the physical and metaphysical level, a man and a woman truly become two in one *flesh*. The sexual complementarity of a man and a woman allows them to unite in this comprehensive way.

In the marital act, the husband and wife engage in a single act with a single function: coordination toward a common end unites them. They form a single organism as a mated pair with a single biological purpose, which the couple performs together as a unity. Note the parallel: The muscles, heart, lungs, stomach, and intestines of an individual human body cooperate with each other toward a single biological end—the continued life of that body. In the same way, a man and a woman, when they unite in the marital act, cooperate toward a single biological end—procreation. A particular marital act may or may not result in the fusion of a sperm with an egg. Nevertheless, the union that this act brings about is so complete that frequently, nine months later, it requires a name. The lovemaking act is also the life-giving act. The act that unites a man and a woman as husband and wife is the same act that can make them mother and father. This begins to tell us something about what the marital relationship is ordered toward.

In the same way that academic communities engage in academic actions that are ordered toward the academic goods of the pursuit of truth and knowledge, the marital relationship is (like the act that embodies it) ordered toward the marital good of procreation and rearing and education of children. The good toward which the marital act is ordered is not a one-time good like winning the next football game or passing the next test. The marital act is comprehensive—it unites the spouses in heart, mind, and body—and is thus oriented toward a comprehensive good—the procreation and education of new persons who can appreciate human goodness in all its dimensions. Marriage is unlike any other community in being comprehensive.

Now it should be clear why marriage requires the comprehensive commitments of both exclusivity and permanency. Let's start with exclusivity. What sort of exclusivity does marriage call for? *Sexual* exclusivity. You don't cheat on your spouse by attending a lecture with someone else. You don't cheat on your spouse by playing football with someone else. But you do cheat on your spouse if you sleep with someone else. It is the sexual act that transforms an ordinary friendship, a union of hearts and minds, into the comprehensive community of marriage, and so the marital norm of exclusivity focuses on sexual fidelity. The act that is distinctive to marriage—which we therefore call the "marital act"—must be reserved exclusively for the spouses. To unite comprehensively with your spouse requires that you pledge not to unite sexually with others. It requires you, in the words of the traditional marriage vow, to forsake all others.

Something similar is true for the other comprehensive commitment of marriage. Because marriage is a comprehensive union, it requires the comprehensive commitment of permanency. To unite comprehensively, spouses can't hold anything back. If they have a sunset clause, if they have an escape date, if they have a way out, then they're not really uniting comprehensively. Comprehensive union requires an open-ended commitment. So marriage requires "forsaking all others" not only for the time being but also into the future—"till death do us part." Ordered toward the comprehensive good of procreation, marriage must be permanent. The families that marriage produces—not only parents and children but also grandparents, nieces and nephews, aunts and uncles and cousins—will be stable only if the marital union itself is stable. Again, the comprehensive nature of marriage explains its comprehensive act, good, and norms.

The Comprehensive View of Marriage Is Based on Human Nature, Not Anti-Gay Animosity

We find this comprehensive view of marriage (often without the Aristotelian accoutrements) in the ancient Hebrews, Greeks, and Romans. We find it in the canon law of the Church, the civil law of Europe, and the common law of England and America. We find it in Christian thinkers like Augustine, Aquinas, Luther, and Calvin, in Enlightenment thinkers like Locke and Kant, and in Eastern thinkers like Gandhi. The world's various political, philosophical, and theological traditions—each with its own vocabulary and with differences around the margins—have all articulated something like the comprehensive view of marriage.

They have arrived at this truth, moreover, by grappling with basic human realities, not out of animosity toward same-sex relationships. Indeed, cultures that had no concept of "sexual orientation" and cultures that took homoeroticism for granted have understood that the union of husband and wife is a distinct and uniquely important relationship.[6] Citing the historical consensus, Justice Alito asked during oral arguments:

> How do you account for the fact that, as far as I'm aware, until the end of the twentieth century, there never was a nation or a culture that recognized marriage between two people of the same sex? Now, can we infer from that that those nations and those cultures all thought that there was some rational, practical purpose for defining marriage in that way, or is it your argument that they were all operating independently based solely on irrational stereotypes and prejudice?

Support for marriage as the union of a man and a woman can't simply be the result of anti-gay animus, Justice Alito pointed out, because "there have been cultures that did not frown on homosexuality....Ancient Greece is an example. It was well accepted within certain bounds." The justice added that "people like Plato wrote in favor of that." And yet, the ancient Greeks, including Plato, never thought a same-sex relationship was a marriage.

As Chief Justice John Roberts explained in his dissenting opinion in *Obergefell*, marriage as the union of husband and wife is about serving the common good, not excluding anyone:

> This universal definition of marriage as the union of a man and a woman is no historical coincidence. Marriage did not come about as a result of a political movement, discovery, disease, war, religious doctrine, or any other moving force of world history—and certainly not as a result of a prehistoric decision to exclude gays and lesbians. It arose in the nature of things to meet a vital need: ensuring that children are conceived by a mother and father committed to raising them in the stable conditions of a lifelong relationship.[7]

Defying the universal consensus about marriage requires breathtaking presumption. Whatever arguments there may be in favor of doing so, that consensus cannot be dismissed as a relic of irrational animus against men and women attracted to members of their own sex.

Why Marriage Matters for Public Policy

If you've followed the argument to this point, you might be willing to say that marriage, properly understood, is a comprehensive union, that it unites a man and a woman in a comprehensive act, ordered toward the comprehensive good of procreating and raising new life in a family, and requiring of them a comprehensive—exclusive and permanent—bond.

But even if I have persuaded you that this is the philosophical truth about marriage, you might ask why any of this matters. Maybe I'm right about the nature of marriage. Why should anyone care? More specifically, why should the *state* care?

Virtually every political community has regulated male-female sexual relationships. This is not because government is a sucker for romance. If marriage were just about consenting adult love, the state wouldn't be in the marriage business. Government recognizes male-female sexual relationships because these alone produce new human beings. For highly dependent infants, there is no path to physical, moral, and cultural maturity—no path to personal responsibility—without a long and delicate process of ongoing care and supervision to which mothers and fathers bring unique gifts. Unless children mature, they never will become healthy, upright, productive members of society. Marriage exists to make men and women responsible to each other and to any children that they might have. Let me explain.

Marriage Benefits Society in a Way No Other Relationship Does

Marriage is society's least restrictive means of ensuring the well-being of children. Government recognition of marriage protects children by encouraging men and women to commit themselves to each other and to take responsibility for their children.

From a public policy perspective, marriage is about uniting a man and a woman with each other as husband and wife to be father and mother to any children their sexual union produces. Marriage is based on the anthropological truth that men and women are complementary, the biological fact that reproduction depends on a man and a woman, and the social reality that children deserve a mother and a father.

Whenever a baby is born, there is always a mother nearby. She's normally in the same room. That's a fact of biology. The question is whether a father will be close by and, if so, for how long. Marriage increases the odds that the father of a child will be committed to the child's mother and that the two of them, committed to each other, will be committed to their child. It connects persons and goods that otherwise tend to fragment. As the late sociologist James Q. Wilson put it, "Marriage is a socially arranged solution for the problem of getting people to stay together and care for children that the mere desire for children, and the sex that makes children possible, does not solve."[8]

Connecting sex, babies, and moms and dads is the irreplaceable social function of marriage. Laws and social expectations can strengthen or weaken marriage in this role, and that's why the government is rightly involved in this aspect of our lives. Maggie Gallagher develops this idea:

> The critical public or "civil" task of marriage is to regulate sexual relationships between men and women in order to reduce the likelihood that children (and their mothers, and society) will face the burdens of fatherlessness, and increase the likelihood that there will be a next generation that will be raised by their mothers and fathers in one family, where both parents are committed to each other and to their children.[9]

As strong as the government's interest is in the marriages of its citizens, however, it is important to remember that the government does not *create* marriage, it *recognizes* marriage. Marriage is a natural institution that predates government. Society as a whole, not merely any given set of spouses, benefits from marriage. This is because marriage helps to channel procreative love into a stable institution that provides for the orderly bearing and rearing of the next generation.

There's No Such Thing as "Parenting"

The complementarity that defines marriage as the union of a man and a woman is crucial as well for the raising of children. There is no such thing as "parenting." There is mothering, and there is fathering, and children do best with both. It does not detract from the many mothers and fathers who have of necessity raised children alone, and done so successfully, to insist that mothers and fathers bring distinct strengths to the task.

In a summary of the "best psychological, sociological, and biological research to date," W. Bradford Wilcox, a sociologist at the University of Virginia, finds that "men and women bring different gifts to the parenting enterprise, that children benefit from having parents with distinct parenting styles, and that family breakdown poses a serious threat to children and to the societies in which they live."[10] Wilcox finds that "most fathers and mothers possess sex-specific talents related to parenting, and societies should organize parenting and work roles to take advantage of the way in which these talents tend to be distributed in sex-specific ways."[11] These differences are not the result of gender roles or sex stereotypes. They are a matter of what comes naturally to moms and dads, what moms and dads enjoy doing with their children.

Dads play important roles in the formation of both their sons and their daughters. As the sociologist David Popenoe of Rutgers University explains, "The burden of social science evidence supports the idea that gender-differentiated parenting is important for human development and that the contribution of fathers to childrearing is unique and irreplaceable."[12] Popenoe concludes:

We should disavow the notion that "mommies can make good daddies," just as we should disavow the popular notion…that "daddies can make good mommies." … The two sexes are different to the core, and each is necessary—culturally and biologically—for the optimal development of a human being.[13]

What are the distinctive gifts of mothers and fathers? Wilcox reports, "Among the many distinctive talents that mothers bring to the parenting enterprise, three stand out: their capacity to breastfeed, their ability to understand infants and children, and their ability to offer nurture and comfort to their children."[14] And fathers, Wilcox writes, "excel when it comes to discipline, play, and challenging their children to embrace life's challenges."[15] As Popenoe explains:

The complementarity of male and female parenting styles is striking and of enormous importance to a child's overall development.…[F]athers express more concern for the child's long-term development, while mothers focus on the child's immediate well-being (which, of course, in its own way has everything to do with a child's long-term well-being.)…[T]he disciplinary approach of fathers tends to be "firm" while that of mothers tends to be "responsive." While mothers provide an important flexibility and sympathy in their discipline, fathers provide ultimate predictability and consistency. Both dimensions are critical for an efficient, balanced, and humane childrearing regime.[16]

Children of each sex, moreover, benefit from the distinct and complementary attention of a mother and father. Consider what dads do for their sons and daughters. Fathers tend to be the ones who engage in what sociologists call "rough and tumble play"—teaching their boys that it's all right to put people in headlocks but not to bite, pull hair, or gouge eyes. Fathers help their boys channel their distinctively masculine tendencies into productive activities. When this doesn't happen, social costs run high. Wilcox writes:

> For boys, the link between crime and fatherlessness is very clear....
>
> Boys learn self-control...from playing with and being disciplined by a loving father. As importantly, boys also learn to control their own aggressive instincts when they see a man they respect and love—their father—handling frustration, conflict, and difficulty without resorting to violence. By contrast, boys who do not regularly experience the love, discipline, and modeling of a good father are more likely to engage in what is called "compensatory masculinity," where they reject and denigrate all that is feminine and instead seek to prove their masculinity by engaging in domineering and violent behavior.
>
> Studies of crime indicate that one of the strongest predictors of crime is fatherless families. Princeton University sociologist Sara McLanahan found in one study that boys raised outside of an intact nuclear family were more than twice as likely as other boys to end up in prison, even controlling for a range of social and economic factors. Another review of the literature on delinquency and crime found that criminals come from broken homes at a disproportionate rate: 70 percent of juveniles in state reform schools, 72 percent of adolescent murderers, and 60 percent of rapists grew up in fatherless homes.[17]

Fathers matter for their boys. They also matter for their daughters. Because dads, on average and for the most part, tend to be larger than moms and have deeper voices than moms, they tend to be better at scaring away bad boyfriends. And because dads were boys themselves, they know what the wrong sort of boy might be looking for in their daughter. As a result, dads are more likely to police whom their daughter is dating. A married father and mother are models of a good male-female relationship for their daughter. Wilcox explains:

> Fathers who are affectionate and firm with their daughters, who love and respect their wives, and who simply stick around can play a crucial role in minimizing the likelihood that their daughters will be sexually active prior to marriage. The affection that fathers bestow on their daughters makes those daughters less likely to seek attention from young men and to get involved sexually with members of the opposite sex. Fathers also protect their daughters from premarital sexual activity by setting clear disciplinary limits for their daughters, monitoring their whereabouts, and by signaling to young men that sexual activity will not be tolerated.
>
> ... [F]athers send a biological signal through their pheromones—special aromatic chemical compounds released from men's and women's bodies—that slows the sexual development of their daughters; this, in turn, makes daughters less interested in sexual activity and less likely to be seen as sexual objects.
>
> Consequently, girls who grow up in intact families are much less likely to experience puberty at an early age, to be sexually active before marriage, and to get pregnant before marriage. Indeed, the longer fathers stick around, the less likely girls are to be sexually active prior to marriage. One study found that about 35 percent of girls in the United States whose fathers left before age 6 became pregnant as teenagers, that 10 percent of girls in the United States whose fathers left them between the ages of 6 and 18 became pregnant as teenagers, and that only 5 percent of girls whose fathers stayed with them throughout childhood became pregnant.[18]

Social science confirms the importance of marriage for children. According to the best available sociological evidence, children fare best according to virtually every indicator examined when reared by their wedded biological parents. Studies that control for other factors, including poverty and even genetics, suggest that children reared in intact homes do best in measurements of educational achievement, emotional health, familial and sexual development, and delinquency and incarceration.[19]

A study published by the left-leaning research institution Child Trends concluded:

> [I]t is not simply the presence of two parents...but the presence of *two biological parents* that seems to support children's development [emphasis in original]....
>
> ... [R]esearch clearly demonstrates that family structure matters for children, and the family structure that helps children the most is a family headed by two biological parents in a low-conflict marriage. Children in single-parent families, children born to unmarried mothers, and children in stepfamilies or cohabiting relationships face higher risks of poor outcomes.... There is thus value for children in promoting strong, stable marriages between biological parents.[20]

According to another study, "The advantage of marriage appears to exist primarily when the child is the biological offspring of both parents."[21] Literature reviews conducted by the Brookings Institution, the Woodrow Wilson School of Public and International Affairs at Princeton University, the Center for Law and Social Policy, and the Institute for American Values corroborate the importance of intact households for children.[22]

The social scientific evidence of the importance of fathers is so compelling that even President Barack Obama refers to it as a truism:

> We know the statistics—that children who grow up without a father are five times more likely to live in poverty and commit crime; nine times more likely to drop out of schools and twenty times more likely to end up in prison. They are more likely to have behavioral problems, or run away from home, or become teenage parents themselves. And the foundations of our community are weaker because of it.[23]

Fathers matter, and marriage helps to connect fathers to mothers and children. Citing President Obama is an opportunity to point out that a child who grows up without a married mom and dad can defy the odds. President Obama is a tremendous example of that. But he would be the first to acknowledge that, on average and for the most part, children who grow up without their married mother and father have a more difficult road to travel. To the all-male graduating class of the historically black Morehouse College, the president said: "I was raised by a heroic single mom....But I sure wish I had had a father who was not only present, but involved. Didn't know my dad. And so my whole life, I've tried to be for Michelle and my girls what my father was not for my mother and me. I want to break that cycle."[24] I agree with President Obama, and I am grateful that he's breaking that cycle.

Marital Breakdown Costs Everyone

Marriage benefits everyone because separating childbearing and childrearing from marriage burdens innocent bystanders—not just children, but the whole community. When parents are unable to care for their children, someone has to step in, and that "someone" is often the state. By encouraging the marriage norms of monogamy, sexual exclusivity, and permanence, the state strengthens civil society and reduces its own role.

By recognizing marriage, the government supports economic well-being. Summarizing a study from the University of Virginia's National

Marriage Project, Professor Wilcox writes, "The core message...is that the wealth of nations depends in no small part on the health of the family."[25] The same study suggests that marriage and fertility trends "play an underappreciated and important role in fostering long-term economic growth, the viability of the welfare state, the size and quality of the workforce, and the health of large sectors of the modern economy."[26]

It should surprise no one, then, that the decline of marriage most hurts the least well-off. A leading indicator of whether someone will know poverty or prosperity is whether, growing up, he or she knew the love and security of having a married mother and father. "Being raised in a married family reduce[s] a child's probability of living in poverty by about 82 percent," my colleague at the Heritage Foundation Robert Rector has found.[27]

The erosion of marriage harms not only the immediately affected families but society as a whole. A Brookings Institution study found that $229 billion in welfare expenditures between 1970 and 1996 can be attributed to the breakdown of the marriage culture and the resulting exacerbation of social ills: teen pregnancy, poverty, crime, drug abuse, and health problems.[28] A 2008 study found that divorce and unwed childbearing cost taxpayers $112 billion each year,[29] and Utah State University's David Schramm has estimated that divorce alone costs local, state, and federal governments $33 billion each year.[30]

Marriage protects children from poverty. It increases the likelihood that they will enjoy social mobility. It steers them away from crime and relieves the state of having to pick up the pieces of their families. If you care about social justice or limited government, if you care about the poor or about freedom, you should care about a strong marriage culture. Civil recognition and support of the marriage union of a man and a woman is the most effective and least intrusive way to pursue freedom and prosperity.

What about Infertility?

Perhaps the most common objection to this basic argument involves infertility. If infertile couples can marry—and no one has ever denied that they can—how can the definition of marriage be linked to procreation? Proponents of same-sex marriage usually regard this argument as a "silver bullet" that destroys the traditional understanding of marriage—as if no one in the previous millennia has realized that some couples (and any woman above a certain age) can't conceive a child. But there are four responses to this argument.

First, as a policy matter, the state is in the business of recognizing marriage not because every marriage will produce a child but because every child has a mother and a father. Through its marriage policy, the state respects the natural bonds that unite the parents who brought a child into the world and encourages them to commit to each other permanently and exclusively. Public policy must consider the big picture, not individual cases. It is the procreative *nature* of marriage rather than the actual procreative results of individual marriages that explains government policy in this area. (And would anyone really want the government to require fertility tests or to ask couples if they intend to have children?)

Second, as a practical matter, many couples who think they are infertile end up conceiving or adopting children. Many who say they never want children change their minds. It's important to keep these men and women united with each other. Indeed, infertility rarely strikes *both* husband and wife, and marital fidelity ensures that the fertile spouse doesn't procreate children with someone else, children who will be deprived of a fully committed mother and father. The fifty-year-old husband whose wife has gone through menopause will never beget children with another woman if he's faithful to his marriage vows. The state has a general interest in channeling their sexual desire into marriage.

Third, as a philosophical matter, an infertile marriage is fully a marriage. A marriage is a comprehensive union marked by one-flesh union—the coordination of the spouses' two bodies toward the single biological end of reproduction. That coordination—and thus the one-flesh union—takes place *whether or not* it achieves its biological end in the fertilization of an egg by a sperm some hours later. The union, like the act that seals it, is still oriented toward family life. This explains why in common, civil, and canon law, infertility has never nullified a marriage. Impotence, by contrast—which prevents a couple from consummating their union in the one-flesh marital act—*has* been grounds for declaring that a marriage was never completed.

Fourth, as a pedagogical matter, recognizing marriages in spite of infertility teaches that marriage is a comprehensive union, not merely an instrument for baby making. That teaching benefits society by encouraging genuine devotion—and hence stability—in all opposite-sex marriages. By contrast, redefining marriage to include same-sex relationships will teach that marriage (gay or straight) is an instrument for gratifying the emotions of adults. The stability that guarantees children a mom and a dad is not a component of such a union.

In sum, then, public policy is about the rule not the exception, marital norms benefit society even when lived out by infertile couples, infertile marriages are still marriages, and state recognition of infertile marriages has the benefit of reinforcing the truth about marriage without any disadvantages.

Marriage Doesn't Violate Anyone's Liberty

Defining marriage as the union of a husband and a wife does not violate anyone's liberty. If the government rightly recognizes, protects, and promotes marriage as the ideal institution for childbearing and childrearing, adults remain perfectly free to make choices about their relationships. A redefinition by the state of the unique institution of marriage is not necessary for citizens to live in another relationship of their choosing. As we'll see in chapter 3, Justice Clarence Thomas devotes his entire dissenting opinion in *Obergefell* to making this point.

The government should not be in the business of affirming our love lives but should leave consenting adults free to live and love as they choose. Despite the increasingly heated rhetoric from the advocates of "marriage equality," there was no ban on same-sex marriage in the decade before *Obergefell* anywhere in the United States. In all fifty states, two persons of the same sex could live together, join a religious community that would bless their relationship, and choose from a multitude of employers that offered them the same benefits available to married couples. Chief Justice Roberts highlighted this in his dissent: "[T]he marriage laws at issue here involve no government intrusion. They create no crime and impose no punishment. Same-sex couples remain free to live together, to engage in intimate conduct, and to raise their families as they see fit." No government license or sanction was necessary for any of this.

But isn't the government's refusal to bestow the name of "marriage" on same-sex relationships demeaning to the persons in those relationships? In the *Obergefell* oral arguments, Justice Kennedy, dismissing the universal and immemorial comprehensive view of marriage, declared that "the whole purpose of marriage" is to bestow "dignity" on a couple. If he were right, then withholding that "dignity" from same-sex couples would indeed be demeaning. But John Bursch, the lawyer defending the State of Michigan's marriage laws, explained that the institution of marriage "did not develop to deny dignity or to give second-class status to anyone. It developed to serve purposes that, by their nature, arise from biology."

Justice Kennedy wrote the majority opinion, however, and as far as the state is concerned, biology now has nothing to do with it. Americans—many of whom thought same-sex marriage would have no effect on them—are about to learn that the Supreme Court's redefinition of marriage will have consequences for everyone, to which we now turn.

TWO

THE CONSEQUENCES
OF REDEFINING
MARRIAGE

I n the last chapter I argued that marriage is a comprehensive—
permanent and exclusive—union of sexually complementary
spouses who engage in a comprehensive act that is inherently
ordered toward a comprehensive good: the procreation and rearing of
new human life. Marriage matters because that union of a man and a
woman can produce a child, and children deserve a mother and a father.
When children are missing a parent, social costs run high. So we need
to encourage men and women to make the comprehensive commitment
that's specially tailored for their comprehensive union, that is, a commitment that is permanent and exclusive.

So how does same-sex marriage affect the public purpose of marriage? The first step in answering that question is to understand that the
Supreme Court's ruling didn't *expand* marriage; it *redefined* marriage.
As Chief Justice John Roberts remarked during oral arguments, "Every
definition that I looked up, prior to about a dozen years ago, defined

marriage as unity between a man and a woman as husband and wife." So, he continued, "you're not seeking to join the institution, you're seeking to change what the institution is. The fundamental core of the institution is the opposite-sex relationship and you want to introduce into it a same-sex relationship."

This is not simply an opinion held by opponents of same-sex marriage. Consider these candid remarks of the writer and gay rights activist Masha Gessen from 2012:

> It's a no-brainer that [same-sex couples] should have the right to marry, but I also think equally that it's a no-brainer that the institution of marriage should not exist.... Fighting for gay marriage generally involves lying about what we are going to do with marriage when we get there—because we lie that the institution of marriage is not going to change, and that is a lie.
>
> The institution of marriage is going to change, and it should change. And again, I don't think it should exist. And I don't like taking part in creating fictions about my life. That's sort of not what I had in mind when I came out thirty years ago.
>
> I have three kids who have five parents, more or less, and I don't see why they shouldn't have five parents legally.... I met my new partner, and she had just had a baby, and that baby's biological father is my brother, and my daughter's biological father is a man who lives in Russia, and my adopted son also considers him his father. So the five parents break down into two groups of three.... And really, I would like to live in a legal system that is capable of reflecting that reality, and I don't think that's compatible with the institution of marriage.[1]

Did you follow that? Whatever you call the tangle of relationships that Ms. Gessen and her children inhabit, it is not "marriage" as we have understood it until today.

Law teaches. It shapes ideas, which shape what people do. A radical change in the law of marriage will have at least four harmful consequences that we can foresee. The needs and rights of children will be subordinated to the desires of adults. The marital norms of monogamy, exclusivity, and permanence will be weakened. Unborn children will be put at even more risk than they already are. And religious liberty—Americans' "first freedom"—will be threatened.

Serving the Desires of Adults, Not the Needs—or Rights—of Children

Now that the court has redefined marriage to eliminate the norm of sexual complementarity, no institution in our legal and political system upholds the principle that every child deserves both a mother and a father. Redefining marriage as a genderless institution sends the signal that men and women—mothers and fathers—are interchangeable. That's a lie, but as people absorb these lies from the law, more children will be denied the benefit of their own parents' committed love for life.

The consent-based view of marriage now enshrined in law teaches that marriage is more about the desires of adults than about the needs—or rights—of children. It re-centers the marital relationship on the intense emotional union of adults—their romance—rather than on the procreation of new lives and the durability of the union on which they depend. When fathers who have absorbed the law's new lessons about marriage face the ordinary temptations to leave, they'll be likelier to leave. That means more kids growing up without their own mother and father in a committed bond for life.

If you doubt the teaching power of the law, recall how Americans redefined marriage the first time with the introduction of no-fault divorce. In the common-law tradition, marriage enjoyed a strong presumption of permanence. You could receive a divorce under certain rather strict conditions—the "three As": abuse, abandonment, and adultery. If a spouse could show a court that his or her marriage had suffered one of these serious injuries, the marital relationship that was expected to be permanent could be legally dissolved.

With the introduction of no-fault divorce, one spouse could abandon the other for any reason or for no reason at all. That's the idea behind no-fault divorce; you don't have to cite fault. Some scholars refer to it as *unilateral* no-fault divorce because the consent of both parties is not required. There's nothing like this for other contracts. You can't tear up your plumbing contract without obtaining your plumber's consent or proving he installed leaky pipes.

How much domestic stability do we expect when a man is under a more serious legal obligation to his plumber than to his wife? In the decades after the introduction of no-fault divorce, the divorce rate more than doubled. There have always been people who wanted to get out of their marriages, of course, but now the law was telling husbands and wives that they need not even aspire to permanence in their marriage. By providing easy exits from marriage and its responsibilities, no-fault divorce helped to change the perception of marriage from a permanent institution designed for the needs of children to a temporary one designed for the desires of adults. As it became not only legally much easier to leave one's spouse but also psychologically and socially easier, the percentage of children growing up with just one parent skyrocketed. The law shapes our culture, which shapes our beliefs, which shape our actions. The law is a teacher.

Think back fifty years, to when Daniel Patrick Moynihan wrote his famous report for President Lyndon Johnson on the state of the black family. Back then, Moynihan was concerned that the rate of births to single mothers was approaching 25 percent among blacks, which he warned would spell disaster for that beleaguered population. (By way of comparison, the percentage of births to unwed mothers in the general population was in the single digits.) Today, 40 percent of all births in America are out of wedlock; the rate is 50 percent among Hispanics and 70 percent among blacks. These children have done nothing wrong, but their prospects in life are much bleaker than those of children born to married parents. They will bear the social costs of the breakdown of the family.

Many scholars and policymakers have concluded, unsurprisingly, that America's most pressing social problem is absentee fathers. Before he "evolved" to his present position on marriage, President Obama was among them. But how will we insist that fathers are essential when the law has redefined marriage to make fathers optional? If the law tells a man that his presence in his child's life is entirely optional, when the going gets tough his motive for sticking around will be weaker.

Laws that reflected the truth about marriage reinforced the idea that the home of a married mother and father is the most appropriate environment for rearing children. That ideal has not only been abolished but condemned as bigotry.

Weakening Marital Norms

The problem with redefining marriage isn't that a few thousand additional households will get additional economic and other benefits. It's that giving them those benefits will require changing the public meaning of marriage, which will weaken its stabilizing norms.

Now that the law has changed to teach that marriage is whatever consensual relationship you find most emotionally fulfilling, people will start to believe it, and then they'll start to live accordingly. They will be more receptive to sexually open relationships, or temporary ones, or multiple-partner ones, as their appetites and fancies dictate. You don't have to take my word for it. Many *proponents* of same-sex marriage are gleefully predicting just that. The result will be less family stability, which hurts children and women and especially the poor.

Leading lesbian, gay, bisexual, and transgender (LGBT) advocates admit that redefining marriage changes its meaning. E. J. Graff cheerfully acknowledges that redefining marriage changes the "institution's message," which will "ever after stand for sexual choice, for cutting the link between sex and diapers." Same-sex marriage, she argues, "does more than just fit; it announces that marriage has changed shape."[2] And, as we saw in chapter 1, Andrew Sullivan says that marriage has become "primarily a way in which two adults affirm their emotional commitment to one another."[3]

Some advocates of redefining marriage embrace the goal of weakening the institution of marriage *in these very terms*. "[Former President George W.] Bush is correct," says Victoria Brownworth, "when he states that allowing same-sex couples to marry will weaken the institution of marriage....It most certainly will do so, and that will make marriage a far better concept than it previously has been."[4] Professor Ellen Willis is delighted that "conferring the legitimacy of marriage on homosexual relations will introduce an implicit revolt against the institution into its very heart."[5]

Michelangelo Signorile urges same-sex couples to "demand the right to marry not as a way of adhering to society's moral codes but rather to debunk a myth and radically alter an archaic institution."[6] Same-sex couples should "fight for same-sex marriage and its benefits and then, once granted, redefine the institution of marriage completely, because the most subversive action lesbians and gay men can undertake...is to transform the notion of 'family' entirely."[7]

Government needs to get marriage policy right because it shapes the norms associated with this most fundamental relationship. The Supreme Court's redefinition of marriage abandoned the norm of male-female sexual complementarity as an essential characteristic of marriage. As a logical matter, making that essential characteristic optional makes others—such as monogamy, exclusivity, and permanence—optional as well.[8]

As the law now teaches a falsehood about marriage, it will be harder for people to live out the norms of marriage, because they make no sense, in principle, if marriage is merely a matter of intense emotional feeling. No reason of principle requires an emotional union to be permanent or even limited to two persons, much less sexually exclusive. There is no reason it must be oriented to family life and shaped by its demands. A couple might choose to live out these norms for their own reasons, but there is no reason of principle to demand that they do so. Legally enshrining a radical consent-based view of marriage will undermine the norms whose link to the common good is the basis for state recognition of marriage in the first place. As society weakens the rational foundation for the norms of marriage, fewer people will observe them, and fewer people, therefore, will reap the benefits of the marriage institution. This will affect not only same-sex households raising children but all marriages and all children.

The state, then, cannot achieve the purpose that is the only reason for its recognition of marriage—the responsible procreation and care of children—if it obscures *what marriage is*. And yet weakening marital norms and severing the connection of marriage to responsible procreation are the admitted goals of many prominent advocates of redefining marriage.

The Norm of Monogamy

Professor Judith Stacey of New York University has expressed hope that redefining marriage will give marriage "varied, creative, and adaptive contours," leading some to "question the dyadic limitations of Western marriage and seek...small group marriages."[9] In their statement "Beyond Same-Sex Marriage," more than three hundred "LGBT and allied" scholars and advocates call for legally recognizing sexual relationships involving more than two partners.[10]

Professor Elizabeth Brake of Arizona State University thinks that justice requires using legal recognition to "denormalize[] heterosexual monogamy as a way of life" and "rectif[y] past discrimination against homosexuals, bisexuals, polygamists, and care networks." She supports "minimal marriage," in which "individuals can have legal marital relationships with more than one person, reciprocally or asymmetrically, themselves determining the sex and number of parties, the type of relationship involved, and which rights and responsibilities to exchange with each."[11]

In 2009, *Newsweek* reported that the United States already had over five hundred thousand polyamorous households, concluding that perhaps the practice is more natural than we think: a response to the challenges of monogamous relationships, whose short-comings…are clear. Everyone in a relationship wrestles at some point with an eternal question: can one person really satisfy every need? Polyamorists think the answer is obvi-ous—and that it's only a matter of time before the monoga-mous world sees there's more than one way to live and love.[12]

Now that the court has eliminated sexual complementarity as an essen-tial characteristic of marriage, no principle limits civil marriage to monogamous couples. And in fact the legal challenges to monogamy have already begun. A federal judge in Utah has allowed a legal challenge to anti-bigamy laws.[13] A bill that would allow a child to have three legal parents passed both houses of the California state legislature in 2012 before it was vetoed by the governor, who claimed he wanted "to take more time to consider all of the implications of this change."[14] The impe-tus for the bill was a lesbian same-sex relationship in which one partner was impregnated by a man. The child possessed a biological mother and father, but the law recognized the biological mother and her same-sex spouse, a "presumed mother," as the child's parents.[15]

Justice Samuel Alito voiced concerns about the norm of monogamy during oral arguments in *Obergefell*. If "equality" requires redefining marriage to include same-sex couples, what else does "equality" require? If the fundamental right to marry is simply about consenting adult romance and caregiving, what limits could the state ever place on it? Justice Alito posed the hypothetical of "a group consisting of two men and two women apply[ing] for a marriage license" and asked, "Would there be any ground for denying them a license?" Pursuing this line of thought further, he asked about other types of couples. How about siblings?

They've lived together for twenty-five years. Their financial relationship is the same as the same-sex couple. They share household expenses and household chores in the same way.

They care for each other in the same way. Is there any reason why the law should treat the two groups differently?

It was a good question, and one that the lawyers to whom it was directed could not answer. Nor could the court. As we'll see in the next chapter, Chief Justice Roberts points out that every argument the court made to redefine marriage to include same-sex couples could be used to redefine it to include multi-person relationships: "Although the majority randomly inserts the adjective 'two' in various places, it offers no reason at all why the two-person element of the core definition of marriage may be preserved while the man-woman element may not." Roberts continues: "It is striking how much of the majority's reasoning would apply with equal force to the claim of a fundamental right to plural marriage." Not once did the court explain why marriage was limited to twosomes once they got rid of male-female complementarity.

The same week as oral arguments, the London *Telegraph* reported that the British "Green Party is 'open' to the idea of three-person marriages."[16] Indeed, a party leader said "she was 'open to further conversation and consultation' about the prospect of the state recognising polyamorous relationships." The issue came up precisely because a constituent had asked about "marriage equality" for threesomes:

> At present those in a "trio" (a three-way relationship) are denied marriage equality, and as a result face a considerable amount of legal discrimination.
>
> As someone living with his two boyfriends in a stable long-term relationship, I would like to know what your stance is on polyamory rights. Is there room for Green support on group civil partnerships or marriages?

Will there be room for such support in America's political parties? In the month leading up to the *Obergefell* ruling, the *Emory Law Journal* published a symposium exploring the constitutional right to polygamy.[17] And in the spring of 2015, the Cambridge University Press published *In Defense of Plural Marriage*,[18] promising that the author, a political scientist in California, shows "how the constitutional arguments that support the option of plural marriage are stronger than those against."[19] The day that the Supreme Court redefined marriage everywhere, *Politico* magazine ran an essay titled: "It's Time to Legalize Polygamy: Why Group Marriage Is the Next Horizon of Social Liberalism."[20] These are mainstream publications.

But if you suspect that all this talk about polygamy and polyamory is just conservative scaremongering, consider that the advocates of same-sex marriage have been enthusiastically exploring new family forms. The liberal online magazine Salon in August 2013 posted a woman's account of her shared life with a husband, boyfriend, and daughter under the headline "My Two Husbands." The subhead: "Everyone wants to know how my polyamorous family works. You'd be surprised how normal we really are."[21]

These adventurers have even coined a new word—"throuple"—to denote one of the new domestic arrangements. *New York* magazine profiled one such group:

> Their throuplehood is more or less a permanent domestic arrangement. The three men work together, raise dogs together, sleep together, miss one another, collect art together, travel together, bring each other glasses of water, and, in general, exemplify a modern, adult relationship. Except that there are three of them.[22]

Are those inclined to such relationships being treated unjustly when their consensual romantic bonds go unrecognized? Are their children unconscionably "stigmatized"? We have just witnessed a successful lawsuit demanding "marriage equality" for same-sex couples. But on what basis could the court deny marriage equality to same-sex throuples? Or mixed-sex quartets? Monogamy's privileged place in Western law and culture, after all, was based on the belief that the one man and the one woman who unite in the comprehensive act that produces a child should form a stable family. But if the male-female nature of marriage is utterly arbitrary, what's so special about the number two? What is the principled reason for denying "marriage equality" to threes and fours and more?

The Norm of Exclusivity

The journalist Andrew Sullivan, who has extolled the "spirituality" of "anonymous sex," also thinks that the "openness" of same-sex unions could enhance the bonds of husbands and wives:

> Same-sex unions often incorporate the virtues of friendship more effectively than traditional marriages; and at times, among gay male relationships, the openness of the contract makes it more likely to survive than many heterosexual bonds.... [T]here is more likely to be greater understanding of the need for extramarital outlets between two men than between a man and a woman.... [S]omething of the gay relationship's necessary honesty, its flexibility, and its equality could undoubtedly help strengthen and inform many heterosexual bonds.[23]

"Openness" and "flexibility" are Sullivan's euphemisms for sexual infidelity. The *New York Times* recently reported on a study finding that exclusivity was not the norm among gay partners: "'With straight people, it's called affairs or cheating,' said Colleen Hoff, the study's principal investigator, 'but with gay people it does not have such negative connotations.'"[24]

A writer in the *Advocate* candidly admits where the logic of redefining marriage to include same-sex relationships leads: "We often protest when homophobes insist that same sex marriage will change marriage for straight people too. But in some ways, they're right."[25] The article continues:

> Anti-equality right-wingers have long insisted that allowing gays to marry will destroy the sanctity of "traditional

marriage," and, of course, the logical, liberal party-line response has long been "No, it won't." But what if—for once—the sanctimonious crazies are right? Could the gay male tradition of open relationships actually alter marriage as we know it? And would that be such a bad thing?[26]

A 2011 *New York Times Magazine* profile of Dan Savage, headlined "Married, with Infidelities," introduced Americans to the term "monogamish," referring to relationships in which the partners allow sexual infidelity provided they are honest about it.[27] The article explained, "Savage says a more flexible attitude within marriage may be just what the straight community needs." After all, sexual exclusivity "gives people unrealistic expectations of themselves and their partners." Savage seems inclined to keep monogamy, but he wants to get rid of the requirement of sexual exclusivity, which he finds outdated and inhumane. No one can have all his sexual needs fulfilled by one person for the rest of his life. This is what's wrong with marriage. Spouses who discuss their sexual relationships openly and honestly, says Savage, with no coercion and no deceit, should be free to have a sexually open relationship.

Indeed, a monogamish relationship may actually enhance the emotional bond of spouses. One of the reasons that spouses get divorced, Savage argues, is that their sexual needs are not being fulfilled inside of marriage. Because Americans have this outdated and unrealistic expectation of sexual exclusivity, when the other spouse finds out about an affair his or her heart is broken. Marriage would work much better, Savage says, if spouses could focus their marriage on their romantic caregiving relationship while being free to fulfill sexual needs outside of it. If marriage is really just about deep romantic feeling and personal fulfillment, it's hard to fault his logic.

The Norm of Permanence

The activists who are questioning the norms of monogamy and exclusivity don't have much use for permanence either. Going far beyond no-fault divorce, which simply weakened this norm, they would eliminate it all together. And they've come up with a name for the new arrangement—*wedlease*—which Paul Rampell introduced in an August 2013 op-ed in the *Washington Post*.[28] Why, he wondered, should marriage be permanent when so little else in life is? Why not have temporary marriage licenses, as with other contracts? "Why don't we borrow from real estate and create a marital lease?" Rampell proposed. Just as you can lease a house, you should be able to lease a spouse. "Instead of wedlock, a 'wedlease.'" He continues:

> Here's how a marital lease could work: Two people commit themselves to marriage for a period of years—one year, five years, 10 years, whatever term suits them. The marital lease could be renewed at the end of the term however many times a couple likes.... The messiness of divorce is avoided and the end can be as simple as vacating a rental unit.

Apparently, the expectation of a permanent commitment in marriage is unrealistic and inhumane. The reason that divorce causes so much heartbreak and disruption is that spouses have unrealistically expected to live with and love one other person for the rest of their lives. The trouble starts when this proves impossible. But if they only signed up for a "wedlease" in the first place, they would avoid the trauma of shattered expectations. Their five- or ten-year "wedlease" could be renewed if they wished, but if it weren't going well, the sunset clause would bring the relationship to a peaceful end.

What's in a Name?

The state is interested in marriage and marital norms because they protect children, strengthen civil society, and make limited government possible. Good marriage laws embody and promote a true vision of marriage, which makes sense of those norms as a coherent whole. There is nothing magical about the word "marriage." Applying the title to a relationship that is not in fact a marriage will not produce adherence to marital norms.

Whatever you think about the morality of "throuples," "monoga-mish" relationships, and "wedleases," the social costs of sexually open marriages, multi-partner marriages, and intentionally temporary mar-riages will be high. And yet the radical change represented by each of these new words follows logically once we abandon the notion that marriage requires a man and a woman. If marriage is just about consent-ing adult romance, then consenting adults will have it on whatever terms they like. Love equals love, after all.

The evidence is simply overwhelming that the marital norms of monogamy, sexual exclusivity, and permanence make a difference for society—and those norms are based on sexual complementarity. If a man does not commit to a woman in a permanent and exclusive relationship, the likelihood of his begetting fatherless children and leaving fragmented families in his wake increases. The more sexual partners a man has and the shorter those relationships are, the more likely he is to have children with multiple women to whom he is not committed. His attention and resources thus divided, the predictable consequences unfold for the moth-ers, the children, and society.

Government promotes marriage to make men and women respon-sible to each other and to any children they might have. The marital norms of monogamy and sexual exclusivity serve the same purpose, because they encourage childbearing within a context that makes it most likely that children will be raised by their mother and father. These norms also encourage shared responsibility and commitment between spouses, ensure that children receive sufficient attention from both their mothers and their fathers, and exclude sexual and kinship jealousy from the family. The norm of permanence ensures that chil-dren will at least be cared for by their mother and father until they reach maturity. It also promotes interaction across the generations as elderly parents are cared for by their adult children and as grandparents help to care for their grandchildren without the complications of frag-mented stepfamilies.

Someone might object that it hardly matters if a small percentage of marriages are open, group, or temporary. The same argument was made during the no-fault divorce debate. No-fault divorce was for the relatively small number of people suffering in unhappy marriages and would be irrelevant for everyone else. But the change in the law changed everyone's expectations of marital permanence. The breakdown of the marriage culture that followed made it possible in our generation to consider removing sexual complementarity from the legal definition of marriage. And that redefinition may lead to further redefinition.

Pretending as a matter of law that men and women are interchangeable, that "monogamish" relationships work just as well as monogamous relationships, that "throuples" are the same as couples, and that "wedlease" is preferable to wedlock will only lead to more broken homes, more broken hearts, and more intrusive government. Americans should reject such revisionism and work to restore the essentials that make marriage so important for societal welfare: sexual complementarity, monogamy, exclusivity, and permanence.

Putting Unborn Children at Risk

Redefining marriage will also put more unborn children at risk. The best protectors of unborn children are a strong marriage culture and people who take the virtue of chastity seriously. But the new consent-based view of marriage reduces marriage to a mere contract. Redefining marriage will also make a culture of chastity harder to foster. Without a culture of chastity, we will never have a pro-life culture.

Indeed, both the pro-choice movement and the movement to redefine marriage reduce human community to contract and consent and limit our obligations to other human beings to those we have freely chosen. Consider their slogans: "My body, my choice." "I consented to sex, not to having a baby!" "Love makes a marriage." "Marriage should last as long as the love lasts." They all reflect the belief that consenting adults should do whatever they want to do, a belief that puts adult desire before the needs of children. And weakening marriage will lead to a culture with more nonmarital sex, thus more nonmarital pregnancy, and sadly more abortion.

Redefining marriage will also increase the use of assisted reproductive technologies. The movement to redefine marriage insists that there are "no differences" between the marital union of husband and wife and the union of two people of the same sex, yet a same-sex couple cannot conceive a child naturally. To achieve full "marriage equality," then, it will be necessary to turn to modern technology. Same-sex couples must use assisted reproductive technologies—with the assistance of sperm donors, egg donors, surrogate wombs, etc.—so they can "have children of their own." In fact, scientists hope eventually to eliminate the need for such outside help. In March 2015, *Time* magazine ran a story titled "Get Ready for Embryos from Two Men or Two Women," trumpeting the possibility that stem cells could create eggs from men and sperm from women.[29] And, of course, there are efforts to create artificial wombs.

The misuse of technology should concern us. The more children that are conceived for same-sex couples through assisted reproductive technology, the more children that will be conceived *explicitly and intentionally* outside of a relationship with both their mother and father. A just society makes sacrifices to ensure that children are known and loved by their own mother and father, while doing what it can to help children denied that blessing by misfortune. But misusing technology turns those priorities upside down, *deliberately* increasing the number of children who grow up fatherless or motherless and subordinating children's needs to adult desires.

The pro-life concern here, of course, is that the assisted reproduction industry destroys massive numbers of human embryos. Anyone familiar with these processes knows that they produce many more embryos than will ever be implanted in a womb, and of the embryos implanted, only a few will survive.

Redefining marriage redefines parenthood. Adults must have what they want, including children. If those children cannot be conceived through a natural act of love, they must be manufactured. Far more children will be destroyed than will be born, of course, but we have decided that adult desires come first.

Giving people the right to get what they want, even a baby, sounds like an expansion of freedom. Activities that were once prohibited are now acceptable, protected, and even privileged. The Supreme Court ensured the legalization of contraception and abortion, for example. And now the government mandates that other people promote them. Obamacare requires employers to provide free contraception and abortifacients, and the State of California and the District of Columbia are attempting to require insurance coverage of elective surgical abortion.[30]

From the contraception mandate, we are moving on to a conception mandate, with California leading the way. All healthcare plans in that state must cover reproductive technologies for all people, married or unmarried, gay, lesbian, or straight.[31] "Reproductive medicine is for everybody's benefit," asserts the author of that law. "To restrict fertility coverage solely to heterosexual married couples violates California's non-discrimination laws. I wrote this bill to correct that."[32] The law makes no allowance for a healthcare plan sponsor's conscientious beliefs about life, marriage, or parenting.

Children should be conceived within a relationship that will provide them with the love and care of the man and woman who gave them life. The unborn child has a right to life, yes, and also deserves a mother and father, and where possible the mother and father who brought the child into being. Because of human frailty, it isn't always possible for a child to be raised in his natural family, but that should be the ideal to which our policy aspires. And we should never *intentionally* deprive a child of such an upbringing. And yet redefining marriage does precisely that.

Threatening Religious Liberty

With marriage now redefined, we can expect to see the marginalization of those with traditional views and the erosion of religious liberty. The law and culture will seek to eradicate such views through economic, social, and legal pressure. With marriage redefined, believing what virtually every human society once believed about marriage will increasingly be deemed a malicious prejudice to be driven to the margins of culture. The consequences for religious believers are becoming apparent.

Some of the justices pointed to this threat during the oral arguments before the Supreme Court in *Obergefell*. When pressed by Justice Alito, the solicitor general, Donald Verrilli, admitted that religious schools that affirm marriage as the union of a man and a woman might lose their nonprofit tax status if marriage were redefined: "It's certainly going to be an issue. I don't deny that. I don't deny that, Justice Alito. It is—it is going to be an issue."

Justice Antonin Scalia asked how a constitutional right to same-sex marriage might affect religious liberties. When counsel replied that religious liberties had not been constricted in the states that have already redefined marriage through legislation, Justice Scalia objected: "They are laws. They are not constitutional requirements. That was the whole point of my question. If you let the states do it, you can make an exception.... You can't do that once it is a constitutional proscription." This concern is repeated in all four of the dissenting opinions, and we will further explore it in the next chapter.

But here's what we can expect. The administrative state may require those who contract with the government, receive governmental money, or work directly for the state to embrace and promote same-sex marriage even if doing so violates their religious beliefs. Nondiscrimination laws may make even private actors with no legal or financial ties to the government—including businesses and religious organizations—liable to civil suits for refusing to treat same-sex relationships as marriages. Finally, private actors in a culture that is now hostile to traditional views of marriage may discipline, fire, or deny professional certification to those who express support for traditional marriage.[33] The Becket Fund for Religious Liberty reports that "over 350 separate state anti-discrimination provisions would likely be triggered by recognition of same-sex marriage."[34]

The attack on religious liberty has in fact already begun, as I describe in more detail in chapter 4. It is important to understand the conceptual framework for this attack.

In 2013 a bill was proposed in the Illinois legislature to redefine marriage while supposedly protecting religious liberty. The Catholic bishop of Springfield explained why the protections of the Religious Freedom and Marriage Fairness Act were meaningless:

> [The bill] would not stop the state from obligating the Knights of Columbus to make their halls available for same-sex "weddings." It would not stop the state from requiring Catholic grade schools to hire teachers who are legally "married" to someone of the same sex. This bill would not protect Catholic hospitals, charities, or colleges, which exclude those so "married" from senior leadership positions.... This "religious freedom" law does nothing at all to protect the consciences of people in business, or who work for the government. We saw the harmful consequences of deceptive titles all too painfully last year when the so-called "Religious Freedom Protection and Civil Union Act" forced Catholic Charities out of foster care and adoption services in Illinois.[35]

In fact, the lack of religious liberty protection seems to be a feature of such bills:

> There is no possible way—none whatsoever—for those who believe that marriage is exclusively the union of husband and wife to avoid legal penalties and harsh discriminatory treatment if the bill becomes law. Why should we expect it [to] be otherwise? After all, we would be people who, according to the thinking behind the bill, hold onto an "unfair" view of marriage. The state would have equated our view with bigotry—

which it uses the law to marginalize in every way short of criminal punishment.[36]

Georgetown University law professor Chai Feldblum, a member of the U.S. Equal Employment Opportunity Commission, argues that "equality" in matters sexual must trump religious liberty:

> [F]or all my sympathy for the evangelical Christian couple who may wish to run a bed and breakfast from which they can exclude unmarried, straight couples and all gay couples, this is a point where I believe the "zero-sum" nature of the game inevitably comes into play. And, in making that decision in this zero-sum game, I am convinced society should come down on the side of protecting the liberty of LGBT people.[37]

Indeed, for many supporters of redefining marriage, such infringements on religious liberty are not flaws but virtues of the movement.

In 2013 the Supreme Court struck down the federal Defense of Marriage Act in an opinion, written by Justice Kennedy, notable for its intemperate rhetoric. Justice Scalia, in dissent, warned of the dangers lurking in the majority opinion:

> To defend traditional marriage is not to condemn, demean, or humiliate those who would prefer other arrangements.... To hurl such accusations so casually demeans this institution. In the majority's judgment, any resistance to its holding is beyond the pale of reasoned disagreement.... All that, simply for supporting an Act that did no more than codify an aspect of marriage that had been unquestioned in our society for most of its existence—indeed, had been unquestioned in virtually all societies for virtually all of human history. It is one thing for a society to elect change; it is another for a court of law to impose change by adjudging

those who oppose it *hostes humani generis*, enemies of the human race.[38]

Those dangers have been amplified by the court in *Obergefell*. To that we now turn.

THREE

JUDICIAL TYRANNY

The Supreme Court's ruling in *Obergefell v. Hodges* is a serious setback for Americans who believe in the Constitution, the rule of law, self-government, and marriage as the union of husband and wife. The Supreme Court has not simply decided a case incorrectly—it has damaged the common good and harmed our republic.

The ruling is as clear an example of judicial usurpation as we've had in a generation. Nothing in the Constitution justifies the redefinition of marriage by judges. In imposing on the American people its judgment about a policy matter that the Constitution leaves to citizens and their elected representatives, the court has inflicted serious damage on the institution of marriage and the Constitution.

In the majority opinion, written by Justice Anthony Kennedy, the court declares: "The limitation of marriage to opposite-sex couples may long have seemed natural and just, but its inconsistency with the central meaning of the fundamental right to marry is now manifest."

Manifest to five unelected and unaccountable judges, that is. Not to the American citizens who, in state after state, voted to uphold the true definition of marriage, and certainly not to the Americans who ratified the Fourteenth Amendment, on which the court relies. The majority of the court has simply replaced the people's opinion about what marriage is with its own—without any constitutional basis whatsoever.

Professor Robert P. George of Princeton University proposes that we respond to the court's abuses by standing up for the truth:

> We must, above all, tell the truth: *Obergefell v. Hodges* is an illegitimate decision. What Stanford Law School Dean John Ely said of *Roe v. Wade* applies with equal force to *Obergefell*: "It is not constitutional law and gives almost no sense of an obligation to try to be." What Justice Byron White said of *Roe* is also true of *Obergefell*: It is an act of "raw judicial power." The lawlessness of these decisions is evident in the fact that they lack any foundation or warrant in the text, logic, structure, or original understanding of the Constitution. The justices responsible for these rulings, whatever their good intentions, are substituting their own views of morality and sound public policy for those of the people and their elected representatives. They have set themselves up as superlegislators possessing a kind of plenary power to impose their judgments on the nation. What could be more unconstitutional—more anti-constitutional—than that?
>
> The rule of law is not the rule of lawyers—even lawyers who are judges. Supreme Court justices are not infallible, nor are they immune from the all-too-human temptation to unlawfully seize power that has not been granted to them. Decisions such as *Dred Scott*, *Roe v. Wade*, and *Obergefell* amply demonstrate that. In thinking about how to respond to *Obergefell*, we must bear in mind that it is not only the institution of marriage that is at stake here—it is also the principle of self-government.[1]

In this chapter, I explain why Professor George is right. First I dissect the argument of the majority opinion striking down conjugal (male-female) marriage laws. Then I turn to the four dissenting opinions, which expose the utter failure of the majority opinion as a work of constitutional law. To conclude, I assess the harms that this act of judicial usurpation is likely to produce.

What the Court Said (and How It Got It Wrong)

The question before the Supreme Court in *Obergefell* was not whether government recognition of same-sex marriages is a good policy but whether anything in the Constitution removes from the people their authority to decide their marriage policy. Yet the court's majority speaks almost exclusively about its "new insights" into marriage and says almost nothing about the Constitution. It could not have done otherwise, because our Constitution is silent on what marriage is. It protects specific fundamental rights and provides the structure of deliberative democracy by which we the people, retaining our authority as full citizens and not subjects of oligarchic rule, decide important questions of public policy, such as the proper understanding of marriage and the structure of laws defining and supporting it.

The court purports to explain why the marriage policy that the United States has followed for all its history is now prohibited by the Constitution. But what it actually does is to *assume* that marriage is an essentially genderless institution and then announce that the Constitution requires states to adopt that same vision of marriage in their laws.

This assumption is all the more remarkable given Justice Kennedy's observation in oral arguments that the definition of marriage as the union of man and woman "has been with us for millennia. And it—it's very difficult for the Court to say, oh, well, we—we know better."[2] Suggesting that he was reluctant to redefine marriage from the bench, he noted that same-sex marriage had been around for only ten years. And he added, "Ten years is—I don't even know how to count the decimals when we talk about millennia."

Even the liberal Justice Stephen Breyer acknowledged that marriage understood as the union of man and woman "has been the law everywhere for thousands of years among people who were not discriminating even against gay people, and suddenly you want nine people outside the ballot box to require states that don't want to do it to change…what marriage is." He asked the solicitor general, "Why cannot those states at least wait and see whether in fact doing so in the other states is or is not harmful to marriage?" And yet he joined Justice Kennedy's majority opinion redefining marriage everywhere.

The incoherence of the majority opinion is evident in its first paragraph:

> The Constitution promises liberty to all within its reach, a liberty that includes certain specific rights that allow persons, within a lawful realm, to define and express their identity. The petitioners in these cases seek to find that liberty by marrying someone of the same sex and having their marriages deemed lawful on the same terms and conditions as marriages between persons of the opposite sex.[3]

As Justice Clarence Thomas makes clear in his dissenting opinion, though, constitutional protections of liberty can hardly require government *recognition*. The liberty that the Constitution protects is a freedom *from* government interference. Gays and lesbians enjoyed full liberty "to define and express their identity" and to exercise their "liberty by marrying someone of the same sex" in the house of worship or wedding hall of their choice. Yet Justice Kennedy writes as if governmental recognition of any consensual relationship is a guaranteed form of *liberty*.

What support does he offer for such a conclusion? He starts with a paean to "the transcendent importance of marriage": The "lifelong union of a man and a woman always has promised nobility and dignity to all persons," and the "centrality of marriage to the human condition makes it unsurprising that the institution has existed for millennia and across civilizations." Citing theological, philosophical, literary, and artistic treatments of marriage, he admits that it "is fair and necessary to say these references were based on the understanding that marriage is a union between two persons of the opposite sex." Indeed, he points out that for the states defending their marriage laws, marriage "is by its nature a gender-differentiated union of man and woman. This view long has been held—and continues to be held—in good faith by reasonable and sincere people here and throughout the world."

So why, exactly, does the U.S. Constitution require a redefinition of marriage? Justice Kennedy turns to the Due Process Clause of the Fourteenth Amendment, which says that no state shall "deprive any person of life, liberty, or property, without due process of law." And why does that clause require states to recognize same-sex relationships as marriages? Because the fundamental liberties that the Due Process Clause protects extend to "certain personal choices central to individual dignity and autonomy, including intimate choices that define personal identity and beliefs." And these choices, Justice Kennedy asserts, now require not merely the absence of government coercion but affirmative recognition by the government. Who decides which "intimate choices" require such recognition and when and how much? The Supreme Court, of course.

Here is the central thesis of Justice Kennedy's argument:

> The nature of injustice is that we may not always see it in our own times. The generations that wrote and ratified the Bill of Rights and the Fourteenth Amendment did not presume to know the extent of freedom in all of its dimensions, and so they entrusted to future generations a charter protecting the right of all persons to enjoy liberty as we learn its meaning. When new insight reveals discord between the Constitution's central protections and a received legal stricture, a claim to liberty must be addressed.

Yes, such claims must be addressed, and yes, one generation may detect an injustice to which an earlier generation was blind. But when a policy considered unjust by some nonetheless has *some* reasonable basis, and when the Constitution is silent about this particular policy, judges should not strike down the policy merely because of their own "new insights." For they, too, could be wrong. Far from rectifying an injustice, they may be committing one. And in purporting to vindicate a newly discovered constitutional right, they may be violating the Constitution by usurping the authority of the people and their elected representatives in Congress and the state legislatures. In the case of marriage, the Constitution empowers the people of future generations to make the necessary judgment calls through the political process. In *Obergefell*, the court usurped that role by imposing a decision in a contest between two reasonable policy views on which the Constitution is silent.

Justice Kennedy acknowledges that all of the Supreme Court's previous decisions about the right to marry "presumed a relationship involving opposite-sex partners." But now, he writes, the court sees that that presumption was wrong, and the majority opinion identifies four principles that "demonstrate that the reasons marriage is fundamental under the Constitution apply with equal force to same-sex couples." Let us examine those four principles.

First, "the right to personal choice regarding marriage is inherent in the concept of individual autonomy." This is because "two persons together can find other freedoms, such as expression, intimacy, and spirituality. This is true for all persons, whatever their sexual orientation." We might ask why this isn't also true for all persons, whatever their *number*. Justice Kennedy does not explain why two but not three or four "persons together can find other freedoms." We might also wonder how "autonomy" gives rise to a right to government recognition.

Second, "the right to marry is fundamental because it supports a two-person union unlike any other in its importance to the committed individuals." (Again, why just two?) Here Justice Kennedy is describing, nearly verbatim, the view of marriage as an intense emotional union that I discussed in chapter 1. "Marriage," he writes, "responds to the universal fear that a lonely person might call out only to find no one there. It offers the hope of companionship and understanding and assurance that while both still live there will be someone to care for the other." It's all about consenting adult romance and care. Marriage just is, on Justice Kennedy's account, legally recognized companionship.

This principle—that marriage is the only relationship that ultimately matters—is particularly harmful because it implies that other relationships are necessarily less important. It would condemn the unmarried—whatever their sexual orientation—"to live in loneliness." I return to this point in chapter 8, when I explore how society can help meet the needs for community of all the unmarried, especially those with same-sex attractions. But the idea that they are condemned to live in loneliness unless marriage is redefined is outrageous.

Justice Kennedy's third principle is that marriage "safeguards children and families and thus draws meaning from related rights of childrearing, procreation, and education." Same-sex couples, then, have "rights of childrearing, procreation, and education." These rights entail a right to marriage since, as a prior decision held, "the right to 'marry, establish a home and bring up children' is a central part of the liberty protected by the Due Process Clause."[4] Here Justice Kennedy discusses children reared by same-sex couples without once acknowledging that some might want a mother and a father. (In chapter 7 I offer compelling evidence for this.) He asserts an adult's right to have children but says nothing about a child's right to a mother and a father.

"Fourth and finally, this Court's cases and the Nation's traditions make clear that marriage is a keystone of our social order." Well, yes, marriage—a union of man and woman, husband and wife, father and mother—is a keystone of our social order *precisely because* of its procreative character, which same-sex couples lack. So this is actually a point *against* Justice Kennedy's view. He asserts—without argument—that "[t]here is no difference between same- and opposite-sex couples with respect to this principle." As he writes, "[s]ame-sex couples, too, may aspire to the transcendent purposes of marriage and seek fulfillment in its highest meaning." Unless, of course, those purposes and that meaning have something to do with uniting as one flesh—comprehensively—in the sort of bond apt for generating new human beings and binding them to their mothers and fathers. Remarkably, Justice Kennedy not once seriously engages with *that* argument.

The opinion concludes, almost as an afterthought, that the right to government recognition of same-sex marriages is derived not only from the Fourteenth Amendment's Due Process Clause but from its Equal Protection Clause as well. The reasoning here is even cloudier. "The Due Process Clause and the Equal Protection Clause are connected in a profound way," writes Justice Kennedy, and in "any particular case one Clause may be thought to capture the essence of the right in a more accurate and comprehensive way, even as the two Clauses may converge in the identification and definition of the right." He concludes that "[t]his interrelation of the two principles furthers our understanding of what freedom is and must become. The Court's cases touching upon the right to marry reflect this dynamic." This passage, devoid of any legal argument, is as clear an instance of the court's legislating from the bench as you will find.

Apparently to buttress his opinion, Justice Kennedy cites ways in which the social practice and legal regulation of marriage have changed over time. He mentions the doctrine of coverture, which treated "a married man and woman...as a single, male-dominated legal entity," bans on interracial marriage, and legal barriers to marriage for persons who owed child support or were in prison. What he fails to acknowledge is that none of these practices or regulations redefined *what marriage is*—a comprehensive union of sexually complementary spouses. The court's majority never addresses arguments of the sort I presented in the first two chapters of this book, even though many amici curiae presented such arguments and some dissenting justices deployed them.[5]

The only argument of the states that Justice Kennedy addresses—quite briefly—is that redefining marriage will change the institution for everyone in ways that could lead to a decrease in the marriage rate (for evidence, see chapter 7). He first misstates this argument ("an opposite-sex couple [might] choose not to marry simply because same-sex couples may do so") and then dismisses it as resting on a "counterintuitive view of opposite-sex couple's decisionmaking [*sic*] processes regarding marriage and parenthood."

The *actual* argument (as opposed to the straw man that Justice Kennedy sets up) is that legally redefining marriage changes its social meaning for everyone—a change that will shape people's behavior over time. The recognition of same-sex marriage, the court says, involves "only the rights of two consenting adults whose marriages would pose no risk of harm to themselves or third parties." But that is *precisely* what the debate is all about—whether redefining marriage causes harm—and in chapter 2, I offered abundant evidence of the likely harm. Justice Kennedy merely assumes his answer to the question and declares victory, offering no evidence or argument.

The Dissents

The court's most basic error is its failure to interpret and apply the Constitution to the case at hand. It simply offers amateur philosophizing about what marriage should be and what freedom "must become." Chief Justice John Roberts opens his dissenting opinion by noting that the Supreme Court "is not a legislature. Whether same-sex marriage is a good idea should be of no concern to us. Under the Constitution, judges have power to say what the law is, not what it should be." As Chief Justice Roberts notes later in his opinion, "There is, after all, no 'Companionship and Understanding' or 'Nobility and Dignity' Clause in the Constitution."

How did the court get it so wrong? The chief justice explains:

> Although the policy arguments for extending marriage to same-sex couples may be compelling, the legal arguments for requiring such an extension are not. The fundamental right to marry does not include a right to make a State change its definition of marriage. And a State's decision to maintain the meaning of marriage that has persisted in every culture throughout human history can hardly be called irrational. In

short, our Constitution does not enact any one theory of marriage. The people of a State are free to expand marriage to include same-sex couples, or to retain the historic definition.

He continues, "The majority's decision is an act of will, not legal judgment. The right it announces has no basis in the Constitution or this Court's precedent." Assuming the powers of a legislature, the majority has acted "on its desire to remake society according to its own 'new insight' into the 'nature of injustice.'" Chief Justice Roberts criticizes the majority for its lack of judicial humility:

> [T]he Court invalidates the marriage laws of more than half the States and orders the transformation of a social institution that has formed the basis of human society for millennia, for the Kalahari Bushmen and the Han Chinese, the Carthaginians and the Aztecs. Just who do we think we are?

Justice Antonin Scalia makes a similar point:

> Hubris is sometimes defined as o'erweening pride; and pride, we know, goeth before a fall. The Judiciary is the "least dangerous" of the federal branches because it has "neither Force nor Will, but merely judgment; and must ultimately depend upon the aid of the executive arm" and the States, "even for the efficacy of its judgments." With each decision of ours that takes from the People a question properly left to them—with each decision that is unabashedly based not on law, but on the "reasoned judgment" of a bare majority of this Court—we move one step closer to being reminded of our impotence.

Chief Justice Roberts also faults the majority for its sloppy use of history. Justice Kennedy's opinion, as we have seen, recites a list of marriage laws that have changed with the times. These changes

did not, however, work any transformation in the core structure of marriage as the union between a man and a woman.
If you had asked a person on the street how marriage was
defined, no one would ever have said, "Marriage is the union
of a man and a woman, where the woman is subject to coverture." The majority may be right that the "history of marriage is one of both continuity and change," but the core
meaning of marriage has endured.

The chief justice continues:

> In *Loving*, the Court held that racial restrictions on the right
> to marry lacked a compelling justification. In *Zablocki*,
> restrictions based on child support debts did not suffice. In
> *Turner*, restrictions based on status as a prisoner were deemed
> impermissible.
>
> None of the laws at issue in those cases purported to change
> the core definition of marriage as the union of a man and a
> woman. The laws challenged in *Zablocki* and *Turner* did not
> define marriage as "the union of a man and a woman, *where
> neither party owes child support or is in prison.*" Nor did the
> interracial marriage ban at issue in *Loving* define marriage as
> "the union of a man and a woman *of the same race.*" ...Remov-
> ing racial barriers to marriage therefore did not change what a
> marriage was any more than integrating schools changed what
> a school was. As the majority admits, the institution of "mar-
> riage" discussed in every one of these cases "presumed a rela-
> tionship involving opposite-sex partners."

The problem with the analogy to interracial marriage is that it
assumes what is in dispute: that sex is as irrelevant to marriage as race
is. It's clear by any reasonable standard—and so, the court was right to
hold—that race has nothing to do with marriage. Racist laws kept the

races apart to keep whites at the top. Marriage has everything to do with men and women, husbands and wives, mothers and fathers and their children, and that is why principle-based policy has defined marriage as the union of one man and one woman.

Marriage can and should be color-blind, but it cannot be blind with regard to the two sexes. The color of two persons' skin has nothing to do with whether they can unite in the sort of comprehensive union naturally oriented to family life, in which the lovemaking act is also a life-giving act—the kind of union that demands permanence and exclusivity. Race has nothing to do with whether they can give any children born of their union the love and knowledge of their own mother and father. Race has nothing to do with society's orderly reproduction, which the court's preceding cases recognize as central to the fundamental right to marry. The sexual difference between a man and a woman, however, is central to each of these concerns. Men and women, regardless of their race, can unite in marriage, and children, regardless of their race, need their mom and dad. To acknowledge such facts requires an understanding of what most fundamentally makes a marriage.

Chief Justice Roberts can therefore conclude:

> In short, the "right to marry" cases stand for the important but limited proposition that particular restrictions on access to marriage *as traditionally defined* violate due process. These precedents say nothing at all about a right to make a State change its definition of marriage, which is the right petitioners actually seek here.

Justice Kennedy's four-principles-of-due-process jurisprudence, then, is nonsense:

> Stripped of its shiny rhetorical gloss, the majority's argument is that the Due Process Clause gives same-sex couples a fundamental right to marry because it will be good for them and for society. If I were a legislator, I would certainly consider

that view as a matter of social policy. But as a judge, I find the majority's position indefensible as a matter of constitutional law.

Indeed, this freewheeling due process jurisprudence, the chief justice points out, was first deployed by the Supreme Court in *Dred Scott v. Sandford*, in which "the Court invalidated the Missouri Compromise on the ground that legislation restricting the institution of slavery violated the implied rights of slaveholders. The Court relied on its own conception of liberty and property in doing so." Fifty years later the court again gave free rein to its own conception of liberty and property in *Lochner v. New York*, in which it "struck down a New York law setting maximum hours for bakery employees, because there was 'in our judgment, no reasonable foundation for holding this to be necessary or appropriate as a health law.'" Chief Justice Roberts quotes Justice Oliver Wendell Holmes Jr.'s dissent: "'The Fourteenth Amendment does not enact Mr. Herbert Spencer's Social Statics,' a leading work on the philosophy of Social Darwinism." Nor does the Fourteenth Amendment enact Andrew Sullivan's vision of marriage.

After a few decades of legislating from the bench, Roberts explains, the court eventually

> recognized its error and vowed not to repeat it. "The doctrine that...due process authorizes courts to hold laws unconstitutional when they believe the legislature has acted unwisely," we later explained, "has long since been discarded. We have returned to the original constitutional proposition that courts do not substitute their social and economic beliefs for the judgment of legislative bodies, who are elected to pass laws."

Until *Obergefell*, that is.

As for the supposed "synergy" between the Due Process Clause and the Equal Protection Clause to which the majority appeals, Chief Justice Roberts simply observes that "the majority fails to provide even a single sentence explaining how the Equal Protection Clause supplies independent weight for its position." Think of a student who can't find good support for a claim in a term paper and so adds dozens of tangential references—as if many weak arguments somehow combine to yield a strong one. "In any event," the chief justice writes, "the marriage laws at issue here do not violate the Equal Protection Clause, because"—and here he quotes Justice Sandra Day O'Connor—"distinguishing between opposite-sex and same-sex couples is rationally related to the States' 'legitimate state interest' in 'preserving the traditional institution of marriage.'"

We should also consider the central argument of Justice Thomas's dissent. I cite this because too many self-professed libertarians have come to the conclusion that a commitment to liberty requires judges to redefine marriage. In a persuasive response to this assertion, Justice Thomas argues that "the majority invokes our Constitution in the name of a 'liberty' that the Framers would not have recognized, to the detriment of the liberty they sought to protect."

In "the American legal tradition," he writes, "liberty has long been understood as individual freedom *from* governmental action, not as a right *to* a particular governmental entitlement." And the liberty of people in same-sex relationships wasn't being infringed:

> [T]hey have been able to cohabitate and raise their children in peace. They have been able to hold civil marriage ceremonies in States that recognize same-sex marriages and private religious ceremonies in all States. They have been able to travel freely around the country, making their homes where they please. Far from being incarcerated or physically restrained, petitioners have been left alone to order their lives as they see fit.

Even in states that hadn't redefined marriage, persons were free "to enter same-sex relationships, to engage in intimate behavior, to make vows to their partners in public ceremonies, to engage in religious wedding ceremonies, to hold themselves out as married, or to raise children."

The government was restricting no one's liberty. But some people had a desire *for* government recognition:

> Petitioners claim that as a matter of "liberty," they are entitled to access privileges and benefits that exist solely *because of* the government. They want, for example, to receive the State's *imprimatur* on their marriages—on state issued marriage licenses, death certificates, or other official forms.

This can't be a "liberty" claim. As Justice Thomas argues, "receiving governmental recognition and benefits has nothing to do with any understanding of 'liberty' that the Framers would have recognized."

So nothing in the Fourteenth Amendment—nothing in the Due Process Clause or the Equal Protection Clause—authorized five unelected judges to redefine marriage for the nation. As Justice Scalia puts it: "We have no basis for striking down a practice that is not expressly prohibited by the Fourteenth Amendment's text, and that bears the endorsement of a long tradition of open, widespread, and unchallenged use dating back to the Amendment's ratification." Yet the majority somehow "discovered in the Fourteenth Amendment a 'fundamental right' overlooked by every person alive at the time of ratification, and almost everyone else in the time since."

What the Dissenting Justices Had to Say about the Harms This Ruling Would Cause

Judicial activism is harmful. The *Obergefell* ruling will likely harm the body politic in four distinct ways: it will harm constitutional democratic self-government, it will harm marriage itself, it will harm civil harmony, and it will harm religious liberty.

Harm to Constitutional Democratic Self-Government

The ruling has already harmed constitutional democratic self-government and will continue to do so. In his dissent Justice Scalia says that it is not important to him what marriage policy a state adopts. "It is of overwhelming importance, however, who it is that rules me. Today's decree says that my Ruler, and the Ruler of 320 million Americans coast-to-coast, is a majority of the nine lawyers on the Supreme Court." Constitutional democratic self-government is vitally important; indeed it is our first political right. Scalia continues: "This practice of constitutional revision by an unelected committee of nine, always accompanied (as it is today) by extravagant praise of liberty, robs the People of the most important liberty they asserted in the Declaration of Independence and won in the Revolution of 1776: the freedom to govern themselves."

Of course, democratic self-government isn't unlimited. That's why I've referred to *constitutional* democratic self-government. For we the people placed limits on the authority we delegated to the political branches of government. That's what a constitution is all about. Justice Scalia therefore notes that the "Constitution places some constraints on self-rule—constraints adopted *by the People themselves* when they ratified the Constitution and its Amendments." But apart from the limits we the people placed on ourselves, "those powers 'reserved to the States respectively, or to the people' can be exercised as the States or the People desire." So the question before the court was "whether the Fourteenth Amendment contains a limitation that requires the States to license and recognize marriages between two people of the same sex. Does it remove *that* issue from the political process?" Justice Scalia's response: "Of course not." And that's why this decision involved judicial activism—a harm to self-government.

He concludes, "This is a naked judicial claim to legislative—indeed, *super*-legislative—power; a claim fundamentally at odds with our system of government....A system of government that makes the People subordinate to a committee of nine unelected lawyers does not deserve to be called a democracy [emphasis in original]." Chief Justice Roberts is likewise dismayed by the court's arrogance:

> The role of the Court envisioned by the majority today, however, is anything but humble or restrained. Over and

over, the majority exalts the role of the judiciary in delivering social change. In the majority's telling, it is the courts, not the people, who are responsible for making "new dimensions of freedom...apparent to new generations," for providing "formal discourse" on social issues, and for ensuring "neutral discussions, without scornful or disparaging commentary."

The court's super-legislative power should trouble anyone concerned with *representative* government, because it is not representative of the American people. Justice Scalia notes that the Supreme Court "consists of only nine men and women, all of them successful lawyers who studied at Harvard or Yale Law School." Besides their elite professional training, he observes,

[f]our of the nine are natives of New York City. Eight of them grew up in east- and west-coast States. Only one hails from the vast expanse in-between. Not a single Southwesterner or even, to tell the truth, a genuine Westerner (California does not count). Not a single evangelical Christian (a group that comprises about one quarter of Americans), or even a Protestant of any denomination. The strikingly unrepresentative character of the body voting on today's social upheaval would be irrelevant if they were functioning as *judges*, answering the legal question whether the American people had ever ratified a constitutional provision that was understood to proscribe the traditional definition of marriage. But of course the Justices in today's majority are not voting on that basis; *they say they are not.* And to allow the policy question of same-sex marriage to be considered and resolved by a select, patrician, highly unrepresentative panel of nine is to violate a principle even more fundamental than no taxation without representation: no social transformation without representation.

No social transformation without representation: our constitutional democracy in a nutshell.

Harm to Marriage

The ruling will harm marriage itself. Chief Justice Roberts notes that marriage "arose in the nature of things to meet a vital need: ensuring that children are conceived by a mother and father committed to raising them in the stable conditions of a lifelong relationship." But the court's redefinition of marriage makes it about the romantic desires of consenting adults rather than about the needs of children and their right to a relationship with their mother and father.

Justice Samuel Alito was the most sensitive of the dissenters to *how* the court was presenting marriage. The court's argument, he observes, "is that the fundamental purpose of marriage is to promote the well-being of those who choose to marry. Marriage provides emotional fulfillment and the promise of support in times of need." But there's no reason to think the revisionist view of marriage is the correct one, and there's certainly nothing in the Constitution requiring government to adopt it. Professor Helen Alvaré of George Mason University Law School has compiled the terms the court uses to describe the purpose of marriage:

> [T]he Supreme Court rules...that marriage is about adults' "defin[ing] and express[ing] their identity," adults' desire for "nobility," "fulfillment," "aspirations," "autonomy," "self-definition," avoiding of "loneliness," and desire for "companionship and understanding". The list goes on.[6]

As Justice Alito explains, "This understanding of marriage, which focuses almost entirely on the happiness of persons who choose to marry, is shared by many people today, but it is not the traditional one. For millennia, marriage was inextricably linked to the one thing that only an opposite-sex couple can do: procreate."

But obscuring the truth about marriage has consequences. Summarizing the argument of the states in defense of their historical marriage laws, Justice Alito writes that "States formalize and promote marriage, unlike other fulfilling human relationships, in order to encourage potentially procreative conduct to take place within a lasting unit that has long been thought to provide the best atmosphere for raising children." But as the expectations associated with marriage were weakened, so were the benefits that marriage provides.

> If this traditional understanding of the purpose of marriage does not ring true to all ears today, that is probably because the tie between marriage and procreation has frayed. Today, for instance, more than 40% of all children in this country are born to unmarried women. This development undoubtedly is both a cause and a result of changes in our society's understanding of marriage.

Justice Alito is right. As the sexual revolution began to undermine the family, more bad ideas—and bad laws—led to more breakdown. Now we have entered a new stage of the sexual revolution by completely redefining marriage, formally establishing the lie that mothers and fathers are interchangeable. We have yet to see where this new stage will take us, but the court's exclusion of the marital norm of sexual complementarity raises the question of what other marital norms may be excluded. Chief Justice Roberts wonders "whether States may retain the definition of marriage as a union of two people." He continues:

> Although the majority randomly inserts the adjective "two" in various places, it offers no reason at all why the two-person element of the core definition of marriage may be preserved while the man-woman element may not. Indeed, from the standpoint of history and tradition, a leap from opposite-sex marriage to same-sex marriage is much greater than one from a two-person union to plural unions, which have deep roots

in some cultures around the world. If the majority is willing to take the big leap, it is hard to see how it can say no to the shorter one.

It is striking how much of the majority's reasoning would apply with equal force to the claim of a fundamental right to plural marriage. If "[t]here is dignity in the bond between two men or two women who seek to marry and in their autonomy to make such profound choices," why would there be any less dignity in the bond between three people who, in exercising their autonomy, seek to make the profound choice to marry? If a same-sex couple has the constitutional right to marry because their children would otherwise "suffer the stigma of knowing their families are somehow lesser," why wouldn't the same reasoning apply to a family of three or more persons raising children? If not having the opportunity to marry "serves to disrespect and subordinate" gay and lesbian couples, why wouldn't the same "imposition of this disability," serve to disrespect and subordinate people who find fulfillment in polyamorous relationships?

The *Obergefell* court has no answer.

Harm to Civil Harmony

The ruling will undermine civil harmony. Fundamental policy changes imposed by judicial rulings with no basis in the Constitution are harder for people to accept. Scalia notes that American self-government was working:

> Until the courts put a stop to it, public debate over same-sex marriage displayed American democracy at its best. Individuals on both sides of the issue passionately, but respectfully, attempted to persuade their fellow citizens to accept their views. Americans considered the arguments and put the

question to a vote. The electorates of 11 States, either directly or through their representatives, chose to expand the traditional definition of marriage. Many more decided not to. Win or lose, advocates for both sides continued pressing their cases, secure in the knowledge that an electoral loss can be negated by a later electoral win. That is exactly how our system of government is supposed to work.

But the court, observes Chief Justice Roberts, has now put an end to all of that:

> Supporters of same-sex marriage have achieved considerable success persuading their fellow citizens—through the democratic process—to adopt their view. That ends today. Five lawyers have closed the debate and enacted their own vision of marriage as a matter of constitutional law. Stealing this issue from the people will for many cast a cloud over same-sex marriage, making a dramatic social change that much more difficult to accept.

The court, writes the chief justice, "seizes for itself a question the Constitution leaves to the people, at a time when the people are engaged in a vibrant debate on that question. And it answers that question based not on neutral principles of constitutional law, but on its own 'understanding of what freedom is and must become.'" This will make the redefinition of marriage more contested in the United States. He elaborates:

> The Court's accumulation of power does not occur in a vacuum. It comes at the expense of the people. And they know it. Here and abroad, people are in the midst of a serious and thoughtful public debate on the issue of same-sex marriage.... This deliberative process is making people take seriously questions that they may not have even regarded as questions before.

When decisions are reached through democratic means, some people will inevitably be disappointed with the results. But those whose views do not prevail at least know that they have had their say, and accordingly are—in the tradition of our political culture—reconciled to the result of a fair and honest debate.

But today the Court puts a stop to all that.

The court had no reason—no basis in the Constitution—to short-circuit the democratic process. No reason to end the national discussion we were having about the future of marriage. Roberts continues, "There will be consequences to shutting down the political process on an issue of such profound public significance. Closing debate tends to close minds. People denied a voice are less likely to accept the ruling of a court on an issue that does not seem to be the sort of thing courts usually decide."

The chief justice quotes from a law review article by Justice Ruth Bader Ginsburg, who joined the majority opinion, in which she assesses the damage *Roe v. Wade* did to civil harmony:

The political process was moving…, not swiftly enough for advocates of quick, complete change, but majoritarian institutions were listening and acting. Heavy-handed judicial intervention was difficult to justify and appears to have provoked, not resolved, conflict.

Obergefell has now provoked conflict rather than resolved it.

Harm to Religious Liberty

Finally, the ruling, as Chief Justice Roberts warns, "creates serious questions about religious liberty." He observes that "many good and decent people oppose same-sex marriage as a tenet of faith, and their freedom to exercise religion is—unlike the right imagined by the majority—actually spelled out in the Constitution." When marriage was redefined demo-cratically, citizens could accompany it with religious liberty protections, but "the majority's decision imposing same-sex marriage cannot, of course, create any such accommodations." Which is why it is so important now for citizens to demand that their elected representatives do so. I discuss model policy in chapter 5.

In addition to Chief Justice Roberts's procedural point—that courts, unlike lawmakers, can't forge compromises—Justice Alito points out that activists will use the decision's rhetoric to attack religious liberty:

> It will be used to vilify Americans who are unwilling to assent to the new orthodoxy. In the course of its opinion, the major-ity compares traditional marriage laws to laws that denied equal treatment for African-Americans and women. The implications of this analogy will be exploited by those who are determined to stamp out every vestige of dissent.

Justice Alito sees dark days ahead: "I assume that those who cling to old beliefs will be able to whisper their thoughts in the recesses of their homes, but if they repeat those views in public, they will risk being labeled as bigots and treated as such by governments, employers, and schools." And we have the court to blame: "By imposing its own views on the entire country, the majority facilitates the marginalization of the many Americans who have traditional ideas."

Most alarmingly, the majority opinion never discusses the free exercise of religion. Chief Justice Roberts wryly notes, "The majority graciously suggests that religious believers may continue to 'advocate' and 'teach' their views of marriage." But the First Amendment, he says, "guarantees...the freedom to '*exercise*' religion. Ominously, that is not a word the majority uses."

Justice Thomas picks up on this as well, noting that the majority opinion "indicates a misunderstanding of religious liberty in our Nation's tradition."

Religious liberty is about more than just the protection for "religious organizations and persons...as they seek to teach the principles that are so fulfilling and so central to their lives and faiths." Religious liberty is about freedom of action in matters of religion generally, and the scope of that liberty is directly correlated to the civil restraints placed upon religious practice.

Although our Constitution provides some protection against such governmental restrictions on religious practices, the People have long elected to afford broader protections than this Court's constitutional precedents mandate. Had the majority allowed the definition of marriage to be left to the political process—as the Constitution requires—the People could have considered the religious liberty implications of deviating from the traditional definition as part of their deliberative process. Instead, the majority's decision short-circuits that process, with potentially ruinous consequences for religious liberty.

In chapter 5 we will explore what can be done *now* to protect religious liberty. And protect religious liberty we must, for as Chief Justice Roberts notes, "Unfortunately, people of faith can take no comfort in the treatment they receive from the majority today." Why not? Because "the most discouraging aspect of today's decision is the extent to which the majority feels compelled to sully those on the other side of the debate." Over and over, the majority attacks Americans who stand for marriage as the union of husband and wife. And as the chief justice writes, "These apparent assaults on the character of fair minded people will have an effect, in society and in court. Moreover, they are entirely gratuitous."

Indeed, "It is one thing for the majority to conclude that the Constitution protects a right to same-sex marriage; it is something else to portray everyone who does not share the majority's 'better informed understanding' as bigoted."

Just How Bad Is It?

All things considered, how bad was the court's ruling? Let me conclude this discussion of *Obergefell v. Hodges* with these thoughts.

First, there is the breathtaking arrogance of the majority, which Justice Scalia excoriates:

> These Justices *know* that limiting marriage to one man and one woman is contrary to reason; they *know* that an institution as old as government itself, and accepted by every nation in history until 15 years ago, cannot possibly be supported by anything other than ignorance or bigotry. And they are willing to say that any citizen who does not agree with that, who adheres to what was, until 15 years ago, the unanimous judgment of all generations and all societies, stands against the Constitution.
>
> The opinion is couched in a style that is as pretentious as its content is egotistic.

Second, the reasoning in the opinion is shamefully shoddy. Justice Scalia cannot hide his contempt:

> The world does not expect logic and precision in poetry or inspirational pop-philosophy; it demands them in the law. The stuff contained in today's opinion has to diminish this Court's reputation for clear thinking and sober analysis.

Indeed, Matthew J. Franck, one of our nation's most acute scholars of constitutional law, thinks that *Obergefell* is so poorly reasoned that it will eventually weaken its own case: "The *Roe* [*v. Wade* abortion] decision has often made pro-life converts out of people who actually read it—I know, because I was one of them—and the *Obergefell* ruling, in time, will do similar work in adding strength to the ranks of marriage's defenders."[7]

There is no better way to conclude this analysis of *Obergefell* than by giving Chief Justice Roberts the last word:

> If you are among the many Americans—of whatever sexual orientation—who favor expanding same-sex marriage, by all means celebrate today's decision. Celebrate the achievement of a desired goal. Celebrate the opportunity for a new expression of commitment to a partner. Celebrate the availability of new benefits. But do not celebrate the Constitution. It had nothing to do with it.

FOUR

"BAKE ME A CAKE, BIGOT!"

S exual liberty and religious liberty need not be in tension. Indeed, most Americans don't want them to be in tension. But some activists are trying to force them into conflict. In this chapter I tell about some of the people whose livelihoods and reputations have come under attack because of their conscientious stance for the truth about marriage. In the next chapter I discuss how public policy should defend religious freedom and the rights of conscience. And then in chapter 6, I explain why the frequently invoked analogy between the defense of marriage and racism—an analogy on which most of the attacks on religious freedom are based—is indefensible as a conceptual and historical matter.

Before turning to the politics and the government's actions, let's look at private-sector intolerance. Brendan Eich gave a thousand dollars to the campaign for Proposition 8 in 2008, and six years later, when his donation was made public, he was forced to resign as CEO of the Mozilla Corporation, a company he had cofounded.[1] Proposition 8, which defined marriage in California as the union of a man and a woman, passed with more than seven million votes, but by 2014 that view of marriage was considered unacceptable.

Eich, unlike many of his tech-culture colleagues, seems to have been quite tolerant. Mitchell Baker, the executive chairwoman of the Mozilla Foundation and the Mozilla Corporation, said of Eich's fifteen years at Mozilla, "I never saw any kind of behavior or attitude from him that was not in line with Mozilla's values of inclusiveness."[2] A dangerously distorted version of inclusiveness forced a perfectly decent man, who was never accused of any intolerance, to resign from the company he had founded simply because he had quietly supported the conjugal view of marriage as a citizen and a voter.

A year later, as the controversy over a religious liberty law in Indiana exploded across the country, a techie named Hampton Catlin was gloating on Twitter about Eich's ouster, which he had orchestrated: "It had been a couple weeks since I'd gotten some sort of @BrendanEich related hate mail. How things going over there on your side, Brendan?" Eich tweeted back in reply, "You demanded I be 'completely removed from any day to day activities at Mozilla' & got your wish. I'm still unemployed. How're you?" Catlin gleefully tweeted: "married and able to live in the USA!...and working together on open source stuff! In like, a loving, happy gay married way!"[3]

The Eich story had a bad ending. But consider the case of Phil Robertson of the A&E television series *Duck Dynasty*. After Robertson told *GQ* magazine that he agreed with the biblical teaching that same-sex sexual acts (along with several other nonmarital sex acts) are immoral, the gay advocacy group GLAAD pushed to get Robertson suspended from the show. And suspended he was.[4] The restaurant chain Cracker Barrel then removed his products from its stores.

But within days, A&E and Cracker Barrel had reversed their decisions.[5]

What made Robertson's case different? The simple explanation is that the executives who run A&E and Cracker Barrel learned that they were out of step with their customers—ordinary Americans who enjoy country-fried steak and shows about duck hunters. Elites are intolerant toward people with traditional views on marriage and sexuality, but ordinary Americans practice tolerance. And that includes most supporters as well as opponents of gay marriage.

As these controversies were unfolding, no one suggested that the government should force Mozilla to employ Eich or force A&E to employ Robertson. They were free to give these loyal and effective employees the boot even if most Americans thought their firing was unjust. But the same rules apparently do not apply on the other side of the debate over same-sex marriage.

The Problem:
Intolerance and Government Coercion

I've said that sexual liberty and religious liberty need not be in tension and that most Americans, regardless of their view on gay marriage, don't want them to be. But some activists *do*, and they are working to pass laws that would allow the government to coerce citizens to violate their beliefs about marriage. For years a central argument of those in favor of same-sex marriage has been that all Americans should be free to live and love as they choose. Yet in the name of that freedom some now want to coerce those who disagree into celebrating same-sex relationships. A growing number of incidents demonstrate that the redefinition of marriage and state policies on sexual orientation have created a climate of intolerance toward citizens who believe that marriage is the union of a man and a woman.

Charities and Schools

Perhaps the best-known examples of government discrimination against organizations that believe in male-female marriage involve Christian adoption agencies. In Massachusetts, Illinois, and the District of Columbia, church-sponsored adoption agencies and foster care providers shut down rather than comply with government orders to place children with same-sex couples on an equal basis with mother-and-father couples. Forcing these agencies to close does nothing to help children who need homes or the couples who want to adopt them. All it does is score a point for political correctness. It makes vulnerable children victims in an adult culture war.

Boston Catholic Charities

For more than a hundred years, Catholic Charities in Boston, Massachusetts, had built a successful record of connecting children to permanent families, placing more children in adoptive homes than any other agency.[6] Then in 2003, a decision of the Massachusetts Supreme Judicial Court required the state to recognize same-sex relationships as marriages.[7] This decision, coupled with an earlier state policy on sexual orientation, forced all adoption providers to place children with same-sex couples.[8]

Rather than abandon Catholic teaching about marriage and the family and ignore the evidence that the best place for a child is with a married mother and father, Catholic Charities of Boston ended its foster care and adoption programs, which had helped approximately 720 children to find permanent adoptive homes over the previous twenty years.[9]

D.C. Catholic Charities

In 2010 the local government of the District of Columbia redefined marriage to include same-sex couples.[10] That ordinance, coupled with the district's sexual orientation policy, would have required Catholic Charities' foster care and adoption services to place children with same-sex couples.[11]

Despite requests by the Archdiocese of Washington to respect private organizations' moral and religious beliefs, the D.C. government refused to grant an exemption. Because it would not violate the faith that had inspired and guided its eighty years of service in the capital city, Catholic Charities was forced to transfer its foster care and adoption program to other providers.[12]

Evangelical Child and Family Agency

For decades, the Evangelical Child and Family Agency (ECFA) had contracted with the State of Illinois to provide foster care services. In 2011, however, a new state civil-union law,[13] coupled with an existing sexual orientation policy, forced private agencies to license unmarried, cohabitating couples—including same-sex couples—as foster care parents in order to keep their state contracts. Because foster children are wards of the state, it is virtually impossible to provide foster care services without a state contract. In other words, a state that refuses to contract with faith-based agencies forces them out of helping children.

Because ECFA was convinced that children should have the unique benefits provided by a married mother and father, the state would not renew its foster care contract.[14] ECFA was thus forced to transfer the cases of the foster children it served to different agencies and end the foster care program that had connected children with permanent families.

The Cost of Adoption Intolerance

Pushing out faith-based foster care and adoption providers comes at a very high cost; these organizations provide real—and unique—services. "One of our main things we were looking for in an agency was one that shared our religious and faith beliefs," explains John Shultz, who with his wife, Tammy, adopted four foster care children through ECFA. Without the support of ECFA, he says, "I don't think I could've weathered the storm of the foster care system."[15]

ECFA and other private, faith-based services in Illinois, including numerous Catholic Charities affiliates,[16] were forced to stop serving over two thousand children, transferring their cases to other providers.[17]

Addressing the threat that sexual orientation laws pose to child welfare agencies, Thomas Atwood, the former president of the National Council for Adoption, warns, "Not only do these laws violate religious liberty, they harm children because they force high-quality, compassionate social service agencies to shut down. If all faith-based agencies closed

due to such laws, the adoption and child welfare field would be deci-
mated, depriving thousands of children growing up in families."[18]

We can expect to see more organizations that serve children in the
foster care system run into crippling intolerance.[19] Every year, the foster
care system serves approximately four hundred thousand children, nearly
a quarter of whom are waiting to be adopted.[20] Across the United States,
there are more than a thousand private, licensed foster care and adoption
providers.[21] Many are faith-based organizations whose religious and
moral beliefs motivate their care for some of the most vulnerable children
in society. Killing off these services out of ideological spite will inflict
incalculable harm on those children. Of the roughly seventy-six thousand
unrelated domestic adoptions that occurred in the United States in 2007,
more than twenty thousand were handled by private providers. The work
and success of private, often faith-based, organizations substantially
increases the number of children who find permanent homes every year.

But the value of these faith-based organizations goes beyond their
ability to place vulnerable children in loving homes or to guide families
through the labyrinth of the foster care and adoption systems. Besides
giving legal, administrative, and material support to adoptive families
and birth mothers, private and faith-based organizations often provide
intangible—yet invaluable—spiritual, emotional, and relational support
that large state bureaucracies are ill equipped to offer.

Through compassionate counseling and practical support, faith-
based and private institutions help thousands of women experiencing
unexpected pregnancies. For instance, in 2007, over eighteen thousand
infants found permanent families through adoption. In addition to offering medical and material support for pregnant women, pregnancy centers
also provide education on the adoption process for women seeking loving
homes for the children they carry. Private and faith-based organizations
play an irreplaceable role in connecting families that wish to adopt with
birth mothers who are carrying their children to term.

None of the Christian agencies shut down by antireligious intolerance was preventing same-sex couples from adopting through other
agencies. They are free to adopt from state agencies or from other private

services with principles that are compatible with their own. These agencies simply asked for the freedom to operate in accordance with their beliefs. Shutting them down because of their Christian principles is shamefully intolerant, and given the compelling evidence that children deserve a mother and a father, it's also bad social policy.

Religious Schools

Private schools and universities are also vulnerable to the intolerance of gay activists and their government allies. Last year, the New England Association of Schools and Colleges (NEASC) began threatening the accreditation of Gordon College, an evangelical Christian institution in Massachusetts, because of its conduct standards, which ask all members of the college community to live by the Christian virtue of chastity. As David French, a lawyer who specializes in religious freedom cases, reported, "NEASC announced that it had met to consider whether 'Gordon College's traditional inclusion of "homosexual practice" as a forbidden activity' violated NEASC's standards for accreditation. NEASC gave Gordon one year 'to ensure that the College's policies and procedures are non-discriminatory.'"[22] In March 2015, Gordon released its report, reaffirming its commitment to traditional Christian teaching on same-sex acts. The following month NEASC affirmed the college's accreditation.

Alas, in the interim, local authorities cut ties with Gordon. French writes: "The city of Salem suspended a contract that allowed Gordon College to use its Old Town Hall. The Lynn School Committee, representing a nearby school district, unconstitutionally refused to accept Gordon's education students as student teachers."[23] That's right, a public school district kicked out student teachers from Gordon, once again holding children hostage in an adult culture war.

Religious schools in the nation's capital are also under attack. In January 2015, the mayor of Washington signed the deceptively titled Human Rights Amendment Act. The bill could be used to compel Washington's private religious schools to violate their beliefs about human sexuality by recognizing LGBT student groups or hosting a "gay pride" day on campus. In order to implement this attack on religious freedom, the city rescinded the Nation's Capital Religious Liberty and Academic Freedom Act, popularly known as the Armstrong Amendment. Passed by Congress in 1989, the Armstrong Amendment had protected religious schools in Washington from government coercion of their beliefs about human sexuality.[24]

Each of these violations of religious liberty was easily avoidable. Provided private schools meet basic standards of safety and education, the government should leave them alone. It certainly shouldn't coerce them to violate the moral beliefs of the religious communities they represent. After all, many families send their children to private schools—often at great sacrifice—precisely to escape the troubling moral indoctrination found in many state schools. Government officials should respect the ability of such schools to witness to their faith.

Wedding Professionals

Similarly outrageous government coercion has been brought to bear against citizens trying to pursue their professional vocation in accordance with their reasonable religious belief that marriage is the union of a man and a woman. Before going into the details of these stories, it is essential to point out that none of them involves discrimination against gays and lesbians as such. None of these citizens has ever said, "I don't serve gays." No, each of these cases involves the conscientious decision not to facilitate a same-sex *wedding*.

Elane Photography

Elaine Huguenin and her husband, Jon, run Elane Photography, a small business in Albuquerque, New Mexico. In 2006 the couple declined a request to photograph a same-sex commitment ceremony because, as Elaine explains, "the message a same-sex commitment ceremony communicates is not one I believe."[25] Elane Photography did not refuse to take pictures of gay and lesbian individuals, but they declined to photograph a ceremony that ran counter to the owners' belief that marriage is the union of a man and a woman (which was also the policy of the State of New Mexico at the time). Other photographers in the Albuquerque area were more than happy to photograph the event.[26]

In 2008 the New Mexico Human Rights Commission ruled that by declining to use their artistic and expressive skills to communicate what was said and what occurred at the ceremony, the Huguenins had discriminated on the basis of sexual orientation and ordered them to pay $6,637.94 in attorneys' fees.[27] The ruling cited New Mexico's human rights law, which prohibits discrimination in "public accommodations" (defined as "any establishment that provides or offers its services...or goods to the public") based on race, religion, and sexual orientation, among other protected classes.

At the end of 2013, the New Mexico Supreme Court upheld the Human Rights Commission's ruling, holding that the First Amendment does not protect a photographer's freedom to decline to take pictures of a same-sex commitment ceremony, even if doing so would violate the photographer's religious beliefs. Justice Richard C. Bosson, in a concurring opinion, dismissed the sacrifice of the Huguenins' religious convictions as "the price of citizenship."[28] In 2014 the U.S. Supreme Court declined to review the case, letting the New Mexico Supreme Court's decision against the Huguenins' right to free expression stand.

Sweet Cakes by Melissa

In early 2013 two women asked the Oregon bakery Sweet Cakes by Melissa to prepare a wedding cake for their same-sex commitment ceremony. The bakery's owners, Melissa and Aaron Klein, had always served all customers without discrimination, but now they were being asked to contribute to the celebration of a same-sex relationship, which their consciences would not let them do. Oregon law at the time did not recognize same-sex marriages.[29]

When the Kleins declined the request, the customers filed a complaint under the Oregon Equality Act of 2007, which prohibits discrimination based on sexual orientation. During an investigation of the Kleins by Oregon's Bureau of Labor and Industries, one of the officials, Brad Avakian, commented, "The goal is to rehabilitate. For those who do violate the law, we want them to learn from that experience and have a good, successful business in Oregon."[30] In January 2014, the agency ruled that the Kleins had violated Oregon's sexual orientation law.[31]

The State of Oregon was not the only party to harass the Kleins because of their fidelity to their religious beliefs. They were subjected to violent protests, boycotts organized by gay activists, vicious telephone calls, and death threats.[32] Fearing for the safety of their five children, the Kleins closed Sweet Cakes in September 2013. Having been driven out of business, however, the Kleins still had to face the fury of the Oregon Equality Act.[33]

In April 2015, an administrative law judge for Oregon's Bureau of Labor and Industries ruled that "$75,000 and $60,000 are appropriate awards to compensate [the same-sex couple] for the emotional suffering they experienced."[34] The Kleins' lawyer deplored the financial devastation visited on the family by the state: "An important thing to understand about the damages the state is claiming in this case is that the [$135,000] isn't going to come from liquidating business assets." Why not? "Their business is gone. They don't have business assets, so when we talk about [the fine], it's personal. It means that's money they would have used to feed their children that they can't use anymore."[35]

How could such a ruinous penalty for declining to bake a cake be justified? The two women who filed the complaint cited 178 symptoms of suffering, including "acute loss of confidence," "doubt," "excessive sleep," feeling "mentally raped, dirty and shameful," "high blood pressure," "impaired digestion," "loss of appetite," "migraine headaches," being "pale and sick at home after work," "resumption of smoking habit," "shock," "surprise," "uncertainty," "weight gain," and "worry."[36]

In June 2015, Kelsey Harkness of the Daily Signal (the news service of the Heritage Foundation) uncovered evidence of collusion in the Sweet Cakes case: "[T]he government agency responsible for enforcing Oregon's anti-discrimination law appears to be working closely with a powerful gay rights advocacy group in its case against Aaron and Melissa Klein."[37]

Harkness found e-mails and text messages that linked the plaintiffs, the gay rights advocacy group in the state, and the government agency investigating and adjudicating the complaint. These communications, Harkness notes, "raise questions about potential bias in the state's decision to charge the Kleins with discrimination for refusing to make a cake for a same-sex wedding."

Hans von Spakovsky, a legal expert at Heritage, told Harkness that the coordination between these groups presents "a clear conflict of interest." He added:

> State agencies have a duty to represent the best interests of the general public, not the interests of one particular advocacy group. The relationship shown by these communications is inappropriate and raises basic questions about the objectivity, bias, and fairness of this agency and its proceedings.

If the State of Oregon's goal in persecuting the Kleins was, as Mr. Avakian described it, to make the Kleins "learn from their experience," the message is coming through loud and clear: religious freedom is threatened in Oregon. And because of the miscarriage of justice, the attorney for the Kleins is appealing. As Harkness reports, "Suspicious of potential collusion, Harmon, the Kleins' lawyer, requested the judge allow her to further investigate the state's relationship with Basic Rights Oregon." We will have to see if justice will prevail.

Masterpiece Cakeshop

A wedding cake was the occasion of another attack on religious liberty, this time in Colorado, a state that in 2006 had constitutionally defined marriage as the union of a man and a woman.[38]

A same-sex couple who had received a marriage license in Massachusetts asked Jack Phillips, the owner of the Masterpiece Cakeshop in a Denver suburb, to make a wedding cake for their reception back home in Colorado.[39] Phillips declined, citing his faith: "I don't feel like I should

participate in their wedding, and when I do a cake, I feel like I am participating in the ceremony or the event or the celebration that the cake is for."
The couple obtained a wedding cake with rainbow-colored filling (illustrat-
ing the expressive nature of event cake baking) from another bakery.[40]

The American Civil Liberties Union filed a complaint against Masterpiece Cakeshop with the state, alleging violations of Colorado's public
accommodation law. During a public hearing of the Colorado Civil Rights
Commission, one of the commissioners, Diann Rice, had this to say:

> I would also like to reiterate what we said in...the last meet-
> ing [concerning Jack Phillips]. Freedom of religion and reli-
> gion has been used to justify all kinds of discrimination
> throughout history, whether it be slavery, whether it be the
> Holocaust....I mean, we can list hundreds of situations where
> freedom of religion has been used to justify discrimination.
> And to me it is one of the most despicable pieces of rhetoric
> that people can use—to use their religion to hurt others.[41]

Having been compared to slave owners and Nazis, Phillips was
eventually found to have violated the law by declining service to the
couple "because of their sexual orientation."[42] Phillips responded that he
would happily sell the couple baked goods for any number of occasions
but that preparing a wedding cake was an expression of support that his
religious convictions would not allow him to make. The State of Colorado was declaring, therefore, that he was not free to run his business in
accordance with his faith.[43]

Arlene's Flowers

On March 1, 2013, Robert Ingersoll and Curt Freed asked Barronelle
Stutzman, the owner of Arlene's Flowers and Gifts in Richland, Washington, to arrange the flowers for their same-sex wedding ceremony.
Washington State had redefined marriage the previous year. Ingersoll
had been a regular customer for nearly a decade, and Stutzman knew

him well. As she recalls, "I put my hand on his and said, 'I'm sorry Rob, I can't do your wedding because of my relationship with Jesus Christ.' We talked a little bit, we talked about his mom [walking him down the aisle]...we hugged and he left."[44]

Stutzman's gentle and sympathetic response was not the end of the matter, however. The state attorney general, Bob Ferguson, sued her for violations of the state's sexual orientation law, and in 2015 a judge ruled that Stutzman had violated the state's antidiscrimination and consumer-protection laws.[45] Knowing that the seventy-year-old florist faced financial ruin, Ferguson made her an offer she couldn't refuse: pay a $2,001 fine and agree to provide services to same-sex weddings, and the matter would be dropped.[46] But Stutzman *did* refuse the offer, explaining her decision in an eloquent letter to the attorney general:

> As you may imagine, it has been mentally and emotionally exhausting to be at the center of this controversy for nearly two years. I never imagined that using my God-given talents and abilities, and doing what I love to do for over three decades, would become illegal. Our state would be a better place if we respected each other's differences, and our leaders protected the freedom to have those differences. Since 2012, same-sex couples all over the state have been free to act on their beliefs about marriage, but because I follow the Bible's teaching that marriage is the union of one man and one woman, I am no longer free to act on my beliefs.
>
> Your offer reveals that you don't really understand me or what this conflict is all about. It's about freedom, not money. I certainly don't relish the idea of losing my business, my home, and everything else that your lawsuit threatens to take from my family, but my freedom to honor God in doing what I do best is more important. Washington's constitution guarantees us "freedom of conscience in all matters of religious sentiment." I cannot sell that precious freedom. You are asking me to walk in the way of a well-known betrayer, one who

sold something of infinite worth for 30 pieces of silver. That is something I will not do.

I pray that you reconsider your position. I kindly served Rob for nearly a decade and would gladly continue to do so. I truly want the best for my friend. I've also employed and served many members of the LGBT community, and I will continue to do so regardless of what happens with this case. You chose to attack my faith and pursue this not simply as a matter of law, but to threaten my very means of working, eating, and having a home. If you are serious about clarifying the law, then I urge you to drop your claims against my home, business, and other assets.[47]

Considering her ordeal, Stutzman remains remarkably gracious: "I did serve Rob. It's the event that I turned down, not the service for Rob or his partner." She adds, "I had a good relationship with Rob and I served him for years. We did have a personal relationship, and I think the world of him. We just disagree on what marriage is."[48] As of March 2015, Stutzman's property is still at risk of government seizure.[49]

Görtz Haus Gallery

Betty and Dick Odgaard, a devout Mennonite couple in Iowa, ran an art gallery, restaurant, and gift shop in a seventy-seven-year-old church building, where they also hosted weddings. The Odgaards would arrange everything from flowers, food, and decorations to the wedding ceremony itself. On the day of the wedding, they would oversee all of these details.[50]

In 2013 the Odgaards declined a request to hold a same-sex wedding at their facility because such a ceremony conflicted with "the religious message they seek to convey through the Gallery, a message which includes the importance of living one's faith in all aspects of life."[51] A day after declining to host the wedding, the Odgaards found themselves under investigation by the Iowa Civil Rights Commission—the same-sex couple had filed a discrimination complaint.[52] The commission in turn sought to force the Odgaards to plan, facilitate, and host same-sex wedding ceremonies at their gallery.[53]

"We hire and serve gays and lesbians, and have close friends who are gays and lesbians," said Betty Odgaard. "And we respect that good people disagree with our religious conviction against hosting a ceremony that violates our faith. We simply ask that the government not force us to abandon our faith or punish us for it."[54]

The Odgaards tried to settle the case peacefully, and while not admitting to any discrimination, they paid $5,000 to the complaining same-sex couple and ceased to host weddings of any kind.[55] That wasn't enough. If they did *any* other wedding-related work, they would be liable to another discrimination complaint. Meanwhile, customers who patronized the gallery and restaurant stopped coming, because of the bad press it was receiving. Kelsey Harkness reports:

> Around town, Görtz Haus became known as the business that refuses to serve gays.
>
> If a group of ladies went to lunch and one disagreed with their opinion not to host same-sex weddings, the entire group boycotted the bistro, the Odgaards explained.
>
> "They didn't come in because the people who are against us are more vocal than the people who are in our court," Richard [Odgaard] said.[56]

The Odgaards never really got their day in court, as "complaints are filed—and judged—in the Iowa Civil Rights Commission."[57] Richard Odgaard says, "We knew what the outcome was going to be, the judge knew what the outcome was going to be, but we had to go through it."[58] In June 2015 the Odgaards announced that they would be closing down everything for good. Another victim of a movement that claims to be about tolerance and coexistence.

Hitching Post Wedding Chapel

In October 2014, officials in the town of Coeur d'Alene, Idaho, told ordained ministers that they would have to celebrate same-sex weddings or face fines and jail time.

Donald and Evelyn Knapp, the proprietors of the Hitching Post Wedding Chapel, have been married for forty-seven years.[59] Ministers of the International Church of the Foursquare Gospel, they are "evangelical Christians who hold to historic Christian beliefs" that "God created two distinct genders in His image" and "that God ordained marriage to be between one man and one woman."[60] The Knapps have been celebrating weddings in their chapel since 1989.

Coeur d'Alene has a nondiscrimination ordinance that includes sexual orientation and gender identity. After the Ninth Circuit Court of Appeals struck down Idaho's constitutional amendment defining marriage as the union of a man and a woman, town officials determined that the Hitching Post is a public accommodation subject to the nondiscrimination ordinance[61] and informed the Knapps that they would have to officiate at same-sex weddings there.[62] The Knapps were facing a 180-day jail term and a $1,000 fine for *each day* they declined to celebrate a same-sex wedding. A week of honoring their faith would cost the couple three and a half years in jail and $7,000 in fines.

In this case, however, the city eventually backed down. Why? Because there was a national outcry and lots of media coverage. Even an influential legal blog hosted at the *Washington Post* noticed the story and warned that the city was violating important religious liberty laws.[63]

Liberty Ridge Farm

For over twenty-five years, Cynthia and Robert Gifford have owned and operated Liberty Ridge Farm in Schaghticoke, New York, where their home is on the second and third floors of the barn. Like many farming families, they often open their farm to the public for events like berry picking, fall festivals, and pig racing. They also host weddings and receptions on the first floor of the barn. The Giffords are involved in every aspect of the wedding planning and celebration: they greet and drive guests in their farm trolley, decorate the barn, set up floral arrangements, arrange fireworks displays, and provide catering. The also open up part of their home on the second floor of the barn as a bridal suite. The only service the Giffords don't offer is providing an officiant for the wedding ceremony.[64]

In 2012 Melisa Erwin and Jennifer McCarthy approached the Giffords about renting the barn for their same-sex wedding ceremony and reception. Cynthia Gifford responded that she and her husband could not in good conscience host a same-sex wedding ceremony at their home.[65] New York law, however, establishes special privileges based on sexual orientation that trump the rights of business owners.[66] Because the Giffords' family farm is classified as a "public accommodation," they cannot "discriminate" on the basis of sexual orientation.

In response to a complaint by Erwin and McCarthy, the New York State Division of Human Rights fined Cynthia and Robert Gifford $13,000 for acting on their belief that marriage is the union of a man and a woman.[67] The agency also ruled that "the nature and circumstances of the [Giffords'] violation of the Human Rights Law also warrants a penalty."[68]

Of course the Giffords were not engaging in invidious discrimination—they were acting on their belief about the nature of marriage. They do not object to gay or lesbian customers' attending their fall festivals or going berry picking or participating in any of the farm's other public activities. The Giffords' only objection is to planning and hosting a ceremony that is a serious affront to their religious convictions.

The Giffords were ordered to pay $1,500 apiece to Erwin and McCarthy in compensation for their mental anguish[69] and a $10,000 penalty to New York State.[70] They decided to host no more weddings as a result of this ruling.

Atlanta Fire Chief Kelvin Cochran

In January 2015, the fire chief of Atlanta, Kelvin Cochran, was fired for writing and publishing, on his own time, a book expressing his biblical understanding of sexual morality.

Cochran had been a firefighter since 1981 and was appointed Atlanta's fire chief in 2008. In 2009 President Obama appointed him U.S. fire administrator for the United States Fire Administration in Washington, D.C.[71] He returned to serve as Atlanta's fire chief in 2010.[72]

A devout Christian, Cochran is a deacon and teacher in his Baptist church. In 2013 he wrote and published a book, *Who Told You That You Were Naked?*,[73] for a church group studying authentic manhood. Same-sex sexual acts are mentioned on only one page of the book and are treated as one among many sexual sins from a Christian perspective.[74]

In late 2014 a retired Atlanta Fire Department captain, Cindy Thompson, contacted GA Voice, a Georgian LGBT group, to protest Cochran's book and its treatment of homosexuality.[75] She then brought the book to Mayor Kasim Reed's LGBT liaison. Soon afterward, gay activist groups began demanding that the fire chief be dismissed.[76] Mayor Reed promptly suspended Chief Cochran for a month without pay and ordered him to submit to sensitivity training.[77] After a month's investigation, the mayor dismissed the chief.

Reed defended his action by insisting, "This is about judgment...This is not about religious freedom, this is not about free speech....Judgment is the basis of the problem."[78] Yet a month earlier Reed had released a statement saying, "I profoundly disagree with and am deeply disturbed by the sentiments expressed in the paperback regarding the LGBT community. I will not tolerate discrimination of any kind within my administration."[79] But the mayor never pointed to any acts of discrimination from Cochran. He only disagreed with the book the chief wrote. The mayor stated that Cochran's book might leave the city vulnerable to litigation, although in thirty-four years of service, Cochran had never been accused of discrimination, and Reed did not release any evidence of discrimination after the monthlong investigation.

In terminating Cochran, Reed said that the fire chief had not consulted with him before publishing his book. Cochran, however, had conferred with the city's ethics officer and been granted verbal permission.[80] Cochran also reported that he gave a copy of the book to the mayor's executive assistant in January 2014—ten months before the suspension.[81] It appears, in fact, that Cochran did everything he could to follow protocol and give the city a chance to review his book before it was published.

The Supreme Court has routinely held that government employees' free speech rights are limited if their speech "has some potential to affect the [governmental] entity's operations."[82] But "so long as employees are speaking as citizens about matters of public concern, they must face only those speech restrictions that are necessary for their employers to operate efficiently and effectively."[83] It is obvious that Cochran was speaking in his private capacity (not as fire chief) and that he was speaking on a matter of public concern (biblical faith and human sexuality). But did his speech interfere with his job?

Cochran's spotless record over thirty-four years as a fireman indicates that his religious writing never interfered with his ability to manage the fire department. The only plausible argument against him is that Reed would have faced considerable political heat from gay activist groups if Cochran had been retained. Yet this is hardly Cochran's fault and has almost nothing to do with fire chief's job description. Upholding Cochran's dismissal on this basis would set a dangerous precedent for the free speech rights of public employees.

In response, Cochran has filed a federal lawsuit against the city.[84] In a press release announcing the lawsuit, Cochran explains why he is fighting back and what is at stake for all believers:

> To actually lose my childhood-dream-come-true profession— where all of my expectations have been greatly exceeded— because of my faith is staggering. The very faith that led me to pursue my career has been used to take it from me. All Americans are guaranteed the freedom to hold to their beliefs without the consequences that I have experienced.[85]

The Future of Tolerance

In the decade or so before the *Obergefell* decision, when Americans were debating the definition of marriage, no one was suggesting that gays and lesbians be barred from forming intimate unions. Same-sex marriage was not "illegal" in the way that theft, arson, and littering are illegal. In all fifty states, two people of the same sex could live together, join a religious community that blessed their relationship, and choose a workplace offering joint benefits. They were free to do all of this, as the dissenting opinions in *Obergefell* point out; the state simply didn't recognize their relationship as a marriage.

People like me argued that government can recognize the truth about marriage *and* leave people free to live and love as they choose. While respecting everyone's liberty in romantic matters, government rightly recognized, protected, and promoted the truth about marriage as the ideal institution for childbearing and childrearing. Adults were free to make choices about their relationships, and they didn't need a state license to do so.

At issue was whether the government would recognize such relationships as marriages and then force every citizen, charity, school, and business to do so as well.

None of the stories told in this chapter had to happen. In a tolerant society, citizens would live and let live when it came to these clashes. The state wouldn't coerce people to violate their reasonable, deeply held religious belief that marriage is the union of a man and a woman. Religious charities and schools would be able to operate in accordance with that belief. And the state would allow its citizens to operate a business and participate in the marketplace without abandoning their faith. The next chapter explains how to protect this right in law.

FIVE

RELIGIOUS FREEDOM:
A BASIC HUMAN RIGHT

P art of the genius of the American system of government is its commitment to protecting the liberty of all citizens while respecting their equality before the law. The government protects their freedom to seek the truth about God, to worship according to their conscience, and to live out their convictions in public life. Likewise, citizens are free to enter into contracts and to form associations according to their own values.

While the government must treat everyone equally, people in the private sector are free to make reasonable distinctions—including ones based on good-faith moral convictions—in their economic activities. Government shouldn't impose substantial burdens on sincere religious beliefs unless it can prove that it must—or, as the law puts it, that the burden imposed on those beliefs is the least restrictive means of advancing a compelling government interest.

Those who make decisions based on moral and religious views may well pay a price in the market, perhaps losing customers and qualified employees, but such choices should remain lawful. Freedom of association and freedom of contract are two-way streets. They entail the freedom to choose whom to associate with, when, and on what terms, as well as the freedom to choose whom to do business with and for what goods or services. Governmental mandates that impinge on these freedoms should be imposed only for compelling reasons.

The proprietors of the family businesses discussed in the previous chapter see their professional work as an extension of their faith life. A wedding photographer, for example, doesn't just provide a business service but uses her God-given talents to tell the story of a particular couple and their relationship. Helping to celebrate a same-sex relationship as a marriage affirms that relationship, and it is unreasonable to coerce religious believers to do that.

The government should not be determining who is right or wrong about baking cakes or taking photographs for same-sex weddings. You don't have to share the beliefs of the owners of Sweet Cakes or Elane Photography to recognize that they ought to be free to run their businesses in accordance with their values—and without fear of reprisal from the government. This chapter explains why.

Religious Freedom: The First Freedom

The Founding Fathers of the United States established a political society unlike any other in all of human history. Here we would not merely "tolerate" the religious practice of minorities but would protect the right of all people to liberty of conscience and the free exercise of religion. The Founders recognized that religious liberty is a God-given *natural* right, not the creation of government. States must respect and protect this right, never undermine or attack it.

George Washington, in a letter to the Hebrew congregation of Newport, Rhode Island, perhaps said it best:

The citizens of the United States of America have a right to applaud themselves for having given to mankind examples of an enlarged and liberal policy—a policy worthy of imitation. All possess alike liberty of conscience and immunities of citizenship.

It is now no more that toleration is spoken of as if it were the indulgence of one class of people that another enjoyed the exercise of their inherent natural rights, for, happily, the Government of the United States, which gives to bigotry no sanction, to persecution no assistance, requires only that they who live under its protection should demean themselves as good citizens in giving it on all occasions their effectual support.[1]

In America, religious liberty is not the result of mere "toleration" but an inherent natural right.

A hallmark of true religious liberty is that it is extended to persons of all faiths, even if their beliefs seem unfounded, flawed, implausible, or downright silly. The foundation of religious freedom, however, is not skepticism, relativism, or indifferentism about theological questions. It is the objective value of the religious quest—seeking to understand the truth about ultimate questions and conforming one's life to that truth with integrity.

People have the right to pursue religious truth and, within the limits of justice and the common good, to act on their judgments of what truth demands. They possess this right even when they are, in some respects, in error. Kevin Seamus Hasson captures this truth in the title of his book *The Right to Be Wrong*,[2] where he rightly argues that religious liberty is for everyone from A to Z—Anglicans to Zoroastrians.

It is a fulfillment of human nature to think about the existence of God and what he might demand of us and to aspire to live in accordance with our conclusions. Throughout human history people have sought the truth about ultimate—and divine—reality and have shaped their lives accordingly. Religious freedom respects the right of all persons to pursue these ends. It is not a concession of the government to its subjects but a natural right that the government recognizes, protects, and is *limited* by. We are to render to Caesar what is Caesar's, but to God what is God's, because Caesar is not God. Religion is outside of the jurisdiction of Caesar, who must acknowledge that men's consciences are bound by a higher law.

This view of religious liberty has found a place in our civil law. As James Madison wrote in his *Memorial and Remonstrance*, "The Religion then of every man must be left to the conviction and conscience of every man."[3] It is an "arrogant pretension" to believe that "the Civil Magistrate is a competent Judge of Religious Truth."[4] The First Amendment to the Constitution has been understood to embody this vision of religious liberty for much of our history, even as other aspects of religious free-exercise case law have changed.

The right to religious liberty is the result of a prior *duty* to seek out the truth about God and the cosmos. Indeed, as Madison explained:

> What is here a right towards men, is a duty towards the Creator. It is the duty of every man to render to the Creator such homage and such only as he believes to be acceptable to him. This duty is precedent, both in order of time and in degree of obligation, to the claims of Civil Society.[5]

At the time of its founding, the government of the United States was virtually unique in protecting the space for its citizens to fulfill this duty according to their own best judgment. As Professor Michael McConnell of Stanford Law School explains,

> In the liberal tradition, the government's role is not to make theological judgments but to protect the right of the people to pursue their own understanding of the truth, within the limits of the common good. That is the difference between "the full and free exercise of religion" (Madison's formulation) and mere "toleration." Toleration presupposes a "dominant group" with a particular opinion about religion (that it is "false," or

at least "unwarranted"), who decide not to "eradicate" beliefs they regard as "wrong, mistaken, or undesirable."[6]

Religious liberty is not unlimited. The state can rightly limit it when justice and the common good so require. In such cases, the limitation of religious liberty is an incidental but unavoidable (and thus justified) effect of the government's action to secure justice. This principle is the basis of the federal Religious Freedom Restoration Act (RFRA) and the various state versions of the same statute. These laws require that regulations which curb religious expression serve a compelling government interest and do so by the least restrictive means possible.[7]

As a matter of natural law, the right to religious liberty is based on the moral truth that sincere religious activity, freely undertaken, is valuable in itself—it is a basic component of human well-being—and should be allowed to flourish. In fact, the intrinsic value of religion explains the behavior of agnostics and atheists just as much as that of Muslims, Jews, and Christians. While they come to different conclusions, they are all motivated by a basic (if only implicit) awareness that human beings are better off when they sincerely seek the truth about ultimate questions and then live accordingly. In other words, people realize the good of religion even if they make mistakes about religious truth. Assuming that one's religious act is sincere (and not, say, merely an attempt to satisfy social expectations), even imperfect expressions of religion are valuable.

Religious *liberty* is important because the search for truth about ultimate things and the effort to live according to that truth are valuable *only* if they are *freely undertaken*. The state, therefore, should protect religious freedom. The quest for religious truth, adherence to religious faith and morals, and the pursuit of a relationship with the divine must be free from coercion.

Religious Freedom Restoration Acts

The federal Religious Freedom Restoration Act was passed in 1993 with almost unanimous support in Congress. Although thirty-one states have a state version of RFRA on the books or equivalent protections for religious liberty,[8] the outcry from the media, from gay rights activists, and from many politicians against recent moves by other states to adopt similar protections has been shrill and dishonest.

In February 2014, the state of Arizona considered a minor legislative clarification to its state RFRA, attracting incendiary media coverage. The *New York Times* editorialized that the Arizona legislature had passed "noxious measures to give businesses and individuals the broad right to deny services to same-sex couples in the name of protecting religious liberty."[9]

The *Times* got it wrong. The Arizona bill, an amendment to the state's 1999 RFRA, never even mentioned same-sex couples.[10] It provided that the RFRA protections would extend to any "state action" and would apply to "any individual, association, partnership, corporation, church, religious assembly or institution or other business organization." In other words, the bill would have protected all citizens and the associations they form from undue burdens by the government on their religious liberty and from private lawsuits that would have the same effect.

Kirsten Powers jumped into the fray with a *USA Today* column misleadingly titled "Arizona Latest to Attack Gay Rights."[11] She warned that the law "would result in nothing less than chaos," even though the federal government had operated under the same rules for twenty years and Arizona had had similar protections since 1999. A bipartisan group of law professors set the record straight in a letter to Governor Jan Brewer:

> The bill has been egregiously misrepresented by many of its critics....
>
> We should not punish people for practicing their religions unless we have a very good reason. Arizona has had a RFRA for nearly fifteen years now; the federal government has had one since 1993; and RFRA's standard was the constitutional standard for the entire country from 1963 to 1990....
>
> [The proposed law] would amend the Arizona RFRA to address two ambiguities that have been the subject of

litigation under other RFRAs. It would provide that people are covered when state or local government requires them to violate their religion in the conduct of their business, and it would provide that people are covered when sued by a private citizen invoking state or local law to demand that they violate their religion.[12]

The rhetoric about giving bigots a license not to serve gays and lesbians was simply nonsensical. Indeed, religious liberty claims in connection with same-sex marriage have never been about turning away certain *persons* or *groups*, but about not endorsing certain *actions* or *ceremonies*.

But the lies worked, and Governor Brewer, a Republican, vetoed the bill. Among those applying pressure were Arizona's two Republican senators, John McCain and Jeff Flake, as well as Newt Gingrich and Mitt Romney,[13] showing that both political parties are susceptible to abandoning principle once the media dial up the heat. Or big business. National Football League officials expressed concern about holding the Super Bowl in Arizona, as scheduled, should the religious liberty bill be enacted.

After the success in Arizona, the media campaign against religious liberty moved on to Michigan in December 2014. The target was the Michigan Religious Freedom Restoration Act,[14] which CBS News warned "would let Michigan doctors [and] EMTs refuse to treat gay patients." The constitutional scholar Edward Whelan pointed out that "the bill is modeled on the federal Religious Freedom Restoration Act...and nothing remotely like what CBS News alleges has ever happened anywhere."[15]

Contrary to CBS's report, the Michigan RFRA did not provide "that people do not have to perform an act that would violate their sincerely held religious beliefs." Like every other RFRA, it simply required that religious liberty be balanced against compelling government interests. *Time* magazine attacked the bill with a column titled "Freedom of Religion Shouldn't Be Unconditional."[16] But no one says it should be, and RFRAs do *not* make it unconditional.

Let's consider the test case that CBS misleadingly proposed, that of doctors and emergency medical technicians. RFRA comes into play only if a sincere religious belief is substantially burdened. I have never heard of any sincere religious belief that would prevent EMTs from treating gay people. Which religion requires that? But for the sake of argument, let's suppose one did.

RFRA then asks if the state is pursuing a compelling governmental interest and doing so in the least restrictive way possible. The provision of essential medical care to all citizens is obviously a compelling interest. Forbidding EMTs to pick and choose which patients they will treat may very well be the least restrictive means possible of ensuring emergency care to all patients.[17]

Douglas Laycock, a law professor and authority on religious liberty—and a supporter of same-sex marriage—confirms the narrowness of the protections sought by those opposed to the redefinition of marriage:

> I know of no American religious group that teaches discrimination against gays as such, and few judges would be persuaded of the sincerity of such a claim. The religious liberty issue with respect to gays and lesbians is about directly facilitating the marriage, as with wedding services and marital counseling.[18]

The Michigan bill had nothing to do with giving medical professionals a right to refuse to treat the broken bones of gay people or to refuse to prescribe antibiotics to lesbians. But that didn't stop the media from saying so.

Indiana

The most outrageous of the recent state religious liberty debates took place in Indiana in late March and early April 2015—coinciding with Christian Holy Week and Jewish Passover. Once again, big business, the media, gay rights activists, and craven politicians combined to defeat modest religious liberty protections.

College basketball's Final Four tournament was about to take place in Indianapolis. Mark Emmert, the president of the NCAA (headquartered in Indianapolis), released a statement that was simply preposterous: "We are especially concerned about how this legislation could affect our student-athletes and employees."

The CEO of Salesforce, Marc Benioff, followed suit, announcing on Twitter, "Today we are canceling all programs that require our customers/employees to travel to Indiana to face discrimination."[19] Salesforce even announced that it was offering employees a $50,000 relocation package to get out of Indiana.[20]

Politicians got in on the act too. Hillary Clinton tweeted, "Sad this new Indiana law can happen in America today. We shouldn't discriminate against ppl bc of who they love #LGBT."[21] Senator Chuck Schumer (who had *cosponsored* the federal RFRA) tweeted: "@NCAA if you're looking for a new place to hold 2021 #FinalFour–NY has plenty of great venues that don't discriminate. #final4fairness."[22] And the governor of Connecticut—one of twenty states at the time with its own RFRA—announced an executive order barring official government travel to Indiana.[23] Rahm Emanuel, the mayor of Chicago, proclaimed that "Governor Pence's act is wrong. It's wrong for the people of Indiana, wrong for the individuals who will face new discrimination, and wrong for a state seeking to grow its economy."[24] He urged Hoosiers to "look next door to an economy that is moving forward into the 21st century." He failed to mention that Illinois has a state RFRA—which Barack Obama voted for as a state senator.

The most prominent corporate bully in the pack was probably Tim Cook, the CEO of Apple, who published an op-ed in the *Washington Post* headlined "Pro-Discrimination 'Religious Freedom' Laws Are Dangerous."[25] The truth is that the one favoring discrimination in this debate is Tim Cook. It is Tim Cook who favors laws that discriminate against people who simply ask to be left alone to run their businesses and their schools and their charities in accordance with their reasonable belief that marriage is the union of a man and a woman. It is Tim Cook who would have the state coerce these people into celebrating a same-sex wedding.

"There's something very dangerous happening in states across the country. A wave of legislation, introduced in more than two dozen states, would allow people to discriminate against their neighbors," Cook writes. That charge is false to its core. The question in Indiana and around the country is whether Americans should be free to live in accordance with the truth about marriage in their public lives.

Cook, astonishingly, equates this belief with Jim Crow segregation: "The days of segregation and discrimination marked by 'Whites Only' signs on shop doors, water fountains and restrooms must remain deep in our past." This debate has nothing to do with refusing to serve gay people simply because they're gay, and the Indiana RFRA wouldn't have protected that. In fact, it doesn't even say who will win in a given case where sexual freedom collides with religious freedom—only that a court should review, using a well-established balancing test, and hold the government accountable to justify its action. But should a seventy-year-old grandmother like the florist Barronelle Stutzman, if she wants to make a living, really have to violate her beliefs by participating in a same-sex wedding?

The hypocrisy in the Indiana debate was amazing. By threatening to boycott Indiana over its religious liberty law, people like Mark Benioff were exercising their right to run their businesses in accordance with their beliefs. Yet they failed to recognize that the baker, the photographer, and the florist are simply asking for the same liberty.

Indeed, Apple itself has exercised this freedom (or would Tim Cook prefer to call it "discrimination"?). A Christian organization called the Manhattan Declaration, which bears witness to the dignity of unborn life, the nature of marriage as the union of husband and wife, and the importance of religious liberty, created an app to help its supporters follow its work. Apple didn't like the message of the Manhattan Declaration and removed it from the App Store.[26] No one has suggested that Apple's discrimination, however deplorable, should be illegal. The company should be free to decide its own values and live according to them.

Cook, however, is apparently blind to the irony when he writes, "Our message, to people around the country and around the world, is this: Apple is open. Open to everyone, regardless of where they come from, what they look like, how they worship or who they love." Unless, that is, they are traditional Catholics, Evangelicals, or Orthodox Christians who support the Manhattan Declaration. Then Apple's message is: "Apple is closed. Closed to those with beliefs we disapprove of."

Senator Schumer gamely tried to explain away the obvious contradiction between his sponsorship of the federal RFRA in 1993 and his hostility to the same protection of religious rights now: "[T]he federal RFRA was written narrowly to protect individuals' religious freedom from government interference unless the government or state had a compelling interest.... Second, the federal RFRA was written to protect individuals' interests from government interference, but the Indiana RFRA protects private companies and corporations."[27]

But as the legal scholars Hans von Spakovsky and Andrew Kloster replied, "Schumer's claim that the comparison [of the Indiana RFRA to the federal RFRA] is 'completely false' is itself 'completely false.'"[28] They noted, "These two provisions are virtually identical." The federal statute protects religious liberty in all spheres of life, as the Supreme Court reminded us in 2014 when it protected the owners of Hobby Lobby and Conestoga Wood Specialties against the Department of Health and Human Services' mandate to provide abortifacient birth control. Spakovsky and Kloster write:

> Under 1 U.S.C. § 1, also known as the federal Dictionary Act, the word "person" when used in an "Act of Congress" includes "corporations, companies, associations, firms, partnership, societies and joint stock companies, as well as individuals." It has been this way since the first dictionary act back in 1947.

So Schumer's claim about the federal law only covering individuals is "completely false." He knew what he voted for back in 1993.[29]

Some critics pointed out that the Indiana RFRA provided citizens a defense in a lawsuit between private parties. But this protection represented no departure from the federal law as it has actually been implemented. The constitutional scholar Josh Blackman explains that "four federal courts of appeals and the Obama Justice Department have all taken the position that RFRA can be used as a defense in private suits involving the enforcement of laws that substantially burden free exercise of religion."[30]

Nevertheless, the campaign of big business and big media against religious liberty in Indiana succeeded. Frantic state legislators and the governor rushed to "fix" RFRA by exempting sexual orientation and gender identity laws from its coverage. Indiana law now says that, with certain narrow exceptions, sexual liberty always trumps religious liberty. The "fix," that is, leaves religious liberty in Indiana weaker than it was before RFRA.

The most remarkable part of the debate over these state religious freedom bills is that no such law has ever been successfully used against a gay rights claim. Professor Laycock writes:

> State RFRAs are quite unlikely to affect discrimination claims. I hope they do affect discrimination claims in certain very narrow contexts: very small businesses providing wedding services or marital counseling services. But I am not optimistic. So far, the religious claimants have lost all of those cases, including the wedding photographer under the New Mexico RFRA, and the florist in Washington under a RFRA-like interpretation of the state constitution.
>
> Discrimination cases in other contexts simply don't come up. The florist in Washington had served her gay customer for years, knowing that the flowers were for his same-sex

partner; she had had gay employees. She didn't object to any of that; she objected to serving the wedding, because she understands weddings and marriages to be inherently religious. She sees civil marriage as resting on the foundation of religious marriage.[31]

RFRA's discouraging track record in cases of wedding services raises the question of just what compelling state interest is served by requiring religious believers to violate their consciences. And whatever that interest might be, how is forcing every photographer, florist, and baker to serve same-sex weddings the least restrictive way of serving that interest? Declining to perform these services doesn't violate anyone else's sexual freedom. If a citizen concludes that he cannot in good conscience participate in a same-sex ceremony, the government should not force him to choose between his religious beliefs and his livelihood. Competitive markets can harmonize Americans' range of values without government interference.

Religious Freedom and Marriage

Government should respect the rights of those who stand for marriage as the union of a man and a woman. Even now that the Supreme Court has redefined marriage, Americans who believe marriage is between a man and a woman should be free to live and work in accord with their moral and religious convictions.

When he "evolved" on the issue in 2012, President Barack Obama insisted that there were reasonable people of goodwill on both sides of the marriage debate. Supporters of marriage as the union of a man and a woman "are not coming at it from a mean-spirited perspective," he insisted. "They're coming at it because they care about families." He added that "a bunch of 'em are friends of mine...you know, people who I deeply respect."[32] The stories recounted in the last chapter, however, reveal that there are considerable grounds to worry about the government's respect for the beliefs of all Americans.

Respecting religious liberty in the marketplace is particularly important. After all, as the first lady, Michelle Obama, put it, religion "isn't
just about showing up on Sunday for a good sermon and good music and
a good meal. It's about what we do Monday through Saturday as well."[33]
And that's precisely why religious liberty protections in the economy are
so essential.

I don't want to suggest that there is a "war" on Christianity or that
Christians are being persecuted in the United States. We're not. Christians are suffering severe persecution for their faith in many parts of the
world, and we shouldn't trivialize it. None of the injustices I have
described here comes close to the atrocities committed in the Middle
East, Africa, and elsewhere.

But what happens in the United States still matters. The citizens of
a self-governing republic should pursue laws and public policies that serve
the common good. We should work to ensure respect for the religious
liberty of all Americans, not just for ourselves. In particular, we should
work to protect the rights of individuals and the associations they form—
businesses and charities, schools and social services—to speak and act
in the marketplace in accordance with their belief that marriage is the
union of a man and a woman.

Government Policy

Respect for religious liberty takes several forms. Charities, schools,
and other organizations that interact with the government should be held
to the same standards of competence as other groups, but their view that
marriage is the union of a man and a woman should not exclude them
from government programs. Government rightly withholds taxpayer
dollars from certain organizations—those that perform abortions, for
example, or those with racist policies—but upholding marriage as the
union of a man and a woman is not like killing or like racism, and the
cases should be treated differently.

Government policy—especially with respect to grants and contracts—should not trample on the consciences of goodwilled citizens

who dissent from official policies on sexuality. Government contracts should not seek to enforce monolithic liberal secularism. Government policy that discriminates against faith-based social service providers that believe marriage is a male-female relationship undermines our nation's commitment to reasonable pluralism and diversity. All citizens and the associations they form should be free to participate in government programs according to their reasonable beliefs.

Educational institutions, for example, should be eligible for government contracts, student loans, and other forms of support as long as they meet the relevant *educational* criteria. Adoption and foster care agencies that meet basic requirements for the welfare of children should be eligible for government contracts without having to abandon their values, especially their religiously informed beliefs about marriage. Protecting the conscience rights and religious liberty of private adoption providers takes nothing away from others. Not every private provider needs to perform every service, and state-run agencies can provide a complete array of services. Protecting the diversity of private providers, each serving families that share its values, will increase the number of children who are connected with permanent, loving families.

Government employees deserve similar protection. Consider a county clerk who has served in her job for decades issuing marriage licenses. Now the government has redefined marriage—and her job. Should she be forced in all circumstances to violate her beliefs? Or consider a police officer asked to ride his motorcycle at the front of a gay pride parade—not to provide security for the parade but to be a part of it on the department's behalf. Should he be forced to violate his beliefs?[34] Everyone deserves the protection of the police department. And of course an officer on patrol can't pick and choose which calls to respond to. In particular, all officers need to respond in *emergencies*. But none of this requires every police officer to accept every assignment ahead of time if his religious beliefs are at stake, alternatives are available, and accommodating him would compromise no one's safety. Indeed, Title VII of the Civil Rights Act of 1964 requires the government to accommodate conscientious objectors as best it can.[35]

The law of religious accommodation for public employees is complicated, but perhaps not as difficult as we sometimes make it. Professor Robin F. Wilson of the University of Illinois Law School, who supports same-sex marriage as a policy matter, writes, "A common refrain is that religious objectors in government service should do all of their job or resign. This stance conflates the public receipt of a service offered by the state with the receipt of that service from each and every employee in the office who is available to do it."[36] In other words, citizens have a claim to receive certain "services from the state, but they do not necessarily have a claim to receive the service from a particular public servant." Sometimes courts may find that there is no burden on the employee. Sometimes the employee may turn down a reasonable accommodation, or there might be no reasonable accommodation available. Employees often lose these disputes. Religious objection is not a trump card, but employees' religious objections should be accommodated when possible. Our law demands a careful—and possibly subtle—balancing of interests.

Specific Protections for Beliefs about Marriage

If we're going to disagree over the nature and purpose of marriage, then protecting the religious liberty rights to dissent—to speak that dissent and to act on that dissent—is essential. The federal government and the states must protect the rights of Americans and the associations they form—both nonprofit and for-profit—to speak and act in the public square in accordance with their beliefs. The stories in the previous chapter illustrate the growing conflict between religious liberty rights and laws that grant special privileges based on sexual orientation and gender identity.[37] We have learned that Religious Freedom Restoration Acts are inadequate to the task of protecting the free exercise of religion against the powerful campaign of big business, big media, and big government to force the entire nation to show approval of same-sex marriage. This coercion of conscience is outrageous in a nation founded on religious freedom, and further measures are necessary.

The recently proposed First Amendment Defense Act would prevent the federal government from engaging in such coercion. It would enact a bright-line rule that government can never penalize someone just for acting on his belief that marriage is the union of husband and wife.[38] The bill is sponsored in the House of Representatives by Republican Raul Labrador of Idaho and in the Senate by Republican Mike Lee of Utah.[39] Congress should pass the bill, and citizens should be given similarly specific protection at the state level.

Predictably, the Left has attacked this bill. The Sunday after the Supreme Court's ruling in *Obergefell*, the *New York Times* religion columnist, Mark Oppenheimer, wrote a column for *Time* magazine titled "Now's the Time to End Tax Exemptions for Religious Institutions."[40] Taking issue with Senator Lee, Oppenheimer argues, "Rather than try to rescue tax-exempt status for organizations that dissent from settled public policy on matters of race or sexuality, we need to take a more radical step. It's time to abolish, or greatly diminish, their tax-exempt statuses." But as Americans once understood, the power to tax is the power to destroy. We clearly have work to do.

America is in a time of transition. The court has redefined marriage, and beliefs about human sexuality are changing. Will the right to dissent be protected? Will our right to speak and act in accord with what Americans had always believed about marriage—that it's a union of husband and wife—be tolerated?

Most Americans say yes, they want to be a tolerant, pluralistic nation. They want peaceful coexistence. I agree with them. It's only ideologues and activists who want to sow the seeds of disharmony by having the government coerce those with whom they disagree. We must work together to protect these cherished American values.

The First Amendment Defense Act is one way of achieving civil peace even amid disagreement. To protect pluralism and the rights of all Americans, of whatever faith they may practice, this bill is good policy. Liberals committed to tolerance should embrace it.

We Must Protect Religious Liberty

Religious liberty is one of the natural rights that governments are instituted to secure. While Americans are free to live as they wish, they should not use the force of government to impose their sexual values on others.

Barronelle Stutzman, Elaine Huguenin—these people were not looking for a fight. They were just trying to remain true to their faith as their consciences directed them. They wanted to find a way to live and let live. They weren't going to prevent their customers from having their ceremony. They weren't going to prevent other professionals from lending a hand. They only asked not to be coerced into violating their consciences. They weren't interested in the culture war—but the culture war was interested in them. And it's interested in the rest of us, too.

SIX

ANTIDISCRIMINATION LAW: WHY SEXUAL ORIENTATION IS NOT LIKE RACE

T he U.S. Constitution has traditionally protected such fundamental civil liberties as freedom of speech, religion, and association, as well as the right to vote, own property, and enter
into contracts. The recognition of these civil liberties leaves everyone
equal before the law. But new laws that bestow special privileges on
some persons based on sexual orientation and gender identity (SOGI)
are undermining those same fundamental civil liberties, especially
freedom of speech and the free exercise of religion. These laws tend to
be vague and overly broad without clear definitions of what conduct
can and cannot be penalized. They expose innocent citizens to ruinous
liability, and they foster economically harmful government interference in markets.

But the damage of SOGI laws is not only economic. They threaten
the freedom of citizens, individually and in associations, to affirm their
religious or moral convictions—convictions such as that marriage is the

union of one man and one woman. Under SOGI laws, acting on these beliefs in a commercial context could be actionable discrimination. These are the laws that have been used to penalize the bakers, florists, photographers, and adoption agencies.

Advocates of SOGI laws, however, say they're just like racial antidiscrimination laws. They argue that opposition to same-sex marriage is just like opposition to interracial marriage—and that the government should treat it in the same way. Their refrain for the past decade has been that laws designating marriage as the union of male and female are no more defensible than bans on interracial marriage. And some argue further that laws protecting the freedom of conscience with respect to marriage are indistinguishable from the laws that enforced race-based segregation. These arguments are wrong on several counts.

However the law defines marriage, the state has no compelling interest in forcing every citizen to treat a same-sex relationship as a marriage in violation of his religious or moral convictions. Even people who personally support same-sex marriage can see that the government is not justified in coercing people who do not. After all, it is reasonable for citizens to believe that marriage is the union of man and woman. When citizens lead their lives and run their businesses in accord with this belief, they deny no one equality before the law. They deserve protection against government coercion.

The assumption that marriage is the union of a man and a woman was nearly universal among human societies until the year 2000. Samesex marriage is the work of revisionism in historical reasoning about marriage. Racial segregation laws, including bans on interracial marriage, were, by contrast, aspects of an insidious ideology that arose in the modern period in connection with race-based slavery and denied the fundamental equality and dignity of all human beings. The race of the spouses has nothing to do with the nature of marriage, and it is unreasonable, therefore, to make it a condition of marriage. This chapter explains all of this.

A Presumption of Freedom

The foundational principle of American life is liberty under law. In general, consenting adults are free to enter or refuse to enter relationships of every sort—personal, civic, commercial, romantic—without government interference. Freedom of association and contract is presumed. If the government is going to interfere, it must explain *why*. It has the burden of proof.

These rights of association and contract mean that businesses and charities and civic associations should be generally free to operate by their own values. They should be free to choose their employees and their customers, to choose the terms of employment and the standards of conduct for members of a club. They should be free to advance their own values and to live them out as they see fit. In every state of the union, after all, it's perfectly legal for an employer to fire an employee for all kinds of reasons—reasons someone else may find compelling or trivial or deplorable. To be sure, some people and groups can and do exercise their freedoms in ways of which others may disapprove. But in this country we tolerate such differences for the sake of the benefits of liberty—creativity, innovation, reform, economic vitality, and the like.

So, for example, in chapter 4 I recounted how the A&E television network suspended Phil Robertson and Cracker Barrel removed his products from its stores. The law left them free to do so. They ended up reversing those decisions because their customers didn't like them. Mozilla was free to force Brendan Eich to resign, and its constituency—techies—seemed content. The baker, the florist, and the photographer should be equally free to run their businesses according to their own values. Disagreement with someone's actions is not enough to justify the government's coercing him into conformity with prevailing opinion. Free association and exchange are usually sufficient to sort these things out, *especially* in cases of abuses, without the costs of government interference. How many businesses in America could post a "no gays allowed" sign and still make any money? The power of public opinion expressed in the marketplace would make such a policy intolerably costly—no need for the government to weigh in.

In short, then, any law that would establish special privileges based on a given trait has a high bar to clear. For one thing, it should be hard to imagine any *legitimate* decisions based on the trait. Otherwise, the cost of the law—sacrificing legitimate liberty—outweighs its benefit. Furthermore, the purported injustice targeted by the law must be resistant to market forces to justify *state* intervention, with all its unintended costs. Some people now claim that laws that create special privileges based on sexual orientation and gender identity (SOGI) clear this high bar. They are mistaken.

Americans should respect the equal dignity of their neighbors, but SOGI laws are not narrowly drawn to protect true equality before the law. As we will see, their far-reaching effects unite civil libertarians concerned about free speech and religious liberty, free marketers concerned about freedom of contract, and social conservatives concerned about marriage and culture.

When the Fayetteville, Arkansas, city council adopted a SOGI ordinance, informed citizens raised concerns about its consequences (intended or unintended), including the abridgement of religious liberty and disturbing policies governing transgender persons' access to restrooms. One of the organizers of the successful campaign to overrule the ordinance explained what was at stake:

> It was called the Civil Rights Ordinance, but it was misnamed. It was an ordinance that actually took away civil rights and freedom from people. It criminalized civil behavior. It didn't accomplish the stated purpose of the ordinance, and it was crafted by an outside group. It wasn't something Fayetteville residents put together.[1]

In May 2015, the school board of Fairfax County, Virginia, voted ten to one to add "gender identity" to its list of protected classes—against overwhelming opposition from parents at the school board meeting. The previous November, the board had voted to add sexual orientation.[2] Dustin Siggins, writing at the Federalist, reports what really drove the school board's vote: "Unless the board approved special treatment for transgendered students and teachers, the state's largest school district would lose $42 million in federal funding."[3] Siggins explains the likely consequences of the move, though the policy itself is rather vague:

> The consequences of the board's decision are clear: Boys who think or feel they are girls will be allowed to use restrooms and locker rooms of the opposite sex. If the board follows the example of Minnesota, schools would have to accommodate male transgendered students who want to spend nights at travel games in hotel rooms with female athletes.[4]

Activist organizations like the Human Rights Campaign—an influential, sophisticated, and lavishly funded LGBT activist organization—are pushing SOGI laws on unsuspecting citizens at the federal, state, and local levels. In 2015 HRC launched an initiative—Beyond Marriage Equality—to bring government coercion to bear on all Americans. This proposed legislation would add "sexual orientation and gender identity" to more or less every federal law that protects on the basis of race.[5] It goes well beyond the Employment Non-Discrimination Act (ENDA)—which would have added SOGI only to employment law. ENDA, which was first introduced in Congress in 1994, has been defeated each and every Congress. When it was first introduced, ENDA only included "sexual orientation," but in 2007 "gender identity" was added to the bill. Thankfully, ENDA has never been made law at the federal level. Nevertheless, having expanded the bill from including sexual orientation to also including gender identity, activists are also seeking to extend this misguided policy well beyond employment—to "credit, education, employment, federal funding, housing, jury service and public accommodations."[6] These SOGI laws must be resisted, as I explain now.

Sexual Orientation and Gender Identity Laws Create Unnecessary Problems

SOGI laws can have serious unintended consequences. They threaten small-business owners with liability for alleged "discrimination" based not on objective traits but on subjective and unverifiable identities. They expand state interference in labor markets, potentially discouraging job creation. They endanger religious liberty and freedom of speech. And they mandate employment policies that, with regard to many workplace conditions, violate common sense. In short, SOGI laws regulate commercial decisions that are best handled by private actors, and they regulate educational decisions best handled by parents and teachers, not bureaucrats.

Establishing special privileges based on gender identity is an especially bad idea. Prohibiting schools, businesses, and charities from making decisions about transgender students, faculty, and employees—especially regarding those in positions of role models—could be confusing to children and detrimental to workplace morale.

First, while issues of sex and gender identity are psychologically, morally, and politically controversial, all should agree that children should be protected from having to sort through such questions before they reach an appropriate age. SOGI laws would prevent schools and employers from protecting children from these adult debates about sex and gender identity by forcing employers to accommodate the desires of transgender employees in ways that put them in the spotlight.

Second, while some SOGI laws provide limited (and inadequate) exemptions for religious education, they provide no protection for students in nonreligious schools. These children would be prematurely exposed to questions about sex and gender if, for example, a male teacher returned to school identifying as a woman. Difficulties can also arise when a student identifies as transgender and seeks to use the restrooms and locker rooms that correspond to his or her new gender identity. These situations are best handled at the local level, by the parents and teachers closest to the children.

Finally, whatever the significance of gender identity, society cannot deny the relevance, in many contexts, of biological sex. For example, an employer would be negligent to ignore the concerns of female employees about having to share a bathroom with a biological male who identifies as female. The same is true for students. The implications for the privacy rights of adults and children are extremely serious, and state laws are already stirring up such concerns. Writing about the proposed federal Employment Non-Discrimination Act (ENDA), Hans Bader, a scholar with the Competitive Enterprise Institute, warns:

> ENDA also contains "transgender rights" provisions that ban discrimination based on "gender identity." Similar prohibitions in state laws created legal headaches for some businesses. One case pitted a transgender employee with male DNA who sued after being denied permission to use the ladies' restroom, a denial that resulted from complaints filed by female employees. The employer lost in the Minnesota Court of Appeals, but then prevailed in the Minnesota Supreme Court. Another case involved a male-looking person who sued and obtained a substantial settlement after being ejected from the ladies' room in response to complaints by a female customer who thought that a man had just invaded the ladies' room.[7]

Market competition can provide more nuanced solutions for particular situations that are superior to a coercive, one-size-fits-all government policy on sexual orientation and gender identity. Schools should be free to develop a variety of policies to address the needs of their students, parents, and teachers. The same is true for businesses. For example, competing interests in employment can be secured through bargaining with various employers who hold a variety of moral or religious beliefs. After all, employers all compete with each other for the best employees. They have incentives to consider only those factors that truly matter for their mission. And companies all compete with each other for customers.

So they have every reason to accept business unless it really does conflict with their deepest commitments.

Those who base their business decisions on moral and religious views may well pay a price in the market, perhaps losing customers and qualified employees, but this only weakens the case for costly government intervention. Bader reports that the liberal Center for American Progress admitted that market forces are already at work in this area: "Businesses that discriminate based on a host of job-irrelevant characteristics, including sexual orientation…put themselves at a competitive disadvantage compared to businesses that evaluate individuals based solely on their qualifications and capacity to contribute."[8] Decisions as to what is "job-relevant" should generally be left to employers and the market.

Many companies have their own policies prohibiting consideration of sexual orientation and gender identity in employment. The Human Rights Campaign reports that 88 percent of Fortune 500 companies voluntarily do not consider sexual orientation in employment decisions.[9] "Median LGBT household income," moreover, "is $61,500 vs. $50,000 for the average American household," according to Prudential.[10] It's hard to see what the justification could be for a federal law that would interfere in employment decisions to create special privileges based on sexual orientation and gender identity when the market is already sorting these things out.[11]

A fundamental principle of American labor law is the doctrine of "at-will" employment, which leaves employers free to dismiss employees at any time. In many other countries, a thicket of laws and regulations makes it extremely difficult to terminate a contract with an employee. Businesses do not want to get stuck with unproductive or superfluous workers. If they cannot lay off employees, they are less willing to take the risk of hiring them in the first place.

Studies find that restrictions on layoffs seriously restrict hiring and job creation. The most severe French prohibitions on layoffs apply to businesses with fifty or more employees. One recent study found that more than twice as many French manufacturers have forty-nine employees as have fifty workers.[12] French businesses seem to curtail hiring to avoid being stuck with poor performers.

SOGI laws chip away at the at-will employment doctrine that has made the American labor market so much stronger than European labor markets. The subjective nature of sexual orientation and gender identity magnifies these problems by encouraging employees to threaten a lawsuit against their employer in response to adverse employment decisions. Hans Bader points out, "Since American business seldom discriminates based on sexual orientation, the potential benefits of ENDA are limited, at best. But ENDA would impose real and substantial costs on business, and it could trigger conflicts with free speech and religious freedom."[13]

The threats to speech and religion are serious. Bader notes that the Supreme Court found that Title VII of the Civil Rights Act of 1964 "require[s] employers to prohibit employee speech or conduct that creates a 'hostile or offensive work environment' for women, blacks, or religious minorities."[14] Employers may even be liable for damages and attorney's fees if they are negligent in failing to notice, stop, or discipline employees whose speech or conduct creates such an environment. SOGI laws would extend these restrictions to "actual and perceived sexual orientation or gender identity."

Consequently, employees or employers who express disapproving religious or political views of same-sex marriage could incur enormous legal liabilities. Businesses would likely respond to such potential liability by self-censoring their speech and preventing employees from expressing views such as support for marriage as a union of one man and one woman.

Bader, who supports same-sex marriage, warns of the potential violations of liberty that ENDA threatens for those who hold other views:

> If ENDA were enacted, such liability would also cover "sexual orientation"–based hostile work environments....Thus, to avoid liability, an employer might have to silence employees with political opinions that are perceived as anti-gay, and

prevent such employees from expressing political views such as opposition to gay marriage or gays in the military that could contribute to a "hostile work environment." ...While I have supported gay marriage and the inclusion of gays in the military, I do not think employers should be sued because their employees express contrary views....[S]ome courts have interpreted "disparate treatment" to include speech or conduct by the complainant's co-workers that affects the complainant's work environment, even when the speech is not aimed at the complainant, and is not motivated by the complainant's sex or minority status....

The possibility that ENDA will be used to silence speech about gay issues is very real. Indeed, some supporters of ENDA openly hope to use it to squelch viewpoints that offend them.[15]

In states with their own versions of ENDA—like California and Washington—employers have already started censoring their employees.[16] Regina Redford and Robin Christy, two employees of the City of Oakland, California, responded to the formation of an association of gay and lesbian employees by forming the "Good News Employee Association," which they promoted with flyers that read, "Good News Employee Association is a forum for people of Faith to express their views on the contemporary issues of the day. With respect for the Natural Family, Marriage and Family values." These flyers contained no reference to homosexuality. But their supervisors ordered the flyers removed, announced in an e-mail that they contained "statements of a homophobic nature and were determined to promote sexual orientation based harassment," and warned that anyone posting such materials could face "discipline up to and including termination."[17]

State versions of ENDA have also chilled employer speech. Seattle's Human Rights Commission brought charges against Bryan Griggs for playing Christian radio stations (on which he advertised) in his place of work and posting a letter from his congresswoman expressing reservations about gays in the military. When a self-identified gay employee complained of a hostile work environment, Griggs had to spend thousands of dollars on legal fees before the plaintiff dropped the charges, saying he had made his point.[18]

SOGI laws imperil religious liberty, privacy, economic freedom, and child welfare, creating more problems than they aim to resolve. They are a solution in search of a problem.

Laws Protecting against Racism Were Necessary and Justified, unlike SOGI Laws

Government should never penalize people for expressing and acting on their view that marriage is the union of husband and wife. Some people, however, want the government to penalize actions based on this belief, claiming that it's akin to racism. They're wrong. Here's why.

While protections against racial discrimination have been necessary and justified, antidiscrimination laws based on sexual orientation and gender identity are neither. Likewise, religious liberty protections for those who object to same-sex marriage are profoundly different from legal enforcement of racial segregation.[19] Robin Wilson, a law professor who supports same-sex marriage as a policy matter, writes, "The religious and moral convictions that motivate objectors to refuse to facilitate same-sex marriage simply cannot be marshaled to justify racial discrimination."[20]

To see how racial discrimination was always alien to our liberties, rightly understood, we can look to history. "The most robust of all property rights," writes the law professor Adam MacLeod, "is the right to exclude, which enables an owner to choose which friends, collaborators, and potential collaborators to include in the use of land and other resources."[21] At common law, these protections extend even to the commercial domain: "If a property owner opens his or her domain to the public as a bakery, for example, the owner does not thereby relinquish her right to exclude. Rather, the common law requires the landowner to have a reason for excluding."[22] But there are no such reasons for excluding on the basis of race, MacLeod argues:

> To combat widespread racial discrimination, Congress and state legislatures promulgated rules in the latter half of the twentieth century that prohibit discrimination in public accommodations and large-scale residential leasing on the basis of race....
>
> In essence, these laws established a bright-line rule. Exclusion on the basis of race is always unreasonable, and therefore unlawful. These laws pick out motivations for exclusion that are never valid reasons. This wasn't really a change in the law—it was never reasonable to discriminate on the basis of race—but rather a conclusive statement of what the law requires.[23]

Before the Civil War, a dehumanizing regime of race-based chattel slavery existed in many states. After abolition, Jim Crow laws enforced race-based segregation. Those wicked laws enforced the separation of persons of different races, preventing them from associating or contracting with one another. Even after the Supreme Court struck down Jim Crow laws, integration did not come easily or willingly in many instances. Public policy therefore sought to eliminate racial discrimination, even when committed by private actors on private property.

Racial segregation was rampant and entrenched when Congress intervened to stop it. Today, however, market forces are sufficient to ensure that people identifying as gay or lesbian receive the wedding-related services they seek. In every publicized case of a business owner's declining to facilitate a same-sex ceremony, the service sought by the couple was readily available from other businesses. In other words, a pluralistic civil society is policing itself; no law is needed here.

Furthermore, the right of religious liberty has been invoked not with respect to sexual orientation in general but with respect to marriage.

Citizens have resisted being coerced into celebrating or providing services for same-sex weddings and treating same-sex relationships as marriages in violation of their beliefs.

MacLeod explains how the right to exclude on a reasonable basis applies in these situations:

> Why is it unreasonable for a photographer to serve all people, including those who self-identify as homosexual, but to refuse to endorse by her conduct the claim that a same-sex commitment ceremony is, in fact, a wedding? If a jury or other competent fact-finder determines that the photographer has a sincere moral or religious conviction that marriage is the union of a man and a woman (and therefore does not include a same-sex couple, a polyamorous group, a polygamous family, and so on), then the photographer has a reason not to use her property (in this case, her camera and her business) to endorse what she believes to be a lie.[24]

Running a business in accordance with the view that marriage is a union of husband and wife is reasonable and should be lawful. Running it based on racist views is unreasonable and thus unlawful.

Bans on Interracial Marriage Were Based on Racism and Had Nothing to Do with Marriage

The analogy that opposition to same-sex marriage is akin to racism and bans on interracial marriage simply fails as a historical and conceptual matter, but few people know the relevant history. Interracial marriage bans are the exception in world history. They have existed *only* in societies with a race-based caste system, in connection with race-based slavery. The understanding of marriage as the union of a man and a woman, on the other hand, has been the norm throughout human history, shared by the great thinkers and religions of both East and West and by cultures with a wide variety of viewpoints about homosexuality.

Likewise, many religions, quite reasonably, teach that human beings are created male and female, and that male and female are created for each other in marriage. Nothing even remotely similar is true of race.

And far from having been devised as a pretext for excluding same-sex relationships—as some now charge—marriage as the union of husband and wife arose in many places over several centuries entirely independent of and well before any debates about same-sex relationships. Indeed, it arose in cultures that had no concept of sexual orientation and in some that fully accepted homoeroticism and even took it for granted.[25]

Searching the writings of Plato and Aristotle, Augustine and Aquinas, Maimonides and al-Farabi, Luther and Calvin, Locke and Kant, Gandhi and Martin Luther King Jr., one finds that the sexual union of male and female goes to the heart of their reflections on marriage, but considerations of race with respect to marriage are simply absent.[26] Only late in human history do we see political communities prohibiting interracial marriage. Such bans had nothing to do with the nature of marriage and everything to do with denying racial equality.

The prohibitions of interracial marriage in colonial America were unprecedented, writes the historian Nancy Cott of Harvard:

> It is important to retrieve the singularity of the racial basis for these laws. Ever since ancient Rome, class-stratified and estate-based societies had instituted laws against intermarriage between individuals of unequal social or civil status, with the aim of preserving the integrity of the ruling class.... But the English colonies stand out as the first secular authorities to nullify and criminalize intermarriage on the basis of race or color designations.[27]

Laws banning interracial marriage were virtually unique to America, explains the legal scholar David Upham: "As one jurist explained in 1883...'[m]arriage is a natural right into which the question of color does not enter except as an individual preference expressed by the parties to the marriage. It is so recognized by the laws of all nations except our own.'"[28]

The English common law, which Americans inherited, imposed no barriers to interracial marriage.[29] Antimiscegenation statutes, which first appeared in Maryland in 1661, were the result of African slavery.[30] Slaves, Cott notes, "could *not* marry legally; their unions received no protection from state authorities. Any master could override a slave's marital commitment [emphasis in original]."[31] They were not citizens or even persons in the eyes of the law. "The denial of legal marriage to slaves quintessentially expressed their lack of civil rights," writes Cott. "To marry meant to consent, and slaves could not exercise the fundamental capacity to consent."[32]

Francis Beckwith summarizes the history of antimiscegenation laws:

> The overwhelming consensus among scholars is that the reason for these laws was to enforce racial purity, an idea that begins its cultural ascendancy with the commencement of race-based slavery of Africans in early 17th-century America and eventually receives the imprimatur of "science" when the eugenics movement comes of age in the late 19th and early 20th centuries.[33]

He concludes:

> Anti-miscegenation laws, therefore, were attempts to eradicate the legal status of real marriages by injecting a condition—sameness of race—that had no precedent in common law. For in the common law, a necessary condition for a legitimate marriage was male-female complementarity, a condition on which race has no bearing.[34]

In other words, antimiscegenation laws were but one aspect of a legal system designed to hold a race of people in a condition of economic and political inferiority and servitude. They had nothing to do with the nature of marriage. At their heart was a denial of human dignity.

Race has nothing to do with marriage, but marriage has everything to do with uniting the two halves of humanity—men and women—as husbands and wives and as mothers and fathers committed to any chil-dren they bring into the world. So while marriage must be color-blind, it cannot be blind to sex. The melanin content of a person's skin has nothing to do with his capacity to unite with another in the bond of marriage as a comprehensive union naturally ordered to procreation. The sexual difference between a man and a woman, however, is at the heart of marriage. Men and women, whatever their race, can unite in marriage. Children, whatever their race, deserve a mom and a dad—their own mom and dad wherever possible.

    Although some invoked the Bible to support interracial marriage bans, religious views about marriage helped to eliminate those very laws. Indeed, the first court to strike down an interracial marriage ban did so in light of a religious argument advanced by an interracial Catholic couple. Professor Fay Botham describes the reasoning behind the Cali-fornia Supreme Court's decision in *Perez v. Sharpe* (1948):[35]

> [The argument] hinged upon several key points of Catholic doctrine:...third, that the Catholic Church has no law forbid-ding "the intermarriage of a nonwhite person and a white per-son"; and fourth, that the Church "respects the requirements of the State for the marriage of its citizens as long as they are in keeping with the dignity and Divine purpose of marriage."[36]

Botham continues:

> [The argument] appealed to the highest source of Catholic authority: the Holy Father himself. Citing Pope Pius XI's 1937 encyclical to the church in Germany, *Mit brennender Sorge*, [the lawyer] pointed out that the "Church has condemned the prop-osition that 'it is imperative at all costs to preserve and promote racial vigor and the purity of blood; whatever is conducive to this end is by that very fact honorable and permissible.'"[37]

The court sided with the Catholic plaintiffs and overturned the state's ban on interracial marriage. Part of the argument hinged on what marriage is and its connection to procreation:

> The right to marry is as fundamental as the right to send one's child to a particular school or the right to have offspring. Indeed, "We are dealing here with legislation which involves one of the basic civil rights of man. Marriage and procreation are fundamental to the very existence and survival of the race."[38]

A few years later, the same court again addressed the meaning of marriage, finding that "the institution of marriage" serves "the public interest" because it "channels biological drives that might otherwise become socially destructive" and "ensures the care and education of children in a stable environment."[39]

The U.S. Supreme Court reached a similar conclusion in 1967 when it struck down all bans on interracial marriage in *Loving v. Virginia*. Declaring that such laws were premised on "the doctrine of White Supremacy,"[40] the court found

> no legitimate overriding purpose independent of invidious racial discrimination which justifies this classification. The fact that Virginia prohibits only interracial marriages involving white persons demonstrates that the racial classifications must stand on their own justification, as measures designed to maintain White Supremacy.[41]

The law thus fell as an impermissible racial classification.

As in *Perez*, numerous religious groups argued that racism distorted a clear-eyed understanding of marriage. As Susan Dudley Gold recounts in *"Loving v. Virginia": Lifting the Ban against Interracial Marriage*:

A coalition made up of Catholic bishops, the National Catholic Conference for Interracial Justice, and the National Catholic Social Action Committee filed a fourth amicus brief in favor of the Lovings. The bishops and the nonprofit groups became involved in the case because of their commitment "to end racial discrimination and prejudice" and because of the "serious issues of personal liberty" raised by the Lovings' ordeal.[42]

Catholics were not alone. Southern Baptist theologians also opposed bans on interracial marriage. In 1964, three years before the Supreme Court ruled in *Loving*, T. B. Maston published a booklet for the Christian Life Commission of the Southern Baptist Convention titled *Interracial Marriage*. While Maston thought "interracial marriages, at least in our society, are not wise," he was clear on their biblical status: "A case cannot be made against interracial marriages on the basis of any specific teachings of the Scripture."[43] Indeed, he argued, "The laws forbidding interracial marriages should be repealed."[44]

Sexual Orientation and Gender Identity Are Conceptually Different from Race

The problem with SOGI policies is not merely that they are unnecessary, that they produce unintended but profoundly damaging consequences, or that they are based on a false analogy between same-sex marriage and interracial marriage. The main problem is even deeper—sexual orientation and gender identity are radically different from race and so should not be elevated to a protected class in the way that race is. First, sexual orientation and gender identity are linked to actions, which are a proper subject matter for moral evaluation, and race is not. Second, race manifests itself readily, whereas sexual orientation and gender identity are ambiguous, subjective, and variable traits. Third, special privileges based on sexual orientation and gender identity undermine the common good by weakening a marriage culture, while protections against racism do not. Let's take these three points in turn.

Martin Luther King Jr. dreamed that his children would be judged not by the color of their skin but by the content of their character. A person's character is expressed in his voluntary actions, and it is reasonable to make judgments about actions. Race implies nothing about one's actions. But in practice, sexual orientation and gender identity terms are frequently used with reference to a person's actions. "Gay" comes to mean not simply a man who desires sex with other men but one who voluntarily engages in such sex acts. "Lesbian" comes to mean a woman who engages in sex acts with other women. Meanwhile, "transgender" is used not simply to describe someone who experiences distress at his biological sex but a biological male who voluntarily presents himself to the world as a female or a biological female who voluntarily presents herself as a male.

SOGI laws impugn judgments common to the Abrahamic faith traditions and to great thinkers from Plato to Kant. By the light of religion, reason, or experience, many people of goodwill believe that our bodies are an essential part of who we are and that maleness and femaleness are not arbitrary constructs but objective ways of being human. A person's sex is to be valued and affirmed, not rejected or altered. Our sexual embodiment as male and female goes to the heart of what marriage is: a union of sexually complementary spouses.

SOGI laws threaten these truths in part because the definitions of sexual orientation and gender identity are ambiguous. They make it a crime for citizens to engage in what the government deems to be "discrimination" based on an "individual's actual or perceived sexual orientation or gender identity." "Sexual orientation" is defined as "homosexuality, heterosexuality, or bisexuality," but the laws leave those terms undefined and offer no principle that limits "orientation" to those three. The definition of "gender identity" is likewise elastic: "The gender-related identity, appearance, or mannerisms or other gender-related characteristics of an individual, with or without regard to the individual's designated sex at birth."

Two eminent authorities—Paul McHugh, MD, the university distinguished service professor of psychiatry at the Johns Hopkins University School of Medicine, and Gerard V. Bradley, a professor of law at the University of Notre Dame—explain why antidiscrimination laws based on these categories are problematic as a matter of science and the law:

> [S]ocial science research continues to show that sexual orientation, unlike race, color, and ethnicity, is neither a clearly defined concept nor an immutable characteristic of human beings. Basing federal employment law on a vaguely defined concept such as sexual orientation, especially when our courts have a wise precedent of limiting suspect classes to groups that have a clearly-defined shared characteristic, would undoubtedly cause problems for many well-meaning employers.[45]

McHugh and Bradley caution against elevating sexual orientation and gender identity to the status of protected characteristics because of the lack of clear definition:

> "Sexual orientation" should not be recognized as a newly protected characteristic of individuals under federal law. And neither should "gender identity" or any cognate concept. In contrast with other characteristics, it is neither discrete nor immutable. There is no scientific consensus on how to define sexual orientation, and the various definitions proposed by experts produce substantially different groups of people.[46]

Continuing, they summarize the relevant scholarly scientific research on sexual orientation and gender identity:

> Nor is there any convincing evidence that sexual orientation is biologically determined; rather, research tends to show that

for some persons and perhaps for a great many, "sexual orientation" is plastic and fluid; that is, it changes over time. What we do know with certainty about sexual orientation is that it is affective and behavioral—a matter of desire and/or behavior. And "gender identity" is even more fluid and erratic, so much so that in limited cases an individual could claim to "identify" with a different gender on successive days at work. Employers should not be obliged by dint of civil and possibly criminal penalties to adjust their workplaces to suit felt needs such as these.[47]

Because sexual orientation and gender identity are ambiguous, subjective concepts that may change over time, a law invoking them to define a protected class would be especially ripe for abuse.

It is not clear, moreover, what would prevent the category of "sexual orientation" from expanding to cover a host of inclinations and behaviors. McHugh and Bradley explain this policy problem in the context of the proposed ENDA:

Despite the effort of ENDA's legislative drafters to confine "sexual orientation" to homosexuality, heterosexuality, and bisexuality, the logic of self-defined "orientation" is not so easily cabined....Even polyamory, "a preference for having multiple romantic relationships simultaneously," has been defended as "a type of sexual orientation for purposes of anti-discrimination law" in a 2011 law review article.[48]

No principle limits what will be classified as a sexual orientation or gender identity in the future. Indeed, Wesleyan College has extended the LGBT acronym and created a "safe space" for LGBTTQQFAG-PBDSM: Lesbian, Gay, Bisexual, Transgender, Transsexual, Queer, Questioning, Flexual, Asexual, Genderf—k, Polyamorous, Bondage/Disciple, Dominance/Submission, Sadism/Masochism.[49] Will SOGI laws be used to protect these orientations and identities as well? If not, why not? SOGI, McHugh and Bradley conclude, would "lead to insurmountable enforcement difficulties, arbitrary and even whimsical results in many cases, and it would have an unjustified chilling effect upon all too many employers' decisions."[50]

Compounding these definitional problems is the point made earlier: sexual orientation and gender identity can refer not only to thoughts and inclinations but also to behavior, and it is reasonable for citizens to make distinctions based on actions. Consequently, SOGI laws would prohibit reasonable decisions based on behavior.

Professor John Finnis of the University of Oxford explains why most modern legal systems are right to resist adding sexual orientation (let alone gender identity) to antidiscrimination provisions:

> [T]he standard modern position deliberately rejects proposals to include in such lists the item "sexual orientation." For the phrase "sexual orientation" is radically equivocal. Particularly as used by promoters of "gay rights," it ambiguously assimilates two things which the standard modern position carefully distinguishes: (I) a psychological or psychosomatic disposition inwardly orienting one towards homosexual activity; (II) the deliberate decision so to orient one's public behavior as to express or manifest one's active interest in and endorsement of homosexual conduct and/or forms of life which presumptively involve such conduct.
>
> Indeed, laws or proposed laws outlawing "discrimination based on sexual orientation" are always interpreted by "gay rights" movements as going far beyond discrimination based merely on (i) A's belief that B is sexually attracted to persons of the same sex. Such movements interpret the phrase as extending full legal protection to (ii) public activities intended specifically to promote, procure, and facilitate homosexual conduct.[51]

Rather than merely protecting against unjust discrimination based on involuntary attractions or desires, SOGI policies forbid citizens from considering public actions. As Professor Finnis concludes:

> So, while the standard position accepts that discrimination on the basis of type I dispositions is unjust, it judges that there are compelling reasons both to deny that such injustice would be appropriately remedied by laws against "discrimination based on sexual orientation," and to hold that such a "remedy" would work significant discrimination and injustice against (and would indeed damage) families, associations, and institutions which have organized themselves to live out and transmit ideals of family life that include a high conception of the worth of truly conjugal sexual intercourse.[52]

Finnis's argument highlights one of SOGI policies' most concerning implications: The laws would further weaken the marriage culture and the ability of citizens and their associations to affirm that marriage is the union of a man and a woman and that sexual relations are reserved for marriage so understood. SOGI laws treat these convictions as if they were bigotry.

In sum, SOGI laws are a solution in search of a problem. They pose serious problems for free markets and contracts, free speech and religious liberty, and the health of our marriage culture. The standard justifications used to defend SOGI laws fail as well. Understanding marriage as the union of man and woman is a reasonable position; bans on interracial marriage were not. Marriage as the union of man and woman is witnessed to repeatedly in the Bible; prohibitions on interracial marriage are not. While interracial marriage bans were clearly part of a wider system of oppression, beliefs about marriage as the union of male and female are not.

There are no good historical or philosophical reasons for the law to treat sexual orientation and gender identity as it treats race—and doing so has serious costs.

SEVEN

THE VICTIMS

I n the earlier chapters of this book, I focused on what marriage is and why it matters, and I explored some of the consequences of redefining marriage. I concentrated on marriage as a public institution to show how changing the public definition of marriage changes marriage *for everyone.*

But what about particular couples and their particular households? The gay marriage movement has achieved much of its success by drawing attention to individual stories, building sympathy for the real families— loving, responsible, stable—who long for "marriage equality." And they're right—we *do* need to look at the households of actual same-sex couples, especially those with children. In this chapter, we'll consider the effects of redefining marriage on the children of same-sex couples. If we're going to rebuild a marriage culture, we'll have to respond to the questions about same-sex marriage and same-sex parenting. We will need new ways of presenting the truth, and social science and personal testimonies provide a way forward.

First, I'll briefly review what we know from social science about how marriage does its important work for kids. Then I'll look at what social scientists are discovering about same-sex parenting and how the redefinition of marriage affects the entire marriage culture. What ultrasound has done for the pro-life movement, good social science can do for the marriage movement. Americans need to know about it.

Second, I'll introduce you to some of the newest voices in the marriage debate: gays and lesbians and children of gays and lesbians who are opposed to the redefinition of marriage. Just as the mainstream media want you to think that Nancy Pelosi speaks for all women in the abortion debate, so too they want you to think that the LGBT community speaks with one voice about marriage. That's not true. And just as women speaking for themselves about the evils of abortion are powerful witnesses for the pro-life movement, so gays and lesbians and the children of same-sex couples who, with considerable courage, oppose redefining marriage are powerful witnesses for the marriage movement. Philosophical argument and scientific evidence are essential, but personal testimony changes hearts.

Social Science

Perhaps you've heard that it makes "no difference" for children whether they are raised by a same-sex couple or by their married mom and dad. Don't believe it. A lot depends on how social scientists interpret the data and on their comparison group, but not a single scientifically rigorous study establishes that conclusion. The scientifically rigorous studies of same-sex parenting all conclude that as a rule, the best place for children is in the home of their married mother and father.

A Forty-Year Consensus: Married Mom and Dad Matter

Scientists have only recently started looking at parenting by same-sex couples—we'll look into that below. But prior to the debate over same-sex marriage, the consensus among family sociologists was that a married mother and father were important for child development. I discussed this consensus in chapter 1, but I'd like to repeat a quotation from a review of the literature in 2002 by the left-leaning research institution Child Trends:

> [I]t is not simply the presence of two parents, as some have assumed, but the presence of *two biological parents* that seems to support children's development [emphasis in original].
>
> [R]esearch clearly demonstrates that family structure matters for children, and the family structure that helps children the most is a family headed by two biological parents in a low-conflict marriage. Children in single-parent families, children born to unmarried mothers, and children in step-families or cohabiting relationships face higher risks of poor outcomes than do children in intact families headed by two biological parents. There is thus value for children in promoting strong, stable marriages between biological parents.[1]

This sums up about forty years of robust social science evidence showing the importance of a married mother and father for children.[2] Scholars have studied the married biological mother-and-father family and compared it with several alternatives, including single parenting, cohabitation, divorce, and—most relevant for evaluating the idea that "any two parents" suffice—divorce with remarriage. And on more or less every factor that social science could measure, children living with their married biological mother and father have advantages, as a rule, over children in any of the alternatives. Over and over again, with large random representative samples, many of which were also longitudinal (that is, tracking the same children through time), the results show the importance of the intact married biological family.

The evidence was so strong that we saw something that hardly ever happens in the academy: scholars willing to change their minds on an issue. A sea change in academic opinion usually occurs only when one generation of scholars dies off and a new generation with new ideas takes its place. That didn't happen this time. The evidence was so compelling that liberal scholars and observers who had thought marriage unimportant acknowledged that they had been wrong.

A case in point is the liberal magazine the *Atlantic*. In 1992, you may recall, Vice President Dan Quayle had criticized the television show *Murphy Brown* for glamorizing single motherhood and was roundly mocked for his "old-fashioned" view. But as more and more social scientists looked at the data, they came to agree with Quayle. In April 1993, the *Atlantic* ran a cover story by Barbara Dafoe Whitehead titled "Dan Quayle Was Right."[3]

The magazine's editors acknowledged:

> The social-science evidence is in: though it may benefit the adults involved, the dissolution of intact two-parent families is harmful to large numbers of children. Moreover, the author argues, family diversity in the form of increasing numbers of single-parent and stepparent families does not strengthen the social fabric but, rather, dramatically weakens and undermines society.[4]

Notice that last sentence: *even stepparent families* do not strengthen the social fabric. It's true. It's not just about two incomes or the attention of two people. As a general rule, divorce and remarriage provides a setting that is little better for children than divorce alone. Even when you get a second income and second parent back in the family through remarriage, children tend to be no better off than if the divorced parent had not remarried.[5]

The question, then, is *why*. Over the years, social scientists have identified three factors that seem to explain why marriage matters: biology, sex, and stability.[6]

A biological connection between parents and their children seems to make a difference. Most people understand this intuitively. If you check into a hospital in labor, you care which baby they give you when you check out. You don't want to leave with *a* child but *your* child. If biology didn't matter, who would care which child went home with whom? Likewise, children seem to have an innate desire to know and be known by their natural biological parents. The children's T-shirt emblazoned "My daddy's name is Donor" may be intended as a sassy affirmation of lesbian parenting, but most people read it as the sardonic lament of a child conceived through the services of a sperm bank.[7]

Biology matters not only conceptually, but also empirically. People seem best equipped by nature to raise children to whom they are biologically related. Scientists have a name for this phenomenon: kin altruism. There are measurable differences between a child's being raised by his biological mother and father and his being raised by adoptive parents—even if the child is adopted right after birth.[8] This is not to denigrate adoption, which is indispensable. Adoptive parents do heroic work. They are no less truly their children's parents, and law and culture should recognize that. But the data do suggest that whenever possible, children should be raised by their biological parents.

To give just one example of the differences: The onset of puberty in a girl is delayed on average by about a year if she is raised by her biological father. By contrast, having a non–biologically related male in the house tends to accelerate the onset of puberty.[9] Scientists aren't entirely sure of the reasons for these differences,[10] but they are there, and they matter for children.

So biology matters. Sex does, too. Men and women, mothers and fathers, are not interchangeable. David Popenoe, the Rutgers sociologist whom I quoted in chapter 1, writes:

> We should disavow the notion that "mommies can make good daddies," just as we should disavow the popular notion...that "daddies can make good mommies."... The two sexes are different to the core, and each is necessary—culturally and biologically—for the optimal development of a human being.[11]

Mothers and fathers interact with children in distinct and complementary ways. The complementarity of the sexes in parenting helps explain why intact married biological families are better for children.

Social scientists also know that stability matters and that familial disruptions harm children.[12] Cohabitation, divorce, and divorce and remarriage entail more instability than faithful marriages. We know how traumatic divorce can be for the adults involved, but it is even worse for the children, who internalize it more intensely than adults do.[13]

If the three great advantages of intact married families are biology, sexual complementarity, and stability, what can we expect to be true of same-sex parenting?

The Science of Same-Sex Parenting

After four decades of consensus about the advantages for children of growing up with their married mother and father, the scholarly standards of family studies seemed to decline. The media began to tout a series of methodologically inadequate studies that supposedly found "no differences" between same-sex parenting and parenting by married moms and dads. Major professional associations, such as the American Psychological Association and the American Sociological Association, submitted amicus curiae briefs in litigation over same-sex marriage asserting that "no differences" is now settled science.[14] Indeed, some of these studies concluded that two females raising children produced better outcomes for children than married mothers and fathers.[15]

This politicized science set off alarm bells among some scholars. It was difficult to believe that, though a child who grows up in a divorced and remarried home or in an adopted home with a mom and a dad is more likely to struggle than a child in an intact biological married home, a child growing up with two moms is "no different" or perhaps even better off.[16] The absence of a father harms children being raised by single mothers; the absence of a father harms children being raised by divorced mothers; but the absence of a father makes no difference for children in lesbian households? That didn't seem right.

And indeed it wasn't right. Researchers looked into the fifty-nine studies finding no differences on which the American Psychological Association relied in its amicus briefs and found that they drew primarily from small convenience samples—nonrandom, nonrepresentative samples—that are not appropriate for generalizations to the whole population.[17]

An amicus brief submitted to the Supreme Court in the *Obergefell* case by the American College of Pediatricians, Family Watch International, and professors Loren Marks, Mark Regnerus, and Donald Paul Sullins (the "ACP brief") clarifies what the evidence shows:

> Despite being certified by almost all major social science scholarly associations—indeed, in part because of this—the alleged scientific consensus that having two parents of the same sex is innocuous for child well-being is almost wholly without basis. All but a handful of the studies cited in support draw on small, non-random samples which cannot be extrapolated to the same-sex population at large. This limitation is repeatedly acknowledged in scientific meetings and journals, but ignored when asserted as settled findings in public or judicial advocacy.[18]

The studies favored by the advocates of same-sex marriage relied on convenience, or snowball, sampling. John Londregan, a professor of political science at Princeton University, explains: "Convenience samples are a staple of the literature because same-sex parenting is rare, and so recruiting same-sex parents for a study generally involves placing ads at day-care centers and in publications aimed at the LGBT population, or contacting people by way of their network of friends."[19]

For example, researchers would post notices in gay bookstores or coffee shops inviting people to participate in a study on same-sex parenting. Some of these studies, as a result, were confined to upper-middle-class women living in San Francisco and New York City—households in elite urban areas with two college degrees and two incomes. You can't draw any conclusions about the LGBT population—or their children—as a whole from such a sample. The parenting studies that were behind the forty-year consensus, on the other hand, were based on representative samples and controlled for factors like education, income, and occupation.

At one point, American courts recognized the need for methodological rigor in studies presented as sociological evidence. As recently as a decade ago, the Court of Appeals for the Eleventh Circuit complained about "significant flaws in the studies' methodologies and conclusions, such as the use of small, self-selected samples; reliance on self-report instruments; politically driven hypotheses; and the use of unrepresentative study populations consisting of disproportionately affluent, educated parents."[20]

So the studies being touted in the media and in courtrooms today are flawed. But what do the more recent studies using better methodology show?

As of April 2015, only eight studies have been conducted using rigorous methods and robust samples, and, when properly analyzed, they all support the previous consensus: children do best when raised by a married mother and father. These include the New Family Structures Study by Professor Mark Regnerus of the University of Texas at Austin, a study of Canadian census data by Douglas W. Allen, and two studies by Donald Paul Sullins based on the American Centers for Disease Control's National Health Interview Survey.[21]

Professor Regnerus summarizes the current state of the science:

> [P]opulation-based surveys of same-sex households with children all tend to reveal *the same thing*, regardless of the data source.... Published research employing the New Family Structures Study (NFSS), the ECLS (Early Childhood Longitudinal Study), the U.S. Census (ACS), the Canadian Census, and now the NHIS [National Health Interview Survey] *all* reveal a comparable basic narrative, namely, that children

who grow up with a married mother and father fare best at face value [emphasis in original].[22]

Professor Londregan offers his own summary of the research: "A picture emerges: in a cross-section of children raised by parents in same-sex relationships, life outcomes tend to resemble those of children raised by single and divorced parents."[23] This isn't surprising. While marriage offers the advantages of biological ties, sexual complementarity, and stability, the households of same-sex couples share the deficiencies in these areas of single or divorced family structures.

Same-sex parenting seems to affect children in sex-specific ways. Girls with two fathers and boys with two mothers had the poorest outcomes. Commenting on Allen's study of Canadian census data, Regnerus observes:

> Thus although the children of same-sex couples fare worse overall, the disparity is unequally shared, but is instead based on the combination of the gender of child and gender of parents. Boys fare better—that is, they're more likely to have finished high school—in gay households than in lesbian households. For girls, the opposite is true. Thus the study undermines not only claims about "no differences" but also assertions that moms and dads are interchangeable. *They're not* [emphasis in original].[24]

The ACP brief puts it this way:

> At this time, the three largest statistically representative data-sets used to address the question—Regnerus's New Family Structures Survey, with 3,000 cases; the National Health Interview Survey, with 1.6 million cases; and the National Longitudinal Survey of Adolescent Health, with 20,000 cases—have all found that children with same-sex parents

fare substantially worse—most measures show at least twice the level of distress—than do children with opposite-sex parents on a range of psychological, developmental and emotional outcomes. The longer social scientists study the question, the more evidence of harm is found.[25]

Regnerus makes the point eloquently when he sums up one of Sullins's studies: "[T]here is no equivalent replacement for the enduring gift to a child that a married biological mother and father offer. It's no guarantee of success. It's not always possible. But the odds of emotional struggle at least double without it."[26]

I mentioned that there are only eight studies with sufficient methodological rigor to be useful, and so far I've discussed four of them. What about the other four? The other four studies of same-sex parenting have been used to support the "no differences" thesis, but they suffer from coding and interpretative errors. As the ACP brief explains, "[A]ll four studies suffer from a fatal flaw: a large portion (40–60%) of the children they report as being with same-sex parents are actually children with opposite-sex parents, rendering any application of their findings to same-sex couples invalid, or at least extremely problematic."[27] When this error is corrected, the data in these studies support the conclusion that children do best with their married mom and dad.

Indeed, as these studies were corrected and reanalyzed, something else was discovered: the longer and more formalized the same-sex union, the worse the outcomes for kids. The ACP brief notes:

> [W]hile outcomes for children with opposite-sex parents improved if their parents were married, outcomes for children with same-sex parents were notably worse if their parents were married....
>
> [A]mong opposite-sex parents, moving from an unmarried to a married state improves outcomes for children; but among same-sex parents, moving from an unmarried to a married state substantially degrades child well-being.[28]

What does this all mean? The most recent research from Sullins suggests that the longer children reside with same-sex parents, the worse the outcomes. The ACP brief concludes:

> Contrary to the suggestion that child emotional harm with same-sex parents would be reduced with more stable parents,...the longer the adolescents were with same-sex parents, the worse they fared. Those who resided with married same-sex parents for over ten years, on average, fared much worse than those residing with unmarried, mostly divorced, same-sex parents for only four years, on average. Child harm with same-sex parents may be amplified by a longer time spent with them, or by marriage itself, or both.[29]

The media, of course, have attacked these studies, as has the academy. These attacks, which demonstrate the politicized nature of this debate, have been impressively refuted. The attacks on Sullins's study, for example, focused exclusively (and quite unconvincingly) on process, because they couldn't deny his findings.[30]

But a word is in order about the Regnerus study, which provoked the most hostility. The primary complaint was that Regnerus hadn't identified and studied children who were raised by same-sex parents in a marriage for all eighteen years of their childhood. But Regnerus was clear that the number of persons who have grown up in such a setting is very small, and he was studying social reality as it is, not as some wish it were. Professor Londregan defends Regnerus from one of the chief criticisms leveled at his study: "Some critics have objected to his use of 'gay and lesbian parents' as shorthand for 'the parents...in his sample who had been involved in a same-sex romantic relationship,' but he is very clear about his definition."[31]

No doubt the Regnerus, Allen, and Sullins studies can be improved on. No doubt more research and better scientific study of same-sex parenting is needed. At this time we have only eight useful studies of same-sex parenting because it is a new phenomenon and, for a variety of reasons, difficult to study. For one thing, the number of same-sex couples raising children is small. For another, there is no agreement about how to define, and thus measure, sexual orientation. For example, "bisexual" women have more children than lesbians, but they might be in lesbian relationships—data-collection projects pay little attention to such nuances.

Nevertheless, there's little reason to think that the lessons of forty years of good scientific studies of adoption and stepparenting wouldn't apply, in general, to same-sex parenting. Might biology, sexual complementarity, and stability cease to matter in this particular family form alone? We know by definition that in no same-sex couple's household will a child have a biological connection to both parents. Likewise, by definition there will be no sexual complementarity in parenting. No same-sex household will provide a child with both a mother and a father. So with respect to two of the three main childrearing advantages of marital households, same-sex parenting cannot provide what a married mother and father can.

What about stability? The evidence indicates that lesbian relationships are the shortest lived of all.[32] Researchers suggest that the reason is not sexual orientation, but gender. Women tend to have a stronger preference for emotional satisfaction in their relationships, so they initiate the majority of divorces in America.[33] An entirely female relationship, preliminary evidence suggests, tends to be less lasting. At the same time, the evidence indicates that gay male relationships tend to be the most open.[34] And again, scholars suggest that the reason is not the partners' orientation. Men tend to be more promiscuous, so a double-male relationship is more likely to be sexually nonexclusive.[35] The preliminary social science suggests, therefore, that same-sex romantic relationships, male or female, are less stable than male-female marriages.[36]

There is good reason, then, to think that further studies of same-sex parenting will confirm the forty-year consensus, vindicating Regnerus, Allen, and Sullins. Still, the social science on same-sex parenting is the subject of lively debate. It must be allowed to continue without political preemption.

The Effect of Redefining Marriage on the Institution of Marriage

Before turning to the testimony of people who have been raised in gay and lesbian homes, it is important to understand that redefining marriage will change marriage and parenting for everyone. We have good philosophical reasons for thinking so, and the initial empirical evidence concurs: where marriage has been redefined to be a genderless institution of consenting adult love, the marriage culture falls apart even more, and even more quickly.

An amicus brief filed in the *Obergefell* case by over one hundred scholars of marriage (the "scholars' brief")—their disciplines included "sociology, psychology, economics, history, philosophy, literature, political science, pediatrics and family law"—points out that where marriage has been redefined, the institution of marriage has been damaged, and this damage affects the children of heterosexuals.[37] In a nutshell:

> [I]n every U.S. jurisdiction for which such data are available, after the adoption of same-sex marriage the *opposite-sex* marriage rate declined by [at] least five percent—in comparison to a national marriage rate that, in the past few years, has been fairly stable. And if a forced redefinition of marriage caused only a five percent permanent decline in U.S. opposite-sex marriage rates, under reasonable assumptions and over the next fertility cycle (30 years), that decline would result in nearly 1.3 million fewer women marrying.[38]

That's right, as the national marriage rate remained stable, the marriage rates in states that redefined marriage fell *at least* 5 percent. This is perfectly logical. If marriage is simply a matter of romance between consenting adults, some persons, content simply to cohabit, will not bother to get married. But cohabitation isn't as stable as marriage, and as the authors of the brief observe, a drop in the marriage rate of only 5 percent would mean over a million fewer women marrying.

In the Netherlands—the first country to redefine marriage as a genderless institution—marriage rates for young women dropped an additional 5 percent over the rate at which they were already declining. That is, same-sex marriage is a symptom of a collapsing marriage culture, and it then becomes a cause of further and more rapid decline. The damage to the culture of marriage was uneven. It hit hardest among those who could least afford it.[39] The scholars' brief explains:

> Making marriage genderless may have little impact on those who are now married or who are well educated, well-to-do, religious and/or otherwise committed to the marital norm of sexual intercourse only between husband and wife. But marginal marriage candidates—including the poor, relatively uneducated, irreligious or others who are highly influenced by cultural messages promoting casual and uncommitted sex—likely will be affected. And then the margins will likely expand, as they did with no-fault divorce.[40]

So we can expect the law to remake civil society where countervailing influences are lacking. This is precisely the effect that no-fault divorce had upon the margins of society, where marriage rates dropped and divorce rates rose the fastest.[41]

Redefining marriage has had the same harmful effect in other countries as well. The scholars' brief points out that in the years before Spain redefined marriage, its marriage rate was rising, but in the nine years after the redefinition, the opposite-sex marriage rate fell by 36 percent. Likewise, after marriage redefinition, the overall marriage rate dropped 4.3 percent in Canada and 7.7 percent in Belgium. Since those marriage rates include same-sex marriages, the drop in opposite-sex marriages is likely even higher.[42]

The decline in marriage after redefinition is also taking place in the United States. All of the states that have redefined marriage and keep records, the scholars' brief notes, have seen a decrease in opposite-sex marriage rates, while the marriage rate in the rest of the country has remained stable. The decline in Vermont was 5.1 percent, in Connecticut 7.3 percent, in Massachusetts 8.9 percent, and in Iowa 9.2 percent.[43] As Gene Schaerr, the attorney who submitted the scholars' brief, points out, "[C]orrelation is not causation. But correlation in harmony with theoretical predictions, past experience, and other causal analysis (see the Netherlands study), give cause for grave concern."[44]

The communities with the most serious misunderstanding of the nature and purpose of marriage have been the first ones to redefine it. Redefinition, in turn, leads to further misunderstanding. It is not surprising, then, as two scholars of marriage explained in another amicus brief (the "fertility brief"), that same-sex marriage was adopted in states with the lowest fertility rates:

> As of 2010, five of the seven States (including Washington, D.C.) with the lowest fertility rates all permitted same-sex marriage (or civil union equivalents). In contrast, none of the nine States with the highest fertility rates allowed it before 2010. And while the fertility rates in both groups of States decreased between 2005 and 2010, the percentage decline was almost twice as large in the states that allowed same-sex marriage or its equivalent.[45]

Indeed, the decline has become so serious, the authors of the fertility brief point out, that "every European country that has adopted same-sex marriage has also had to implement some form of pro-natalist policy"[46]—that is, governmental incentives for people to have babies. Same-sex marriage didn't cause this problem, of course, but the common devaluation of marriage itself led to both the redefinition of marriage and the decline in childbirth. Why would any society want to lock in that distorted view of marriage?

Same-sex marriage is a consequence, not a cause, of the collapse of our marriage culture. We have heterosexuals, not gays and lesbians, to blame for decades of marital instability, with the consequent harm to women, to children, and especially to the poor. But we *can* expect same-sex marriage, by ratifying the adult-centric vision of marriage, to accelerate the collapse. As the scholars' brief puts it, "[W]e can reasonably conclude that a nationwide rule mandating recognition of such marriages would likely be followed in each state by some combination of increased abortions and increased nonmarital births."[47] The logic is simple: redefine marriage and weaken the marriage culture, reduce the number of marriages, and thus increase the number of abortions and nonmarital births. Relying on data suggesting that same-sex marriage will lead to a 5 percent reduction in the overall marriage rate, the scholars predict there will be as many as nine hundred thousand more aborted babies and six hundred thousand more fatherless children.[48]

Redefining marriage was sold as an act of compassion for the 240,000 children being raised by same-sex couples.[49] But the preliminary social science suggests that redefining marriage won't help those children. It will instead increase the number of children being raised by same-sex couples, and it risks undermining family stability for the seventy-four million children in America.

Personal Witness

I suggested earlier that good social science could do for the same-sex marriage debate what ultrasound did for the abortion debate by revealing truths that people prefer to ignore. Likewise, what Feminists for Life and Silent No More and Women Speak for Themselves did for the pro-life movement, voices from the LGBT community—especially the children of gays and lesbians—could do for the marriage movement. Just as women could explain why their commitments to feminism made them oppose abortion, so voices of gays and lesbians and their children could explain why their commitments to equality and rights—particularly the equality and rights of children—make them oppose the redefinition of marriage. Philosophy and social science are important, but people are ultimately moved more by stories than by logic or data.

Children of Gays and Lesbians Speak for Themselves

In the past three years, several children of gays and lesbians have spoken out about how redefining marriage has social costs. Their basic story is the same: Same-sex marriage denies them a relationship with either a mother or a father—it denies them *their* mother or *their* father. Even worse, normalizing same-sex parenting by redefining marriage tells children of gays and lesbians who suffer from the absence of their father or mother that the problem is with *them*, that the hurt they feel isn't a legitimate response to objective reality but the result of their own misguided feelings. The following stories explain.

Perhaps the first LGBT voice that came to national prominence opposing the redefinition of marriage was Robert Oscar Lopez, "a bisexual Latino intellectual," who was raised for seventeen years by his mother "and her female romantic partner."[50] He was moved to speak when he heard about the controversy surrounding the Regnerus study, which was the first work of social science that captured his experience. Regnerus's work, he writes, "acknowledges what the gay activist movement has sought laboriously to erase, or at least ignore": people like Lopez and their stories.

The title of Lopez's essay, which he published in the online journal I edit, Public Discourse, was "Growing Up with Two Moms: The Untold Children's View."[51] Lopez movingly recounted the pain he had suffered because of his missing father. While he loved his mother and her partner, who were ideal caregivers, neither could replace an absent father. Most of his peers learned "both traditionally masculine and traditionally feminine social mechanisms," he writes, and they learned them from a man and a woman:

> They learned, typically, how to be bold and unflinching from male figures and how to write thank-you cards and be sensitive from female figures. These are stereotypes, of course, but stereotypes come in handy when you inevitably leave the safety of your lesbian mom's trailer and have to work and survive in a world where everybody thinks in stereotypical terms, even gays.

By contrast, Lopez "had no male figure at all to follow, and [his] mother and her partner were both unlike traditional fathers or traditional mothers." He points out that gays and lesbians pushing for what they call "marriage equality"—and in turn depriving children of a mother or a father—fail to understand how they themselves frequently benefited from their own childhood homes: "Many gays don't realize what a blessing it was to be reared in a traditional home."

You might think that the gay press would be interested in the voice of a Hispanic bisexual, but it's not. Instead, "the first person who contacted me to thank me for sharing my perspective on LGBT issues was Mark Regnerus." Lopez was not part of Regnerus's study, but he posted a comment on an article about the study, and Regnerus e-mailed him about it.

> Forty-one years I'd lived, and nobody—least of all gay activists—had wanted me to speak honestly about the complicated gay threads of my life. If for no other reason than this, Mark Regnerus deserves tremendous credit—and the gay community ought to be crediting him rather than trying to silence him.

Media gatekeepers do not want stories like Lopez's to be heard, and the "gay movement is doing everything it can to make sure that nobody hears them," he writes.

> I cherish my mother's memory, but I don't mince words when talking about how hard it was to grow up in a gay household. Earlier studies examined children still living with their gay parents, so the kids were not at liberty to speak, governed as all children are by filial piety, guilt, and fear of losing their allowances. For trying to speak honestly, I've been squelched, literally, for decades.

Gay activists use intimidation to shut down debate about their agenda, and no one has faced more attacks on their characters than the children of gays and lesbians who oppose gay marriage. In an amicus brief submitted to the Supreme Court in *Obergefell*, Lopez points out that through his scholarly research he has come to know personally over seventy children reared by same-sex parents: "The vast majority of these people will never come forward because of the climate of fear and intimidation that the debate on gay marriage has fostered."[52] As a result, Lopez notes, "when the Court decided *Windsor* [the 2012 decision striking down the federal Defense of Marriage Act] the Justices had heard testimonials almost completely from [children of gays] whose statements aligned perfectly with the political goals of the same-sex marriage movement. These testimonials were extremely one-sided and lacked critical independence from gay guardians."[53] Alas, Justice Kennedy ignored Lopez's amicus brief.

He also ignored Katy Faust, another person raised by two women. In February 2015, Faust published her moving testimony at Public Discourse in the form of a letter to the man known to be the pivotal vote on the Supreme Court: "Dear Justice Kennedy: An Open Letter from the Child of a Loving Gay Parent":

> I write because I am one of many children with gay parents who believe we should protect marriage. I believe you were right when, during the Proposition 8 deliberations, you said "the voice of those children [of same-sex parents] is important." I'd like to explain why I think redefining marriage would actually serve to strip these children of their most fundamental rights.[54]

Faust explains that though she loves her mother, she opposes gay marriage, because "this debate, at its core, is about one thing. It's about children." Her own experience is instructive: "While I did love my mother's partner and friends, I would have traded every one of them to have my mom and my dad loving me under the same roof." Faust subsequently submitted her testimony to the court in an amicus brief.

Faust is clear that "there is no difference between the value and worth of heterosexual and homosexual persons...because we are all humans created in the image of God." But not all *relationships* are equal: "[W]hen it comes to procreation and child-rearing, same-sex couples and opposite-sex couples are wholly unequal and should be treated differently for the sake of the children."

You can believe both of those things. I certainly do. But our culture won't let us say them. Faust explains:

> It's very difficult to speak about this subject, because I love my mom. Most of us children with gay parents do. We also love their partner(s). You don't hear much from us because, as far as the media are concerned, it's impossible that we could both love our gay parent(s) and oppose gay marriage. Many are of the opinion I should not exist. But I do, and I'm not the only one.

Faust takes seriously a basic biological truth and moral reality: "Each child is conceived by a mother and a father to whom that child has a natural right." So what happens "when two adults who cannot procreate want to raise children together"?

> When a child is placed in a same-sex-headed household, she will miss out on at least one critical parental relationship and a vital dual-gender influence. The nature of the adults' union guarantees this. Whether by adoption, divorce, or third-party reproduction, the adults in this scenario satisfy their heart's desires, while the child bears the most significant cost: missing out on one or more of her biological parents.

Despite her painful personal experience, for most of her life Faust publicly supported same-sex parenting: "I could have been the public service announcement for gay parenting." But not anymore: "I cringe when I think of it now, because it was a lie." Only when she herself became a parent did she begin to realize why she was wrong: "Kids want their mother and father to love them, and to love each other." She continues:

> Now that I am a parent, I see clearly the beautiful differences my husband and I bring to our family. I see the wholeness and health that my children receive because they have both of their parents living with and loving them. I see how important the role of their father is and how irreplaceable I am as their mother. We play complementary roles in their lives, and neither of us is disposable. In fact, we are both critical. It's almost as if Mother Nature got this whole reproduction thing exactly right.

Faust does not denigrate the lives or loves of gay parents. "I am not saying that being same-sex attracted makes one incapable of parenting. My mother was an exceptional parent.... This is about the *missing* parent." Family structure matters, and same-sex marriage *institutionalizes* missing parents. Of course two lesbians can be great moms, but neither can be a father. Children of lesbians love their moms, Faust writes, but "ask about their father, and you are in for either painful silence, a confession of gut-wrenching longing, or the recognition that they have a father that they wish they could see more often."

This makes sense, doesn't it? The problem with same-sex parenting is obvious if, as Faust suggests, we consider children in similar situations:

> What is your experience with children who have divorced parents, or are the offspring of third-party reproduction, or the victims of abandonment? Do they not care about their missing parent? Do those children claim to have never had a sleepless night wondering why their parents left, what they look like, or if they love their child? Of course not. We are

made to know, and be known by, both of our parents. When one is absent, that absence leaves a lifelong gaping wound.

Faust points out that the "undisputed social science" shows "that children suffer greatly when they are abandoned by their biological parents, when their parents divorce, when one parent dies, or when they are donor-conceived." And so she asks, "[H]ow can it be possible that they are miraculously turning out 'even better!' when raised in same-sex-headed households?" The politicized science simply doesn't make sense—it doesn't reflect reality. "Every child raised by 'two moms' or 'two dads,'" writes Faust, "came to that household via one of those four traumatic methods. Does being raised under the rainbow miraculously wipe away all the negative effects and pain surrounding the loss and daily deprivation of one or both parents?"

In closing her letter to Justice Kennedy, Faust notes that the court has a duty to protect the freedoms of adults but also to provide equal protection to the most vulnerable among us. Her solution? Freedom for gays and lesbians *and* the truth about marriage: "I unequivocally oppose criminalizing gay relationships. But defining marriage correctly criminalizes nothing." So she urges Justice Kennedy, "The bonds with one's natural parents deserve to be protected. Do not fall prey to the false narrative that adult feelings should trump children's rights. The onus must be on adults to conform to the needs of children, not the other way around." Just as Lopez did, Faust expresses her concern for young people who find themselves attracted to their own sex:

> This is not about being *against* anyone. This is about what I am for. I am *for* children! I want all children to have the love of their mother and their father. Being for children also makes me *for* LGBT youth. They deserve all the physical, social, and emotional benefits of being raised by their mother and father as well.

Another child of two moms, Heather Barwick, expresses the same concern in a public letter of her own: "Dear Gay Community: Your Kids Are Hurting."[55] She begins:

> Gay community, I am your daughter. My mom raised me with her same-sex partner back in the '80s and '90s....Do you remember that book, "Heather Has Two Mommies"? That was my life. My mom, her partner, and I lived in a cozy little house in the 'burbs of a very liberal and open-minded area. Her partner treated me as if I was her own daughter. Along with my mom's partner, I also inherited her tight-knit community of gay and lesbian friends....I still feel like gay people are *my* people. I've learned so much from you.

Why was Barwick writing? "I'm writing to you because I'm letting myself out of the closet: I don't support gay marriage." Her explanation was simple: "It's not because you're gay....It's because of the nature of the same-sex relationship itself"—a relationship that would deprive children of a mom or a dad.

Barwick used to support same-sex marriage:

> Growing up, and even into my 20s, I supported and advocated for gay marriage. It's only with some time and distance from my childhood that I'm able to reflect on my experiences and recognize the long-term consequences that same-sex parenting had on me. And it's only now, as I watch my children loving and being loved by their father each day, that I can see the beauty and wisdom in traditional marriage and parenting.

The problem that Barwick particularly highlights is not only that same-sex parenting deprives a child of a mom or a dad, but that same-sex *marriage* teaches the child that there's nothing wrong with being so deprived, that if a child aches and longs for the missing mom or dad, the problem is with the child, not the relationship. "A lot of us, a lot of your kids, are hurting. My father's absence created a huge hole in me, and I ached every day for a dad. I loved my mom's partner, but another mom could never have replaced the father I lost." Barwick describes it poignantly:

> I grew up surrounded by women who said they didn't need or want a man. Yet, as a little girl, I so desperately wanted a daddy. It is a strange and confusing thing to walk around with this deep-down unquenchable ache for a father, for a man, in a community that says that men are unnecessary. There were times I felt so angry with my dad for not being there for me, and then times I felt angry with myself for even wanting a father to begin with. There are parts of me that still grieve over that loss today.

Redefining marriage redefines parenting. So a legal system that redefines marriage changes a society's culture and the values it promotes—as well as the expectations of its citizens. A society that redefines marriage, writes Barwick, "promotes and normalizes a family structure that necessarily denies us something precious and foundational. It denies us something we need and long for, while at the same time tells us that we don't need what we naturally crave. That we will be okay. But we're not. We're hurting."

Redefining marriage will stigmatize the children of same-sex couples, because they will not be allowed to give voice to their experience of lacking a mom or a dad. Barwick offers a compelling description of the difference between kids of divorce or adoption and kids of same-sex marriage:

> Kids of divorced parents are allowed to say, "Hey, mom and dad, I love you, but the divorce crushed me and has been so

hard...." Kids of adoption are allowed to say, "Hey, adoptive parents, I love you. But this is really hard for me. I suffer because my relationship with my first parents was broken. I'm confused and I miss them even though I've never met them."

But children of same-sex parents haven't been given the same voice. It's not just me. There are so many of us. Many of us are too scared to speak up and tell you about our hurt and pain....If we say we are hurting because we were raised by same-sex parents, we are either ignored or labeled a hater.

Or worse. In his amicus brief, Robert Lopez reports on his research on children of gays ("COGs" for short): "COGs, particularly in the younger generation, have told me stories about therapists or counselors chastising them for feeling sad about not having one parent."[56] Indeed, "one COG, a boy conceived in the 1990s by a surrogate contract with a gay father, was taken to a lesbian psychiatrist who told him that his aching sadness on Mother's Day was the result of homophobia. He was told to apologize to his gay father for having confided in the lesbian psychiatrist about his anger over not having a mother."[57]

In another story, a "teenage girl who was a sperm-donor-conceived child of a lesbian couple laments that she gets a 'lecture' when she longs for a 'normal' family."[58] Lopez is clear that these lectures come in many forms: "[N]ot only from parents but from family friends, relatives, teachers, peers, and all the cultural authorities on television."[59] The basic story is the same: "[I]f we state that our childhood experience was strange, bizarre, or abnormal, we are doing something wrong and told that if we continue making such statements, we will pay terrible consequences."[60]

Lopez agrees with Barwick that same-sex marriage actually makes things worse, as illustrated in the stories of younger, more recently conceived children of gays and lesbians:

It has gotten harder, not easier, for COGs, to the extent that gay marriage has become a broader and more accepted phenomenon. The younger generation of COGs has lived with an enormous amount of surveillance and speech policing by people interested in ensuring that they say nothing to undermine the social prestige of their gay guardians. The younger generation of COGs seems to feel more uprooted from the missing half of their ancestry and more fearful of defying the authority of gay stepparent figures whom they still tend to view as stepparents even if they are fond of them.[61]

While children in straight families are allowed to "express unhappiness about something going on in their home," the same is not true for children in gay families. They are "warned that they are guilty of homophobia if they are unhappy with their home life or, alternatively, told always to direct blame at external homophobia and exonerate their parents' decisions."[62]

For all of Justice Kennedy's concern about conferring the "dignity" of marriage on same-sex couples, there's little concern about conferring suffering on the children raised in such relationships. A relentless focus on adult desire has left us astonishingly calloused.

"I'm Gay and I'm against Gay Marriage"

In addition to *children* of gays and lesbians opposed to gay marriage, there are also gays and lesbians themselves opposed to it. Perhaps none has been braver or more well spoken than Doug Mainwaring. In 2013 he wrote an essay for Public Discourse that attracted wide attention: "I'm Gay and I Oppose Same-Sex Marriage."[63] Though the media portray opponents of gay marriage as thralls to religion and tradition (if not outright homophobia), Mainwaring insists that "neither religion nor tradition has played a significant role in forming my stance. But reason and experience certainly have." It was his experience as a gay man raising children with another man that convinced him that his kids needed their mother.

Mainwaring had been married to a woman and had children with her. But the marriage fell apart, and he decided to explore his same-sex attraction. "At first, I felt liberated," he writes. "I dated some great guys, and was in a couple of long-term relationships." But over the years, "intellectual honesty led" him to "some unexpected conclusions. (1) Creating a family with another man is not completely equal to creating a family with a woman, and (2) denying children parents of both genders at home is an objective evil. Kids need and yearn for both."

This wasn't idle talk. "It took some doing, but after ten years of divorce, we began to pull our family back together. We have been under one roof for over two years now. Our kids are happier and better off in so many ways," and his family is flourishing. "Did we do this for the sake of tradition? For the sake of religion? No. We did it because reason led us to resist selfish impulses and to seek the best for our children."

Mainwaring's courage is admirable, perhaps even heroic, but ordinary people are capable of great virtue when they set aside selfish desire for the sake of someone else. Robert Lopez did it too:

> As a man, though I am bisexual, I do not get to throw away the mother of my child as if she is a used incubator. I had to help my wife through the difficulties of pregnancy and post-partum depression.... Once I was a father, I put aside my own homosexual past and vowed never to divorce my wife or take up with another person, male or female, before I died. I chose that commitment in order to protect my children from dealing with harmful drama, even as they grow up to be adults. When you are a parent, ethical questions revolve around your children and you put away your self-interest...forever.[64]

As Mainwaring and his wife put their family back together for the sake of their children, he noticed "perhaps a hundred different things, small and large, that are negotiated between parents and kids every week. Moms and dads interact differently with their children. To give kids two moms or two dads is to withhold from them someone whom they desperately need and deserve in order to be whole and happy. It is to permanently etch 'deprivation' on their hearts."

If anyone has earned the right to speak out on this issue, it is Doug Mainwaring, who writes with unwavering honesty and compassion:

> Two men or two women together is, in truth, nothing like a man and a woman creating a life and a family together. Same-sex relationships are certainly very legitimate, rewarding pursuits, leading to happiness for many, but they are wholly different in experience and nature.

The Italian fashion designers Domenico Dolce and Stefano Gabbana—both gay—caused a stir in March 2015 when they expressed unfashionable ideas about the family:

> - The only family is the traditional one. No chemical off-spring and rented uterus. Life has a natural flow; there are things that cannot be changed.
> - Procreation must be an act of love.
> - *Dolce*: I call children of chemistry, synthetic children. Uteri for rent, semen chosen from a catalogue.
> - *Gabbana*: The family is not a fad. In it there is a super-natural sense of belonging.[65]

Amid the furious reaction, Doug Mainwaring came to their defense:

> Dolce and Gabbana are bravely standing against a future of state-enforced genderlessness, against a tidal wave of adult selfishness that overwhelms children's rights and their best interests, and against the meddling government jigsaw that has continued to split, carve, and slice family life over the last few decades—especially for the poor, minorities, and the most vulnerable. And the most vulnerable and silent minority is, of course, children.[66]

"Synthetic children" may be an infelicitous phrase, but everyone knew what Dolce was getting at. "It's not the *children* who are synthetic," explained Mainwaring, "for all human beings share equal dignity. Rather, it's the *process* through which they come into the world." And it's an "anything goes" process that violates human dignity at virtually every turn. The adoption process is carefully regulated, but "engineering children through gamete purchase and womb rental falls under no such restrictions." With modern technology and a lack of regulation, writes Mainwaring, "for wealthy white gay males, there are no rules, only endless options for accessorizing their lives with humans."

Using their reason to reflect on experience, Dolce and Gabbana concluded, as Mainwaring did, that children need a married mother and father. Another name for reasoned reflection on experience is "natural law." As Mainwaring puts it:

> Dolce and Gabbana, whether they use the term or not, are strong advocates of *natural law....* [T]hey recognize and honor *complementarity.* The complementarity of man and woman is not a religious construct; it is written on our hearts, spelled out in our DNA, and present everywhere we turn and look at nature. Resisting it requires a truly herculean campaign by academics, politicos, and media personalities advocating the novel idea of genderlessness [emphasis in original].

Two years after his announcement that he was gay but against gay marriage, Mainwaring revealed that he had taken another step. It began when he realized he had made a mistake:

> I eventually came to the conclusion that I had committed a grave injustice against my kids by divorcing my wife and attempting to create a family with another man. They deserved to be raised by both their mom and dad under the same roof. Who was I to deny them this most basic of children's rights?

I became determined to find a way to bring our family back together for the sake of our kids as they finished out their high school years.[67]

But he didn't stop there. "Once I began thinking, reasoning, and examining my life, an extraordinary thing happened: I couldn't stop." Where did this all lead?

Reason led me to acknowledge natural law, which led me to begin rejecting some of my former ways of thinking and acting. Reason alone was enough to lead me to change the direction of my life. Then quite amazingly, natural law and reason working together led me to recognize and acknowledge God's existence. And once I acknowledged God's existence, again there was only one reasonable thing to do: I asked Jesus Christ to take the throne of my life, and I began to reject the emptiness of my self-centered ways.

Some want the church to stay away from the marriage debate because it's not a "seeker-friendly" issue. But Doug Mainwaring's story suggests that the church's countercultural truth telling about the nature of marriage makes its claims about supernatural truth more, not less, credible.

The choice "to remain faithful to my wife predated my embrace of faith by a full two years," writes Mainwaring.

Although I had only hoped for peaceful coexistence with my then ex-wife as we agreed to join forces for a few years for the sake of the kids, I was met with another wonderful surprise. We found our relationship repairing itself day by day, and our love rekindled. And while our kids are now long past high school age, there's no question about the future of our marriage: *'Til death do us part.*

Truth Telling

One of the most important tasks of the pro-marriage movement now is to make it possible for honest social scientists to study the effect of redefining marriage on the institution itself and the effect of same-sex parenting on children. We must also make it possible for children of gays and lesbians to speak freely and honestly about their experiences growing up without a mom or a dad. As Lopez reminds us, "The children of same-sex couples have a tough road ahead of them—I know, because I have been there. The last thing we should do is make them feel guilty if the strain gets to them and they feel strange. We owe them, at the least, a dose of honesty."[68]

And yet, as Lopez has documented in painstaking detail, their stories are rarely welcome:

> COGs are not easily allowed to speak honestly about their families or themselves while they are children or while they are adults.... [COGs who do speak] have dealt with gay activists contacting their employers or professional associates in order to retaliate against them for negative feedback regarding gay parenting. As far as I know, popular pro-gay-marriage groups, including COLAGE [Children of Lesbians and Gays Everywhere], have not come forward to defend any of us from these public humiliations.
>
> [COGs who speak out] have also experienced gay activists contacting friends or relatives to apply pressure on them and alienate them from social support as punishment for discussing their hardships in gay homes. All, as well, have dealt with concerted efforts by groups such as the New Civil Rights Movement, the Human Rights Campaign, and GLAAD to load the Internet with negative press about them, so that their names become permanently associated with labels such as anti-gay, bigots, homophobe, or sometimes more pedestrian brands like "ungrateful," "crazy," or "bitter."[69]

As Mark Regnerus's experience with an academic inquisition at the University of Texas shows, pro-marriage scholars face similar obstacles in telling the truth. The truth about marriage and the family is out of favor among our political, business, academic, and cultural elites. Proclaiming it will require not only courage but teamwork.

EIGHT

BUILDING A MOVEMENT

The redefinition of marriage as a genderless partnership is possible only in a society that has already done serious damage to the institution. Long before there was a debate about same-sex marriage, Americans of every political stripe bought into a sexual ideology that undermined the rational foundations for the marital norms of permanence, exclusivity, and monogamy. Cohabitation, no-fault divorce, recreational sex, nonmarital childbearing, and pornography all contributed to the breakdown of the marriage culture. If marriage is simply about emotional companionship, then *of course* men and women are interchangeable.

What took decades to deconstruct will take a long time to rebuild. Americans dedicated to the truth about marriage need a strategic approach to rebuilding a marriage culture. The place to start, of course, is with our own families. Pope Benedict XVI—a world-class intellectual—reminds us that while intellectual arguments are important, people are moved more by beauty and holiness. The lives of the saints are more inspiring than the arguments of philosophers and social scientists. So the first thing we need to do is live the truth about marriage ourselves.

But we can't ignore our culture-forming institutions—our laws, our churches, our schools, our media—because they will influence the next generation's ability to live the truth of marriage. We must redouble our efforts to explain what marriage is and the consequences of redefining it. Making the case in speeches, books, and articles, no matter how well reasoned, won't be enough. Artists, filmmakers, novelists, and pastors have to share the compelling truth about marriage in ways that speak to the heart.

Every Organization Matters

The redefinition of marriage was not inevitable, but the sexual revolutionaries wanted you to think it was. They didn't succeed because they made a better argument. Most people weren't persuaded that genderless marriage is a better policy. They were harassed and intimidated into silence by the gay advocacy juggernaut. And even then, when it came to the public opinion poll that matters most—elections—gay marriage fared poorly. That's why the activists resorted to another institution of elites— the courts—to set aside the judgment of the people.

The number of LGBT advocacy groups is remarkable, and their success in mainstreaming their cause has meant that *every* liberal institution—think tank, university, Hollywood studio, network newsroom, and court of law—is advancing the ball. We need conservative forces— scholars, religious leaders, media personalities, journalists, politicians, and more—to join the effort to rebuild a marriage culture. We must be bolder, better organized, and more strategic—and exercise greater foresight when engaging on this issue.

Of course, many elites are not with us on social issues generally, and on the marriage issue in particular. These are the people who run our nation's big businesses, the political parties, and much of the press. Simply asking political leaders and media personalities to take us seriously and represent our viewpoints won't be enough. That's not what other groups do. They make it costly for political or media leaders to do the wrong thing.

If you cross the free-market movement or the gun lobby, they will challenge you. If you're a politician, you'll face a challenger in your primary election. Campaign contributions that once came your way will go to your opponent instead. When you see an interest group that has a lot of sway, it's not because politicians naturally agree with it—it's that they've been made to care. And on the marriage issue, we haven't done enough to make our representatives care. There was no cost for those who caved in or stayed silent, while the other side made those who stood up for us pay heavily. We need to find ways to defend our champions and keep weak-willed supporters from jumping ship.

This will, of course, be difficult if we are out-funded. Social conservatives need to think more carefully about philanthropy. Too many "big tent" conservative organizations actively undermine social conservatism. Donating half of your political contributions to one such organization and half to the Family Research Council, for example, effectively cancels out your gift. We need to make it clear that we will not be taken for granted. After all, the Republican Party cannot win an election without the support of social conservatives.

We need to take moneymaking seriously. Organizations that promote a strong marriage culture won't flourish if they're not funded. That means we need funders. Donors to free-market organizations usually are interested in the free market because they have met with success there themselves. Social conservatives, on the other hand, often lack the resources to contribute to any number of social conservative organizations. And it's not only on politics that we are outspent—we lose in the academy and media as well.

We've even lost Fox. Keep in mind that Fox is the home of *Beverly Hills, 90210*; *Melrose Place*; and now *Glee*—each of which has done its part to undermine a healthy vision of marriage and human sexuality. And of course there was *Will and Grace* on NBC and now *Modern Family* on ABC. But what is the conservative alternative to *Glee*? Whether it is the glamorization of premarital sex in *Beverly Hills, 90210* or the normalization of same-sex relationships in *Modern Family*, the media shape our culture, which in turn shapes our laws and our lives.

A two-way street connects law and culture. If we care about the next generation's living out the truth of marriage, then we have to care about how both our law and our culture present marriage. There is opportunity here. Roger Ailes famously described himself as a media genius for discovering a niche market that ABC, NBC, CBS, CNN, and MSNBC were all ignoring: half of the American population. What Ailes did for news media someone needs to do for entertainment. Entrepreneurs in television and the movies who produce high-quality family-friendly content are likely to make a nice profit. There is an audience for entertainment that is well done and reinforces the values that parents are trying to impart to their children.

"High-quality" is the key term here. "Christian" music, TV, and film need to strive for greater excellence. We must remember that piety is no substitute for competency in any walk of life.

This book, for obvious reasons, has focused on philosophy and law. My point in this chapter is not that we need fewer natural-law philosophers or appellate litigators; it's that we need more of *everything*. Christians need to be at the forefront of every human endeavor. Christians used to shape their culture—because God became a man, not just a mind. Much of the best literature, the best art, the best music—for over a thousand years—was produced by Christians: Shakespeare, Dante, and Chaucer; Palestrina, Bach, and Beethoven. Whom do we have today?

Perhaps the most important step will be preventing our own communities, especially our children, from believing a lie. Forming the moral imagination is key. Better cultural products—movies, TV shows, and music—will certainly help. Better church programs, discussed in a moment, will help. Better schools will be key as well. We will therefore have to protect the freedom of our schools to teach and act in accordance with the truth about marriage.

Beyond protecting our right to witness to the truth, we will need to find new ways of communicating our vision of marriage—especially on liberal, secular college campuses. Conservative enclaves on elite campuses—like the James Madison Program at Princeton University, run by Professor Robert George—are a model for this effort. So too are parallel institutions like Hillsdale College, Grove City College, and Christendom College, for example. Conservatives need to protect enclaves of sanity.

How is this public argument to be made? Three great men, whom I have been fortunate to have as teachers, provide an example. As an undergraduate, I attended a summer seminar on natural law led by Professor Hadley Arkes, a great intellect and gifted teacher whose warmth and humor complement the power of his arguments. Some argue that we should soften our stance on controversial issues, that in order to be evangelists we need to be seeker friendly. Not Arkes, who was himself evangelized by teachers who didn't shrink from proclaiming the truth in season and out of season. While we shouldn't be bombastic or imprudent, it is precisely our countercultural witness to what St. Paul called the more excellent way that will win hearts.

Another formative teacher was Professor Robert George of Princeton University. Working as his research assistant for two years after college (mostly on policy debates in bioethics), I learned that bad philosophy must be answered with good philosophy and bad science must be answered with good science. We cannot allow the other side to frame the debate as one of faith *against* reason, of backward superstition against enlightened science. This takes work. We have to work twice as hard as our opponents. We have to understand their arguments better than they do in order to explain, *at the level of reason*, where they've gone wrong.

But we can't stop there. Here's where my third teacher comes in. For two years I worked as an assistant editor at *First Things*, a journal of religion and public life founded by Father Richard John Neuhaus. These turned out to be the last two years of Father Neuhaus's life. He taught me that while we have to respond to bad reason with good reason, we also have to build on that reason with revelation. Nature and natural law are foundational, but grace builds on and perfects nature. And Christ came to make us perfect.

Fr. Neuhaus pursued what he called the high adventure of Christian discipleship. Friendship with Jesus was ultimately the only thing that mattered to him. After all, the only way to live out the truth of the natural law is to know and love the natural-law giver. The courage, strength, and hope we need to fulfill our vocation are the gift of the one who calls us.

A leader in the civil rights movement, Father Neuhaus marched with Martin Luther King Jr. and protested the Vietnam War. And he was an early recruit to the pro-life movement, which he saw as the logical extension of his earlier activism. He hoped that his liberal friends would see it the same way, but they abandoned him, and a life that had seemed destined for liberal accolades and the applause of elites took a new path. The same may happen to us. Many of our friends in politics who have stood with us so far may walk away. It shouldn't change what we do.

The opposition we encounter in defending marriage may be ferocious. In his dissent from Justice Kennedy's 2013 opinion striking down the federal definition of marriage in the Defense of Marriage Act, Justice Scalia noted darkly, "It is one thing for a society to elect change; it is another for a court of law to impose change by adjudging those who oppose it *hostes humani generis*, enemies of the human race."

Hostes humani generis. My Latin isn't very good, but I did a little research into this phrase. It was used in admiralty law to describe persons, such as pirates, who were outside the realm of legal protection. And pagans, including the Roman historian Tacitus, also used the phrase to describe the early Christians.

We needn't pretend that we face anything like Nero's persecution—or the kind of persecution Christians face today in the Middle East and parts of Africa. But we should be concerned. The erosion of religious liberty and the rights of conscience in America matters because America matters. Ours is the only country founded on the proposition that all men are endowed by their Creator with certain unalienable rights—including the free exercise of religion. If America can't get this right, what does that mean for the rest of the world?

Interreligious Witness to the Truth

While my arguments in this book have focused on philosophy and social science, this is not to suggest that religious voices must be silent. No, religious voices are crucial. The global interfaith consensus about the importance of sexual complementarity in marriage was impressively demonstrated at the international Humanum colloquium, which Pope Francis hosted at the Vatican in November 2014.[1] The speakers, gathered from twenty-three countries, represented a remarkable range of faith traditions from all over the earth—Catholic, Evangelical, Pentecostal, Mormon, Jewish, Muslim, Buddhist, Hindu, Jain, Sikh, and Taoist. They all shared an understanding that men and women are created for each other. The speeches can be viewed on the Internet,[2] but five in particular suggest the sort of religious witness needed.

Pope Francis opened the symposium by declaring that "children have a right to grow up in a family with a father and a mother." He also spoke of an ecological crisis of culture and urged participants to care for their social environments. "The crisis in the family has produced an ecological crisis, for social environments, like natural environments, need protection."[3] Cardinal Gerhard Müller, the prefect of the Congregation for the Doctrine of the Faith, echoed the pope, saying that "children have a natural, inherent right to a father and a mother to live with them."[4]

This gets it just right: Marriage unites a man and a woman as husband and wife so that children may have the love of their mother and father. And we have to care about the culture—a marriage culture or a hook-up culture—because social environments need protection.

Jackie Rivers, a doctoral fellow in African and African American studies at Harvard University (where she received her Ph.D.), explained the importance of marriage for social justice. Black children, she said, "have suffered the most as a result of the decline of marriage in the black community."[5] She added:

> The deleterious effects of being raised in single-headed households have been well documented. Children growing up in

female-headed households experience higher rates of poverty. These children underperform in school: they earn lower scores on verbal and math achievement tests and lower grades in their courses. They have more behavioral problems and higher rates of chronic health and psychiatric disorders. Adolescents and young adults raised without stable families experience elevated risks of teenage childbearing, of dropping out of high school, of being incarcerated, and of being idle (being neither employed nor in school).

Efforts to redefine marriage, she argued, will only make matters worse: "The unavoidable message is a profoundly false and damaging one: that children do not need a mother and a father in a permanent complementary bond." Rivers also chided those who misuse the legacy of the civil rights movement: "Those who promote what they call marriage equality have unjustly appropriated the language and the mantle of the black struggle in the United States, the civil rights movement. But there can be no equivalence between blacks' experience of slavery and oppression and the circumstances of homosexuals."

Russell Moore, the president of the Southern Baptist Convention's Ethics and Religious Liberty Commission, noted the unity of the world's faiths in understanding the marriage of a man and a woman as part of the natural order:

We come from different countries, sometimes with tensions between those countries. We hold to different religions, sometimes with great divergences there on what we believe about God and about the meaning of life. But all of us in this room share at least one thing in common. We did not spring into existence out of nothing, but each one of us can trace his or her origins back to a man and a woman, a mother and a father.

We recognize that marriage and family is a matter of public importance, not just of our various theological and ecclesial distinctive communities, since marriage is embedded in the creation order and is the means of human flourishing, not just the arena of individual human desires and appetites. We recognize that marriage, and the sexual difference on which it is built, is grounded in a natural order bearing rights and responsibilities that was not crafted by any human state, and cannot thus be redefined by any human state.[6]

Marriage is a natural institution, so a religiously diverse society can unite in recognizing marriage and its crucial role in human flourishing.

In "the wake of the disappointment sexual libertarianism brings," said Moore, "there must be a new word about more permanent things, such as the joy of marriage as a permanent, conjugal, one-flesh reality between a man and woman." He vowed that "we will not capitulate on these issues because we cannot."

One of America's most famous pastors, Rick Warren of Saddleback Church, insisted, "A lie doesn't become a truth and wrong doesn't become right and evil doesn't become good just because it's popular. Truth is truth."[7] Indeed, promoting truth is the only way to be perennially relevant: "No revolution will last, including the sexual revolution.... [E]very lie eventually crumbles under its own deception."

As for the popular slogan about being on the "right side of history," Warren reminded his audience that "it isn't necessary to be on the side of culture—it's not even necessary to be on the right side of history, it's just important to be on the right side." And the right side is not determined by majority vote: "The dustbins of history are stuffed with conventional wisdom of cultures that proved false, and truth is not decided by a popularity contest."

Lord Jonathan Sacks, the former chief rabbi of the United Kingdom, delivered perhaps the most captivating talk of the entire conference. He began with the foundation of man's dignity:

That is what makes the first chapter of Genesis so revolutionary with its statement that every human being, regardless of class, color, culture or creed, is in the image and likeness of God himself. We know that in the ancient world it was rulers, kings, emperors and pharaohs who were held to be in the image of God. So what Genesis was saying was that we are all royalty. We each have equal dignity in the kingdom of faith under the sovereignty of God. From this it follows that we each have an equal right to form a marriage and have children.[8]

There is "a deep connection between monotheism and monogamy," said Sacks, "just as there is, in the opposite direction, between idolatry and adultery." He continued:

> Monotheism and monogamy are about the all-embracing relationship between I and Thou, myself and one other, be it a human, or the divine, Other.... From monogamy the rich and powerful lose and the poor and powerless gain. So the return of monogamy goes against the normal grain of social change and was a real triumph for the equal dignity of all. Every bride and every groom are royalty; every home a palace when furnished with love.

But what happens when marriage and family break down? Sacks points to the statistics of his own country, where roughly half of all children are born outside of marriage, more than 40 percent of marriages end in divorce, and the average length of cohabitation is less than two years:

> The result is a sharp increase among young people of eating disorders, drug and alcohol abuse, stress-related syndromes, depression and actual and attempted suicides. The collapse of marriage has created a new form of poverty concentrated among single parent families, and of these, the main burden is born by women, who in 2011 headed 92 percent of single-parent households. In Britain today more than a million

children will grow up with no contact whatsoever with their fathers.

This is creating a divide within societies the like of which has not been seen since Disraeli spoke of "two nations" a century and a half ago. Those who are privileged to grow up in stable loving association with the two people who brought them into being will, on average, be healthier physically and emotionally. They will do better at school and at work. They will have more successful relationships, be happier and live longer.

And yes, there are many exceptions. But the injustice of it all cries out to heaven. It will go down in history as one of the tragic instances of what Friedrich Hayek called "the fatal conceit" that somehow we know better than the wisdom of the ages and can defy the lessons of biology and history.

A Fourfold Mission for the Church

How should the church respond? How can it help to rebuild a marriage culture? The church—either through action or inaction—will play a major role in the debate over the meaning of marriage. To be sure, all religious communities have a role to play in the defense of marriage. The view of marriage I defend on the basis of natural law is common, as displayed at the Humanum colloquium, to Judaism, Christianity, Islam, and many other world religions. But it is not my place to tell other religious communities what to do. I can speak only about what my own, Christian, community should do. There are four things the church must do.

First, the church needs to present a case for biblical sexuality that is appealing and that engages the best of modern thought. The virtues of chastity and lifelong marriage are enriching, but after fifty years, the church has still not devised a compelling response to the sexual revolution. The legal redefinition of marriage could take place when and where it did only because the majority of Americans lacked a sound understanding of the nature of man and the nature of marriage.

The church needs to find a way to capture the moral imagination of the next generation. It needs to make the truth about human sexuality and its fulfillment in marriage not only attractive and appealing, but noble and exhilarating. This is a truth worth staking one's life on.

In the face of the seduction of cohabitation, no-fault divorce, extramarital sex, nonmarital childbearing, pornography, and the hook-up culture, what can the church offer as a more fulfilling, more humane, more liberating alternative? Until it finds an answer, the church will make no headway in the same-sex marriage debate, which is the fulfillment of those revolutionary sexual values.

A proper response to the sexual revolution also requires engaging—not ignoring—the best of contemporary thought, especially the best of contemporary secular thought. What visions of the human person and sex, of marriage and personal wholeness do today's thinkers advance? Exactly where and why do their ideas go wrong? The church needs to show that the truth is better than a lie. And that the truth can defeat all lies.

In these efforts, we shouldn't discount the potential of slumbering Christian communities to wake up. It's easy to forget that, in 1973, the Southern Baptists were in favor of abortion rights and supported *Roe v. Wade*. Today they are at the forefront of the pro-life movement. Christians who are on the wrong side of the marriage debate today can change their minds if we help them.

The church's second task is to develop ministries for those who experience same-sex attraction and gender identity conflicts. Such persons, for whom fidelity to the truth about human sexuality requires special courage, need our loving attention. Pope Francis's description of the church as a field hospital after a battle is especially apt here.

These ministries are like the pro-life movement's crisis pregnancy centers. Abortion is sold as the most humane and compassionate response to an unplanned pregnancy. It's not. And pro-lifers' unprecedented grassroots response to women gives the lie to that claim. Likewise, those who believe the truth about marriage should be the first to walk with men and women dealing with same-sex attraction or gender identity conflicts, showing what a truly humane and compassionate response looks like.

Young people experiencing same-sex desire can face isolation and confusion as their peers first awaken to the opposite sex. They suffer humiliation if they say too much, but they bear the heavy burden of a secret if they keep silent. Parents and teachers must be sensitive to these struggles. We should fight arbitrary or abusive treatment of them. As relatives, coworkers, neighbors, and friends, we must remember that social hardship isn't limited to youth.

A shining example of ministry to the same-sex attracted is Courage, an international apostolate of the Catholic Church, which has produced the documentary film *The Desire of Everlasting Hills*.[9] Every community needs groups like this to help their same-sex-attracted neighbors discern the unique life of loving service to which God calls each of them and find wholeness in communion with others. But this work can't just be outsourced to special groups and ministries. Each of us needs to be willing to form deep friendships with men and women who are attracted to their own sex or struggle with their identity, welcoming them into our homes and families, especially when they aren't able to form marriages of their own.

After all, the conjugal view of marriage—that it is inherently ordered to one-flesh union and hence to family life—defines the limits of marriage, leaving room for meaningful nonmarital relationships, especially deep friendships. This is liberating. The same-sex attracted, like everyone else, should have strong and fulfilling relationships. Marriage isn't the only relationship that matters. And the conjugal view of marriage doesn't denigrate other relationships. Those who would redefine marriage as a person's most intense or deepest or most important relationship devalue friendship by implying that it's simply *less*: less meaningful, less fulfilling. The greatest of Justice Kennedy's errors may be his assertion that without same-sex marriage some people are "condemned to live in loneliness." His philosophy of marriage is anemic. And as our society has lost its understanding of marriage, it has suffered a corresponding diminution, even cheapening, of friendship.

We all need community, and those who for whatever reason never marry will know certain hardships that the married are spared. We should bring those left dry by isolation into other forms of community—as friends, fellow worshippers, neighbors, comrades in a cause, de facto members of our families, big siblings to our children, and regular guests in our homes.

The church's third task is to defend religious liberty and to help conscientious Christians understand how to bear witness to the truth when a radical sexual agenda has become a nonnegotiable public policy. What should bakers and florists and photographers do? What should directors of local Catholic Charities or Evangelical schoolteachers do?

There is no one single answer for every circumstance. Each person's situation will require a unique response, based on his vocation and the challenges he faces. The answers for schools and charities and professionals may vary with a thousand particulars, but the church will need to teach Christians the moral principles to apply to their own circumstances.

The church also has to help the rest of society understand the importance of freedom, particularly religious freedom. The national conversation on this important civil liberty hasn't been going well, and Indiana revealed how extreme a position the corporate and media establishments have staked out. They have the money and the megaphones. We have the truth.

The fourth task of the church is the most important and the most challenging. We need to live out the truth about marriage and human sexuality. Husbands and wives must be faithful to one another for better and for worse till death do them part. Mothers and fathers must take their obligations to their children seriously. The unmarried must prepare now for their future marital lives so they can be faithful to the vows they will make. And they need the encouragement of pastors who are not afraid to preach unfashionable truths.

Pope Benedict was right when he said the lives of the saints are the best evangelists. The same thing is true when it comes to marriage. The beauty and splendor of a happy family is our most eloquent testimony.

THE LONG VIEW

I f you've read this far, the situation we're in might seem pretty dire. But that cannot be reason for despair. We must take what we know about marriage and put it to work, helping our fellow citizens to understand why we believe what we do about marriage. Even those who disagree can come to recognize at least that our views are reasonable. Right now, too many equate our beliefs about marriage with the venomous and deplorable "God hates fags" slogan of the Westboro Baptists. If that's the only voice they've heard on the issue, it's hard to blame them. We must work harder so that they hear our voices.

Recently, there have been signs of hope that the truth can prevail before long—and be tolerated even sooner. I'd like to offer a short analysis of how we've gotten where we are and then place the challenges we face within a larger, global framework. In my introduction to this book, I appealed to the lessons of the pro-life movement. Now, in concluding,

Signs of Hope

In the weeks leading up to the Supreme Court's *Obergefell* ruling, several states acted to protect the religious liberty rights of their citizens. Remarkably, on the same day in mid-June, three states—North Carolina on the East Coast, Michigan in the Midwest, and Texas of, well, Texas— all enacted laws that would prevent the government from discriminating against or penalizing citizens or organizations because of their belief that marriage is the union of a man and a woman.

Let's start with Texas. On June 11, Governor Greg Abbott signed into law the Pastor Protection Act. It protects priests, pastors, and rabbis in Texas from having to conduct a wedding that violates their beliefs about marriage.[1] In praising the governor for signing the bill into law, Ken Paxton, the state's attorney general, called on the legislature to pass laws protecting *all* Texans:

> But to be clear, it's not enough. We now have much more work to do to ensure that all Texans can practice their faith and, among other things, recognize traditional marriage without being punished, harassed or discriminated against for their beliefs.
>
> What about the wedding photographer, the event planner, the caterer, the bed and breakfast owner, cake baker or any other Texas small business owner who is threatened or sued for carrying out their work according to their faith? What about the religiously-affiliated adoption agency that believes it should only place a child in a home with traditional marriage? What about the private school that teaches traditional marriage but is told it is an "issue"? Will that school lose its 501(c)(3) tax-exempt status, as was suggested by the U.S.

Solicitor General while arguing against traditional marriage
in the Supreme Court?[2]

Paxton concluded that "the people of Texas and its leadership must not
sit idly by in the face of hostility and harassment at the hands of a small
but loud chorus of activists and the corporate cronies cowed by them
who denounce Texans simply for standing in defense of traditional
marriage."

The same day, 1,300 miles away, the North Carolina legislature
passed religious liberty protections for civil servants.[3] It was, in fact, the
lawmakers' *second* vote for the bill—this time by a supermajority in both
houses to override their governor's veto. No profile of courage, the governor had vetoed the bill apparently to avoid the sorts of attacks directed
at Governor Mike Pence over Indiana's Religious Freedom Restoration
Act. Fortunately, the people of North Carolina wouldn't cower to the
bullies and special interest groups. They insisted their elected representatives protect their rights. And they did.

The North Carolina law protects magistrates who object to performing solemnization ceremonies—and clerks who object to issuing marriage
licenses—for same-sex couples. To be clear, it says that no eligible couple
(same- or opposite-sex) can be denied a marriage license. It just allows
individual magistrates or clerks to recuse themselves from the process
behind the scenes should they have sincere objections to same-sex marriage.[4] Both sides of the marriage debate get something important to them,
and no one loses anything. Government employees, after all, have rights
that should be protected. Had this bill not become law, magistrates and
clerks who declined to take part in same-sex marriages could have been
removed from office and convicted of a crime punishable by up to 120
days in jail.

And finally, on the same day that lawmakers in Austin and Raleigh
were enacting these protections, Michigan governor Rick Snyder signed
into law three bills protecting the freedom of private adoption agencies
to operate in accord with their beliefs, including the belief that children

deserve a married mother and father.[5] After seeing what had taken place in Massachusetts, Illinois, and Washington, D.C., the people of Michigan insisted that their state pass laws to ensure that no private adoption agency would ever be forced to violate its beliefs or stop helping children.

The voters of Michigan had good reason to be concerned. Their state's adoption system is particularly successful, in part because of the state's good relationship with faith-based providers. In 2014 alone, 85 percent of children in the state's foster care system were adopted into permanent, loving families.[6]

Remarkably, the *Detroit Free Press* condemned this piece of legislation, denouncing it as "anti-gay" and a "craven attempt to cloak discrimination in faith" that "leaves the best interests of the 13,000 children in the state's care...entirely out of the equation."[7] That's right, the newspaper actually argued that a law to protect the freedom of adoption agencies to find children homes with married moms and dads ignores the best interests of children. More outrageously, the paper declared that faith-based adoption agencies—which, as the editorial noted, account for 50 percent of adoptions in Michigan—should be forced to provide same-sex adoptions or shut down, to be replaced by more state agencies. Happily, the people of Michigan—and their liberty—prevailed over this breathtaking arrogance.

There's actually a fourth story to share as well. That very same day, back in Washington, D.C., Senator Mike Lee of Utah delivered a vitally important speech about religious liberty at Hillsdale College's Kirby Center, and almost a week later he introduced in Congress the First Amendment Defense Act, which would prevent the federal government from discriminating against or penalizing anyone for believing that marriage is the union of husband and wife.

Now it is our work to see to it that these state laws are replicated in all fifty states, that this proposed federal policy becomes law, and that both begin a broader trend in law and culture.

How We Got Here

In recent political memory, religious liberty was a value that brought together conservatives, libertarians, and progressives. As recently as 1993, the federal Religious Freedom Restoration Act was passed by a nearly unanimous Congress and signed by a Democratic president. Today, the same value is a political liability. Bakers, photographers, and florists are being ruined, adoption agencies shuttered, schools threatened with loss of accreditation and nonprofit status. So what happened? Why is religious liberty now losing so much ground?

Three historical developments explain our current predicament: a change in the scope of our government, a change in our sexual values, and a change in our political leaders' vision of religious liberty. An adequate response will need to address each of these changes.

First, government has changed. The progressive movement gave us the administrative state. Limited government and the rule of law were replaced by the nearly unlimited reach of technocrats in governmental agencies. As government assumes responsibility for more areas of life, the likelihood of its infringing on religious liberty increases. Why should government be telling bakers and florists which weddings to serve in the first place? Why should it tell charities and religious schools how to operate and which values to teach? Only a swollen sense of unaccountable government authority can explain these changes.

Second, sexual values have changed. At the time of the American Revolution, religion and liberty were so closely linked that Thomas Jefferson could affirm, "The God who gave us life, gave us liberty at the same time." Meanwhile, his French contemporary Denis Diderot, expressing sentiments that would culminate in a very different revolution, declared that man "will never be free until the last king is strangled with the entrails of the last priest." In our own time, however, the sexual revolution has shattered the American synthesis of faith and freedom, setting religion at odds with "liberty"—or more accurately, license. Now bakers, florists, adoption agencies, and schools that uphold what Americans have always believed about marriage find themselves at odds with the law.

Third, religious liberty has changed. Our Constitution protects the natural right to the free exercise of religion. But some liberals are trying to drastically narrow that right by redefining it as the mere "freedom of worship." If they succeed, the robust religious freedom that made American civil society the envy of the world will be reduced to Sunday-morning piety confined within the four walls of a chapel. They have even gone so far as to rewrite the U.S. immigration exam to say that the First Amendment protects "freedom of worship" rather than the "free exercise of religion."[8] True religious liberty entails the freedom to live consistently with one's beliefs seven days a week—in the chapel, in the marketplace, and in the public square.

These three changes represent a rejection of the American Founding. Progressive politics and a radical view of human sexuality are combining to coerce compliance at the expense of a bedrock human right. And of course much of this has been enabled by judicial activism, as in *Obergefell*.

So how do we fight against this onslaught? We start by fighting for courts to interpret and apply our laws fairly. Without a sound judiciary, no amount of public debate can ensure sound policy on issues like marriage and religious liberty, for the courts will always be able to refashion or discard what the people (through their representatives) have achieved. This is why the work of groups such as the Federalist Society, which opposes such judicial activism, is so important.

Outside the courtroom, our best strategy for fighting governmental overreach is to fight for more limited government. The less power government has, the less room there is for abuses of power. The alliance between social and economic conservatives is not just a marriage of convenience. They share important principles, and they face a common enemy—the expansion of government beyond its proper scope. This is why the work of an organization such as the Heritage Foundation, which opposes ever-expanding government, is so important.

Limited government and religious liberty are best served when human laws reflect the "laws of nature and of nature's God," as the Declaration of Independence puts it. All men are created equal and are endowed by their Creator with a right to life. Mankind is created male and female, and marriage, by nature, is the union of man and woman. Only by redefining these concepts according to desire rather than nature is it possible to concoct a "right to choose" that extends even to the killing of an unborn child or an endlessly malleable concept of "marriage."

Restoring a sound understanding of human nature and the laws of nature will be the work of the many organizations and groups—churches and synagogues, primary schools and universities, for example—that constitute civil society. Among these groups, public interest law firms such as the Alliance Defending Freedom have an important role. We need groups like this to push back on the sexual revolution and remind people of the law written on their hearts—a law that points the way to true, ordered liberty, not license, when it comes to human sexuality and the family.

Both the Bible's moral principles and reason require us to conform our desires to transcendent moral truths grounded in our nature as human beings, rational animals. The followers of postmodernism seek to re-create nature in accord with their desires, while the followers of progressivism use the power of government to make everyone else conform to the desires of elites, who know best. These ideologies promote the satisfaction of desire even while trampling *true* natural rights and liberties like the free exercise of religion. And that's where the work of groups like the Becket Fund for Religious Liberty proves so crucial. They insist against limiting religion to worship, and they defend its free exercise against encroachment in the name of untrammeled desire.

So the three steps that have undone core elements of the American Founding—progressive government and the administrative state, the sexual revolution's elevation of desire, and the whittling of religious free exercise down to the freedom to worship—all need to be countered. Political organizations, religious and civic organizations, and legal organizations will have to play their roles in empowering the citizenry to reclaim their government and culture.

Without a return to the principles of the American Founding—ordered liberty based on faith and reason, natural rights and morality, limited government and civil society—Americans will continue to face serious and perplexing challenges. The dilemmas faced by bakers and florists and charities and schools are only the beginning.

Some Perspective

I began this book by suggesting that after *Obergefell*, the pro-marriage movement should take its cue from pro-lifers after *Roe v. Wade*. In particular, I highlighted three practical tactics:

1. We must call the court's ruling in *Obergefell* what it is: judicial activism.
2. We must protect our freedom to speak and live according to the truth about marriage.
3. We must redouble our efforts to make the case for it in the public square.

In this book I have tried to flesh out these three strategies. And while the immediately preceding section provides some historical context on how to think about why we are facing these challenges only *now* in American history, I want to suggest a larger framework for thinking about these challenges as a whole. I speak in this section explicitly as a Christian.

The two-thousand-year story of the Christian church's cultural and intellectual growth is a story of challenges answered. For the early church, there were debates about who God is (and who is God). In response, the church developed the wonderfully rich reflections of Trinitarian theology and Christology. In a sense, we have the early heresies to thank for this accomplishment. Arius's errors gave us Athanasius's refinements on Christology. Nestorius's blunders gave us Cyril's insights.

In truth, of course, we have the Holy Spirit to thank for it all. He continually leads the church to defend and deepen its understanding of the truth, against the peculiar errors of the age.

A thousand years later, with the Reformation and Counter-Reformation, the church saw renewed debates about salvation—building on those Augustine had waged with Pelagius, no less. Whichever side you favor in the debates of the sixteenth century, they left the church as a whole with a much richer theology of justification, ecclesiology, and soteriology.

Debates about the nature of God, of salvation, and of the church never disappear, of course. But today, the most pressing heresies—the newest challenges for the church's teaching and mission—center on the nature of man. The tribulations that marked the twentieth century and continue into the twenty-first—totalitarianism, genocide, abortion, and the sexual ideology that has battered the family and redefined marriage—have sprung from a faulty humanism. I don't mean to equate each of these human tragedies with the others, but they all spring from faulty anthropology, a misunderstanding of the nature of man.

Before he became a bishop, a cardinal, and eventually Pope John Paul II, Karol Wojtyła was an academic philosopher. He thought deeply about the crisis of culture then enveloping the West and determined its cause: a faulty understanding of the human person. Shortly after the Second World War, he wrote to a friend about his main intellectual project:

> I devote my very rare free moments to a work that is close to my heart and devoted to the metaphysical sense and mystery of the *person*. It seems to me that the debate today is being played out on that level. The evil of our times consists in the first place in a kind of degradation, indeed in a pulverization, of the fundamental uniqueness of each human person. This evil is even more of the metaphysical order than of the moral order. To this disintegration planned at times

by atheistic ideologies we must oppose, rather than sterile polemics, a kind of "recapitulation" of the inviolable mystery of the person.[9]

Commenting on this passage, John Paul II's biographer George Weigel explains:

That radical humanism—that life-forming commitment to "the inviolable mystery of the person"—was, and is, Karol Wojtyła's response to a century in which false humanisms had created mountains of corpses and an ocean of blood, Auschwitz and the Gulag, abortion as a widespread means of fertility regulation, and the prospect of the biotechnical remanufacture of the *humanum*.[10]

If we are seeing in our own time challenges to the truths that we are created male and female, and that male and female are created for each other in marriage, it is because we have lost sight of the true nature of man. We must respond to false humanisms with a true humanism committed to the unique and irreplaceable value of each person.

This false humanism in John Paul II's time was on powerful display in the political order, where totalitarianism grew. Today, blindness to the truth about the human person has led to a crisis of family and sexuality. But then as now, we see clearly the church's latest intellectual and cultural challenge: not the nature of God or redemption, but of man and morality. Our task is to explain what human persons most fundamentally are, and how we are to relate to one another within families and polities.

For us, as for John Paul II's generation, nothing less than authentic freedom is at stake. For a freedom based on faulty anthropology and morality is slavery. Only a freedom based on the truth is worthy of the name. As Weigel explains:

Freedom untethered from truth is freedom's worst enemy. For if there is only your truth and my truth, and neither one of us recognizes a transcendent moral standard (call it *"the* truth") by which to adjudicate our differences, then the only way to settle the argument is for you to impose your power on me, or for me to impose my power on you. Freedom untethered from truth leads to chaos; chaos leads to anarchy; and since human beings cannot tolerate anarchy, tyranny as the answer to the human imperative of order is just around the corner. The false humanism of the freedom of indifference leads first to freedom's decay, and then to freedom's demise.[11]

In the realm of sex and marriage, we have seen the unfettered desire of the strong—adults, the affluent—pursued at the expense of the vulnerable—children, the poor. To avoid the tyranny of sexual desire, which in the name of freedom and dignity breaks hearts and homes and spawns loneliness, we must commit to witnessing to the truth of human nature. These debates, seen from the inside as they are under way, may seem intractable, but in the long run this is how our age will develop a richer anthropology and a richer morality. As we are challenged to defend the truths of human nature—male and female created for each other in marriage—we will discover a deeper reflection on human nature and our fulfillment.

Another Glimmer of Hope

Allow me to conclude this book with one more story from Passover and Holy Week of 2015 in Indiana. The story shows both that the stakes are high and that the American people are better equipped to determine the way forward than our ruling elites.

The story began when a journalist from ABC57, a local news station in South Bend, went to the rural community of Walkerton and asked the O'Connor family—owners of Memories Pizza—a ridiculous question: what they would do if they were asked to cater a same-sex wedding reception. The O'Connors made it clear that Memories Pizza has no objection to serving gay and lesbian customers. But serving pizza at a same-sex wedding would be celebrating what they believe to be a lie about marriage, and they would have to decline such a request.[12]

ABC57 first reported the story on its website with the headline "RFRA: First Michiana Business to Publicly Deny Same-Sex Service."[13] BuzzFeed reported the story with the outrageous headline "Indiana Pizzeria Owners Say They'd Deny LGBT People Service." (Both ABC57 and BuzzFeed subsequently corrected their headlines.)

As a result of this entirely fabricated media controversy, the O'Connor family received death threats, their business was the target of boycotts, and their social media pages and Yelp reviews were taken over with what Kirsten Powers describes as "obscene and homo-erotic pictures."[14] By the time the media lynch mob was done, the owners felt so unsafe that they had to close their restaurant.

The story might have ended there. But Dana Loesch and Lawrence B. Jones III of TheBlaze launched an online GoFundMe campaign to assist the O'Connors. Ordinary Americans, appalled by the Left's intolerance, responded with overwhelming generosity. Within a week more than thirty thousand people had contributed more than $800,000. The O'Connor family, a class act, decided to reopen their restaurant and donate the money: "They revealed they are set to share their new fortune with disabled children, a women's help group, firefighters, police trusts, Christian churches, and Washington florist Barronelle Stutzman, 70, who was fined after declaring she would not serve a gay wedding."[15]

Countless businesses and lives could be ruined if America responds the wrong way to the Supreme Court's unjust and unconstitutional ruling on same-sex marriage. But most Americans, straight or gay, don't want that to happen. One twenty-dollar donation to Memories Pizza was accompanied by the following message:

> As a member of the gay community, I would like to apologize
> for the mean spirited attacks on you and your business. I know
> many gay individuals who fully support your right to stand up
> for your beliefs and run your business according to those
> beliefs. We are outraged at the level of hate and intolerance

that has been directed at you and I sincerely hope that you are able to rebuild.[16]

That's one grassroots voice. We must make it our business to multiply ones like it.

The Long View

And yet some people seem to think this debate is over. They're wrong. My experience on college campuses over the past few years suggests there is hope. On almost every campus I have visited, including elite law schools like Harvard and Yale, students have told me that they had never before heard a rational case for marriage. Christians have said that they always knew marriage was between a man and a woman but didn't know how to defend that truth as a matter of law and policy. They knew what the Bible reveals and the church teaches but lacked a vocabulary for articulating what God has written on the heart. Now they can explain how faith and reason go together, and how theology and philosophy, the Bible and social science all point to the same truth. It is crucially important to reassure these students so they don't internalize doubt, cower before aggressive opposition, and ultimately cave in.

It's important to help those who haven't made up their minds to see that reasonable people of goodwill are to be found on both sides of this debate. Some are genuinely on the fence, and we should do what we can to keep them from coming down on the wrong side. Indeed, I have received hundreds of notes over the past year from people who decided to come down on the right side because of an argument for marriage they heard from me.

While we may not be able to convert the committed advocates of same-sex marriage, we should seek to soften their resolve to eliminate us from polite society. Again, on campus after campus where I have spoken, students who identify as liberal have admitted that this was the first time they have heard a reasoned case for marriage. They have told me that they respect the argument. Frequently, they're not even sure why it's wrong, even as they insist that it *is* wrong. Winning respect from these students for our religious liberty rights is essential. We do that, in part, by explaining the reasons for our beliefs about marriage.

In the past, nearly all American children received the great gift of being raised to adulthood within the marital bond of the man and the woman whose union gave them life. Today, far fewer than half the children in some communities are so fortunate, and the consequences are tragic. Though same-sex marriage didn't cause this breakdown, it will only make things worse. Indeed, it will lock in the distorted view of marriage as an institution primarily concerned with adult romantic desires and make the rebuilding of the marriage culture much more difficult.

Whatever the law or culture may say, we must commit now to witness to the truths about marriage—that men and women are equal and equally necessary in the lives of children; that men and women, though different, are complementary; that it takes a man and a woman to bring a child into the world; and that marriage policy should maximize the odds that a child will grow up with a mom and a dad.

Long before the debate about same-sex marriage, there was a debate about marriage. From that debate there emerged a "marriage movement" to explain why marriage is good for the men and women who are faithful to its responsibilities and for the children they bring into the world. Over the past decade, a new question has arisen: What does society have to lose by removing sexual complementarity from its definition of marriage?

Many citizens are increasingly tempted to think that marriage is simply an intense emotional union among consenting adults—conventionally two, but maybe more. That union may be sexual or platonic, exclusive or open, temporary or permanent. This understanding leaves marriage with no essential features, no fixed core as a social reality. It is simply whatever consenting adults want it to be.

With such an understanding of marriage, how will society protect its children—the primary victims of our nonmarital sexual culture—without the government's growing more intrusive and more expensive?

Marriage exists to bring a man and a woman together as husband and wife to be father and mother to any children their union produces. Marriage benefits everyone because separating the bearing and rearing of children from marriage burdens innocent bystanders: not just children, but the whole community. Without healthy marriages, the community must step in to provide more directly for children's well-being and upbringing. By encouraging the norms of marriage—monogamy, sexual exclusivity, and permanence—the state strengthens civil society and reduces its own role.

Government has always recognized marriage—always understood as the union of a man and a woman—because marriage benefits society in a way that no other relationship or institution does. Marriage is society's least restrictive means of ensuring the well-being of children. State recognition of marriage protects children by encouraging men and women to commit to each other and take responsibility for their children.

The future of this country depends on the future of marriage, and the future of marriage depends on citizens' understanding what it is and why it matters and demanding that government policies support, not undermine, true marriage.

Some appeal to historical inevitability as a reason to avoid dealing with the question of what marriage is. Public opinion, however, reflects millions of human choices, not blind historical forces. The question is not what will happen, but what we should do.

In this struggle to preserve marriage, as in the pro-life cause, we need to take a long view, not counting the immediate wins or losses, but rebuilding, over decades perhaps, the intellectual and moral infrastructure of a society that can once again appreciate the truth about marriage.

NOTES

Introduction

1. Adam Liptak, "The Case against Gay Marriage: Top Law Firms Won't Touch It," *New York Times*, April 11, 2015, http://www.nytimes.com/2015/04/12/us/the-case-against-gay-marriage-top-law-firms-wont-touch-it.html?_r=0.

2. Transcript of oral arguments for Obergefell v. Hodges, available at the Supreme Court website, "14-556-Question-1. Obergefell v. Hodges," date argued: April 28, 2015, http://www.supremecourt.gov/oral_arguments/argument_transcripts/14-556q1_7l48.pdf. For more, see Ryan T. Anderson, "Obama Administration Says Non-Profit Status 'Going to Be an Issue' for Religious Schools," Daily Signal, April 28, 2015, http://dailysignal.com/2015/04/28/obama-administration-says-non-profit-status-going-to-be-an-issue-for-religious-schools/.

3. Kirsten Powers, "Jim Crow Laws for Gays and Lesbians?," *USA Today*, February 19, 2014, http://www.usatoday.com/story/opinion/2014/02/18/gays-lesbians-kansas-bill-religious-freedom-christians-column/5588643/.

4.   Powers, "Arizona Latest to Attack Gay Rights," *USA Today*, February 25, 2014, http://www.usatoday.com/story/opinion/2014/02/25/arizona-right-refuse-gay-religious-freedom-homosexuality-column/5817555/.

5.   Mark Joseph Stern, "Kansas' Anti-Gay Segregation Bill Is an Abomination," Slate, February 13, 2014, http://www.slate.com/blogs/outward/2014/02/13/kansas_anti_gay_segregation_bill_is_an_abomination.html.

6.   Editorial Board, "A License to Discriminate," *New York Times*, February 24, 2014, http://www.nytimes.com/2014/02/25/opinion/a-license-to-discriminate.html?_r=0.

7.   "Bill Would Let Michigan Doctors, EMTs Refuse to Treat Gay Patients," CBS News, December 11, 2014, http://www.cbsnews.com/news/bill-would-let-michigan-doctors-emts-refuse-to-treat-gay-patients/.

8.   Eric Bradner, "NCAA 'Concerned' over Indiana Law That Allows Biz to Reject Gays," CNN, March 26, 2015, http://www.cnn.com/2015/03/25/politics/mike-pence-religious-freedom-bill-gay-rights/.

9.   Marc Tracy, "Controversial Indiana Law Puts Pressure on N.C.A.A. and Other Leagues," *New York Times*, March 26, 2015, http://www.nytimes.com/2015/03/27/sports/ncaabasketball/controversial-indiana-law-puts-pressure-on-ncaa-and-other-leagues.html.

10.   Brian Eason, "Indianapolis Looks to Limit 'Religious Freedom' Damage," *USA Today*, March 27, 2015, http://www.usatoday.com/story/news/nation/2015/03/27/indiana-religious-freedom-law-fallout/70534200/.

11.   Liptak, "The Case against Gay Marriage."

12.   Frank Bruni, "Bigotry, the Bible and the Lessons of Indiana," *New York Times*, April 3, 2015, http://www.nytimes.com/2015/04/05/opinion/sunday/frank-bruni-same-sex-sinners.html?_r=0&assetType=opinion.

13.   "Our Letters Policy on Same-Sex Marriage—an Explanation and an Apology: John L. Micek," PennLive, June 27, 2015, http://www.pennlive.com/opinion/2015/06/our_letters_policy_on_same-sex.html.

One: Men, Women, and Children: The Truth about Marriage

1.   Sherif Girgis, Ryan T. Anderson, and Robert P. George, *What Is Marriage? Man and Woman: A Defense* (New York: Encounter Books, 2012).

2. United States v. Windsor, No. 12–307, 570 U.S. 13 (and 8) (2013) (Alito, S., dissenting); Girgis, Anderson, and George, *What Is Marriage?*

3. United States v. Windsor, No. 12–307, 570 U.S. 13 (and 8) (2013) (Alito, S., dissenting).

4. John Corvino and Maggie Gallagher, *Debating Same-Sex Marriage* (New York: Oxford University Press). My review of that book is here: "The Marriage Mess," *National Review* 64, no. 14 (July 30, 2012), available online at https://www.nationalreview.com/nrd/articles/309271/marriage-mess.

5. Andrew Sullivan, ed., *Same-Sex Marriage: Pro and Con; A Reader* (New York: Vintage Books, 1997), xvii, xix.

6. Girgis, Anderson, and George, *What Is Marriage?*

7. Obergefell v. Hodges 576 U.S. (2015), available online at http://www.supremecourt.gov/opinions/14pdf/14-556_3204.pdf.

8. James Q. Wilson, *The Marriage Problem* (New York: HarperCollins Publishers, 2002), 41.

9. Corvino and Gallagher, *Debating Same-Sex Marriage*, 96.

10. W. Bradford Wilcox, "Reconcilable Differences: What Social Sciences Show about the Complementarity of the Sexes and Parenting," *Touchstone* 18, no. 9 (November 2005): 32, 36.

11. Ibid.

12. David Popenoe, *Life without Father: Compelling New Evidence That Fatherhood and Marriage Are Indispensable for the Good of Children and Society* (New York: The Free Press, 1996), 146.

13. Ibid., 197. See also Wilcox, "Reconcilable Differences," 36.

14. Wilcox, "Reconcilable Differences."

15. Ibid.

16. Popenoe, *Life without Father*, 145–46.

17. Wilcox, "Reconcilable Differences."

18. Ibid.

19. For the relevant studies, see Witherspoon Institute, *Marriage and the Public Good: Ten Principles* (Princeton: NJ, August 2008), 9–19, http://winst.org/wp-content/uploads/WI_Marriage_and_the_Public_Good.pdf. Signed by some seventy scholars, this document presents extensive evidence from the social sciences about the welfare of children and adults.

20. Kristin Anderson Moore, Susan M. Jekielek, and Carol Emig, "Marriage from a Child's Perspective: How Does Family Structure Affect Children, and What Can We Do about It?," Child Trends Research Brief, June 2002, pp. 1, 6, http://www.childtrends.org/wp-content/uploads/2013/03/MarriageRB602.pdf.

21. Wendy D. Manning and Kathleen A. Lamb, "Adolescent Well-Being in Cohabiting, Married, and Single-Parent Families," *Journal of Marriage and Family* 65, no. 4 (November 2003): 876 and 890.

22. See Sara McLanahan, Elisabeth Donahue, and Ron Haskins, "Introducing the Issue," *Marriage and Child Wellbeing* 15, no. 2 (Fall 2005): available online at http://www.princeton.edu/futureofchildren/publications/docs/15_02_01.pdf; Mary Parke, "Are Married Parents Really Better for Children?," Center for Law and Social Policy, May 2003, http://www.clasp.org/admin/site/publications_states/files/0086.pdf; and Wilcox et al., *Why Marriage Matters: Twenty-Six Conclusions from the Social Sciences*, 2nd ed. (New York: Institute for American Values, 2005), 6, available online at http://americanvalues.org/catalog/pdfs/why_marriage_matters2.pdf.

23. "Obama's Speech on Fatherhood," speech by Barack Obama, Apostolic Church of God, Chicago, June 15, 2008, transcript posted on RealClearPolitics, http://www.realclearpolitics.com/articles/2008/06/obamas_speech_on_fatherhood.html.

24. "Transcript: Obama's Commencement Speech at Morehouse College," speech by Barack Obama, Morehouse College, May 19, 2013, transcript posted on the *Wall Street Journal*, http://blogs.wsj.com/washwire/2013/05/20/transcript-obamas-commencement-speech-at-morehouse-college/.

25. Social Trends Institute, "The Sustainable Demographic Dividend: What Do Marriage and Fertility Have to Do with the Economy?," 2011, http://sustaindemographicdividend.org/articles/the-sustainable-demographic.

26. H. Brevy Cannon, "New Report: Falling Birth, Marriage Rates Linked to Global Economic Slowdown," *UVA Today*, October 3, 2011, https://news.virginia.edu/content/new-report-falling-birth-marriage-rates-linked-global-economic-slowdown.

27. Robert Rector, "Marriage: America's Greatest Weapon against Child Poverty," Heritage Foundation *Special Report* no. 117, September 5, 2012,

http://www.heritage.org/research/reports/2012/09/marriage-americas-greatest-weapon-against-child-poverty.

28. Isabel V. Sawhill, "Families at Risk," in *Setting National Priorities: The 2000 Election and Beyond,* ed. Henry J. Aaron and Robert D. Reischauer (Washington: Brookings Institution Press, 1999), 97, 108. See also Witherspoon Institute, "Marriage and the Public Good," 15.

29. Institute for American Values et al., *The Taxpayer Costs of Divorce and Unwed Childbearing: First-Ever Estimates for the Nation and for All Fifty States* (New York: Institute for American Value, 2008), available online at http://www.americanvalues.org/catalog/pdfs/COFF.pdf.

30. David G. Schramm, "Preliminary Estimates of the Economic Consequences of Divorce," Utah State University, 2003.

Two: The Consequences of Redefining Marriage

1. Robert P. George, "What Few Deny Gay Marriage Will Do," *First Things*, April 16, 2013, http://www.firstthings.com/blogs/firstthoughts/2013/04/what-few-deny-gay-marriage-will-do.

2. E. J. Graff, "Retying the Knot," in *Same-Sex Marriage: Pro and Con; A Reader,* ed. Andrew Sullivan (New York: Vintage Books, 1997), 134, 136, 137.

3. Sullivan, "Introduction," *Same-Sex Marriage*, 17, 19.

4. Victoria A. Brownworth, "Something Borrowed, Something Blue: Is Marriage Right for Queers?," in *I Do/I Don't: Queers on Marriage*, ed. Greg Wharton and Ian Philips (San Francisco: Suspect Thoughts Press, 2004), 53, 58–59.

5. Ellen Willis, "Can Marriage Be Saved? A Forum," *Nation*, July 5, 2004, p. 16, available online at http://www.thenation.com/article/can-marriage-be-saved-0#.

6. Michelangelo Signorile, "Bridal Wave," *Out*, December 1993/January 1994, pp. 68, 161.

7. Ibid.

8. See Sherif Girgis, Ryan T. Anderson, and Robert P. George, *What Is Marriage? Man and Woman: A Defense* (New York: Encounter Books, 2012).

9. See Maggie Gallagher, "(How) Will Gay Marriage Weaken Marriage as a Social Institution: A Reply to Andrew Koppelman," *University of St. Thomas Law Journal* 2, no. 1 (2004): 62, available online at http://ir. stthomas.edu/cgi/viewcontent.cgi?article=1047&context=ustlj.

10. "Beyond Same-Sex Marriage: A New Strategic Vision for All Our Families and Relationships," BeyondMarriage.org, July 26, 2006, http://beyondmarriage.org/full_statement.html.

11. Elizabeth Brake, "Minimal Marriage: What Political Liberalism Implies for Marriage Law," *Ethics* 120, no. 2 (January 2010): 302, 303, 323, 336.

12. Jessica Bennett, "Polyamory: The Next Sexual Revolution?," *Newsweek*, July 28, 2009, http://www.newsweek.com/polyamory-next-sexual-revolution-82053.

13. Julia Zebley, "Utah Polygamy Law Challenged in Federal Lawsuit," Jurist, July 13, 2011, http://jurist.org/paperchase/2011/07/utah-polygamy-law-challenged-in-federal-lawsuit.php.

14. Jim Sanders, "Jerry Brown Vetoes Bill Allowing More Than Two Parents," *Capitol Alert* (blog), *Sacramento Bee*, September 30, 2012, http://blogs.sacbee.com/capitolalertlatest/2012/09/jerry-brown-vetoes-bill-allowing-more-than-two-parents.html.

15. For more on this, see Jennifer Roback Morse, "Why California's Three-Parent Law Was Inevitable," Public Discourse (Witherspoon Institute), September 10, 2012, http://www.thepublicdiscourse.com/2012/09/6197.

16. Matthew Holehouse, "Greens 'Open' to Three-Person Marriage, Says Natalie Bennett," *Telegraph*, May 1, 2015, http://www.telegraph.co.uk/news/general-election-2015/11576818/Greens-open-to-three-person-marriage-says-Natalie-Bennett.html.

17. "Paper Symposium: Polygamous Unions? Charting the Contours of Marriage Law's Frontier," *Emory Law Journal* 64, no. 6, available online at http://law.emory.edu/elj/content/volume-64/issue-6/index.html. See also Eugene Volokh, "*Emory Law Journal* on a Constitutional Right to Polygamy," *Volokh Conspiracy* (blog), *Washington Post*, June 9, 2015, http://www.washingtonpost.com/news/volokh-conspiracy/wp/2015/06/09/emory-law-journal-symposium-on-a-constitutional-right-to-polygamy/.

18. Ronald C. Den Otter, *In Defense of Plural Marriage* (New York: Cambridge University Press, 2015).

19. See, for example, the Cambridge University Press webpage for *In Defense of Plural Marriage*: http://www.cambridge.org/us/academic/subjects/law/family-law/defense-plural-marriage?format=HB.

20. Fredrik DeBoer, "It's Time to Legalize Polygamy: Why Group Marriage Is the Next Horizon of Social Liberalism," *Politico* magazine, June 16, 2015, http://www.politico.com/magazine/story/2015/06/gay-marriage-decision-polygamy-119469.html#.VY_tCBNVhBc.

21. Angi Becker Stevens, "My Two Husbands," Salon, August 3, 2013, http://www.salon.com/2013/08/05/my_two_husbands/. See also Brooke Lea Foster, "Married, but Not Exclusive," *Washingtonian*, July 30, 2013, http://www.washingtonian.com/articles/people/married-but-not-exclusive/.

22. Molly Young, "He & He & He," *New York*, June 29, 2012, http://nymag.com/news/features/benny-morecock-throuple/.

23. Andrew Sullivan, *Virtually Normal: An Argument about Homosexuality* (New York: Vintage Books, 1996), 202–3.

24. Scott James, "Many Successful Gay Marriages Share an Open Secret," *New York Times*, January 28, 2010, http://www.nytimes.com/2010/01/29/us/29sfmetro.html.

25. Ari Karpel, "Monogamish," *Advocate*, July 7, 2011. See the article description here: http://www.advocate.com/arts-entertainment?page=310&fb_xd_fragment=.

26. Karpel, "Monogamish."

27. Mark Oppenheimer, "Married, with Infidelities," *New York Times Magazine*, June 30, 2011, http://www.nytimes.com/2011/07/03/magazine/infidelity-will-keep-us-together.html?pagewanted=all&_r=2&amp.

28. Paul Rampell, "A High Divorce Rate Means It's Time to Try 'Wedleases,'" *Washington Post*, August 4, 2013, http://www.washingtonpost.com/opinions/a-high-divorce-rate-means-its-time-to-try-wedleases/2013/08/04/f2221c1c-f89e-11e2-b018-5b8251f0c56e_story.html.

29. Guy Ringler, "Get Ready for Embryos from Two Men or Two Women," *Time*, March 18, 2015, http://time.com/3748019/same-sex-couples-biological-children/.

30. Alex Anderson, "California Requires Insurers to Cover Abortion Services," Daily Signal, August 25, 2014, http://dailysignal.com/2014/08/25/california-

requires-insurers-cover-abortion-services/; and Ryan T. Anderson and Sarah Torre, "Congress Should Protect Religious Freedom in the District of Columbia," Heritage Foundation *Issue Brief* no. 4364, March 9, 2015, http://www.heritage.org/research/reports/2015/03/congress-should-protect-religious-freedom-in-the-district-of-columbia.

31.   Kathleen Miles, "Gay Couples Will Receive Fertility Coverage under New State Law," Huffington Post, October 9, 2013, http://www.huffingtonpost.com/2013/10/09/gay-couples-fertility-coverage-california_n_4073491.html.

32.   William Bigelow, "CA Law Extends Insurance to Fertility Treatments for Same-Sex, Married Couples," Breitbart, October 10, 2013, http://www.breitbart.com/big-government/2013/10/10/new-ca-law-forces-insurance-companies-to-cover-same-sex-unmarried-couples-fertility/.

33.   For more on this, see Thomas M. Messner, "Same-Sex Marriage and the Threat to Religious Liberty," Heritage Foundation *Backgrounder* no. 2201, October 30, 2008, http://www.heritage.org/research/reports/2008/10/same-sex-marriage-and-the-threat-to-religious-liberty.

34.   Becket Fund for Religious Liberty, *Issues Brief: Same-Sex Marriage and State Anti-Discrimination Laws* (Washington, DC: January 2009), 2, http://www.becketfund.org/wp-content/uploads/2011/04/Same-Sex-Marriage-and-State-Anti-Discrimination-Laws-with-Appendices.pdf. See also Messner, "Same-Sex Marriage and Threats to Religious Freedom," 4.

35.   Thomas John Paprocki, letter to priests, deacons, and pastoral facilitators in the diocese of Springfield, January 3, 2013, http://www.dio.org/blog/item/326-bishop-paprockis-letter-on-same-sex-marriage.html#sthash.CPXLw6Gt.dpbs.

36.   Ibid.

37.   Chai R. Feldblum, "Moral Conflict and Liberty: Gay Rights and Religion," *Brooklyn Law Review* 72, no. 1 (Fall 2006): 119, http://www.brooklaw.edu/~/media/PDF/LawJournals/BLR_PDF/blr_v72i.ashx.

38.   United States v. Windsor, no. 12–307, 570 U.S. 21 (2013) (Scalia, J., dissenting).

Three: Judicial Tyranny

1. Various, "After *Obergefell*: A *First Things* Symposium," *First Things*, June 27, 2015, http://www.firstthings.com/web-exclusives/2015/06/after-obergefell-a-first-things-symposium

2. Transcript of oral arguments for Obergefell v. Hodges, available at the Supreme Court website, "14-556-Question-1. Obergefell v. Hodges," date argued: April 28, 2015, http://www.supremecourt.gov/oral_arguments/argument_transcripts/14-556q1_7l48.pdf.

3. Obergefell v. Hodges, 576 U.S. ___ (2015), available online at http://www.supremecourt.gov/opinions/14pdf/14-556_3204.pdf.

4. Zablocki v. Redhail, 434 U.S. 374, 384 (1978), quoting Meyer v. Nebraska, 262 U.S. 390, 399.

5. Justice Clarence Thomas, for example, cited my amicus brief in his dissent at 576 U.S. ___ (2015) (slip op., at 12).

6. Helen M. Alvare, "A Decision That's Unfair and Disenfranchising," Crux, June 25, 2015, http://www.cruxnow.com/life/2015/06/25/supreme-court-gay-marriage-is-constitutional/#pov2.

7. Matthew J. Franck, "Thanks for Everything, Justice Kennedy," Public Discourse (Witherspoon Institute), June 20, 2015, http://www.thepublicdiscourse.com/2015/06/15235/.

Four: "Bake Me a Cake, Bigot!"

1. Ryan T. Anderson, "Eich Is Out. So Is Tolerance," Daily Signal, April 3, 2014, http://dailysignal.com/2014/04/03/eich-tolerance/.

2. Kara Swisher, "Mozilla Co-Founder Brendan Eich Resigns as CEO, Leaves Foundation Board," Re/code, April 3, 2014, http://recode.net/2014/04/03/mozilla-co-founder-brendan-eich-resigns-as-ceo-and-also-from-foundation-board/.

3. The entire Twitter exchange can be read here: https://twitter.com/hcatlin/status/583790770907439104.

4. Anderson, "A&E, *Duck Dynasty*, and the Climate of Intolerance in America," Daily Signal, December 20, 2013, http://dailysignal.com/2013/12/20/penalizing-hold-biblical-views-marriage/.

5. Ericka Andersen, "A&E Reverses *Duck Dynasty* Decision, Welcomes Phil Robertson Back," Daily Signal, December 28, 2013, http://dailysignal. com/2013/12/28/ae-reverses-duck-dynasty-decision-welcomes-phil-robertson-back.

6. Matthew W. Clark, "The Gospel according to the State: An Analysis of Massachusetts Adoption Law and the Closing of Catholic Charities Adoption Services," *Suffolk University Law Review* 41, no. 4 (2008).

7. Goodridge v. Dept. of Public Health, 798 N.E.2d 941 (Mass. 2003), available online at http://www2.law.columbia.edu/faculty_franke/Gay_Marriage/ Goodridge%20Decision%20edited%20Fundamental%20Right.pdf.

8. Maggie Gallagher, "Banned in Boston: The Coming Conflict between Same-Sex Marriage and Religious Liberty," *Weekly Standard* 11, no. 33 (May 15, 2006), available online at http://www.weeklystandard.com/ Content/Public/Articles/000/000/012/191kgwgh.asp.

9. News release, "Catholic Charities of Boston to Discontinue Adoption Services," statement by Archbishop Sean O'Malley, Archdiocese of Boston, March 10, 2006, http://www.bostoncatholic.org/uploadedFiles/ News_releases_2006_statement060310-1.pdf.

10. District of Columbia Official Code, § 46-401. The D.C. Code can be viewed online at LexisNexis: http://www.lexisnexis.com/hottopics/dccode/.

11. Evangelical Child and Family Agency, *2012 Annual Report* (Wheaton: IL, 2012), 2, available online at http://www.evancfa.org/downloads/ ECFAAnnualReportFY2012.pdf; and Karla Dial, "Illinois Christian Foster Care Group Loses State Contract," CitizenLink, September 14, 2011, http:// www.citizenlink.com/2011/09/14/illinois-christian-foster-care-group-loses-state-contract/.

12. United States Conference of Catholic Bishops, "Discrimination against Catholic Adoption Services," Fact Sheet, 2013, http://www.usccb.org/ issues-and-action/religious-liberty/upload/Catholic-Adoption-Services-Fact-Sheet-Updated.pdf.

13. Illinois Religious Freedom Protection and Civil Union Act, Illinois Compiled Statutes, 750 ILCS 75/.

14. Evangelical Child and Family Agency, *2012 Annual Report*, 2; and Dial, "Illinois Christian Foster Care Group Loses State Contract."

15. Marriage Anti-Defamation Alliance, "Schulz, Craigen, Montague," YouTube video, posted by NationForMarriage, December 15, 2011, http://marriageada.org/schulz-craigen-montague/.

16. Sarah Torre, "Civil Union Law Forces Catholic Charities to Drop Adoption Service," Daily Signal, June 1, 2011, http://dailysignal.com/2011/06/01/civil-union-law-forces-catholic-charities-to-drop-adoption-service/; and Torre, "Charities Become Collateral Damage in the Debate over Marriage," Daily Signal, July 14, 2011, http://dailysignal.com/2011/07/14/charities-become-collateral-damage-in-the-debate-over-marriage/.

17. Manya A. Brachear, "3 Dioceses Drop Foster Care Lawsuit," *Chicago Tribune*, November 15, 2011, http://articles.chicagotribune.com/2011-11-15/news/ct-met-catholic-charities-foster-care-20111115_1_civil-unions-act-catholic-charities-religious-freedom-protection.

18. Thomas C. Atwood, "Foster Care: Safety Net or Trap Door?," Heritage Foundation *Backgrounder* no. 2535, March 25, 2011, p. 12, http://www.heritage.org/research/reports/2011/03/foster-care-safety-net-or-trap-door.

19. See Torre and Anderson, "Adoption, Foster Care, and Conscience Protection," Heritage Foundation *Backgrounder* no. 2869, January 15, 2014, http://www.heritage.org/research/reports/2014/01/adoption-foster-care-and-conscience-protection.

20. Children's Bureau, "Trends in Foster Care and Adoption: FFY2002–FFY2012," U.S. Department of Health and Human Services, Administration for Children and Families, Administration on Children, Youth and Families, accessed April 2015, p. 1, http://www.acf.hhs.gov/sites/default/files/cb/trends_fostercare_adoption2012.pdf; and Children's Bureau, "The AFCARS Report: Preliminary FY 2012 Estimates as of November 2013," U.S. Department of Health and Human Services, Administration for Children and Families, Administration on Children, Youth and Families, no. 20, accessed April 2015, p. 2, https://www.acf.hhs.gov/sites/default/files/cb/afcarsreport20.pdf.

21. Child Welfare Information Gateway, "National Foster Care & Adoption Directory Search," U.S. Department of Health and Human Services, Administration for Children and Families, https://www.childwelfare.gov/nfcad/.

22. David French, "Religious Liberty Is Reaffirmed in the Face of Strong Academic and Cultural Headwinds," *National Review*, May 1, 2015, http://www.nationalreview.com/article/417788/gordon-college-keeps-its-faith-and-its-accreditation-david-french.

23. Ibid.

24. District of Columbia Code, § 2-1402.41, available online at http://law.justia.com/codes/district-of-columbia/2012/division-i/title-2/chapter-14/unit-a/subchapter-ii/part-e/section-2-1402-41.html.

25. Anderson, "Same-Sex Marriage Trumps Religious Liberty in New Mexico," Daily Signal, August 22, 2013, http://dailysignal.com/2013/08/22/same-sex-marriage-trumps-religious-liberty-in-new-mexico/.

26. Willock v. Elane Photography, Decision and Final Order before the Human Rights Commission of the State of New Mexico, HRD No. 06-12-20-0685, available online at http://www.volokh.com/files/willockopinion.pdf, p. 8.

27. Ibid., 9.

28. Elane Photography v. Vanessa Willock, Supreme Court of the State of New Mexico, No. 33,687, August 22, 2013, available online at http://www.adfmedia.org/files/ElanePhotoNMSCopinion.pdf.

29. Leslie Ford, "Intolerance Burns Out Oregon Bakers," Daily Signal, September 5, 2013, http://dailysignal.com/2013/09/05/intolerance-burns-out-oregon-bakers/.

30. Maxine Bernstein, "Lesbian Couple Refused Wedding Cake Files State Discrimination Complaint," *Oregonian/Oregon Live*, August 14, 2013, http://www.oregonlive.com/gresham/index.ssf/2013/08/lesbian_couple_refused_wedding.html.

31. Billy Hallowell, "'We Still Stand by What We Believe': Bakers Who Refused to Make a Gay Wedding Cake Doubled Down Despite Ruling They Violated Couple's Civil Rights," TheBlaze, January 20, 2014, http://www.theblaze.com/stories/2014/01/20/state-rules-oregon-bakery-that-refused-to-make-a-gay-wedding-cake-violated-lesbian-couples-civil-rights/.

32. Hallowell, "'Bible-Thumping…B**ch': Bakers Who Refused to Make Gay Couple's Wedding Cake Shut Down Their Shop Following Threats, Anger," TheBlaze, September 2, 2013, http://www.theblaze.com/

stories/2013/09/02/bible-thumping-bch-bakery-that-refused-to-make-gay-couples-wedding-cake-is-shutting-down-its-shop-following-threats-anger/.

33.   Kelsey Harkness, "Bakers Who Declined Service to Same-Sex Couple Found to Violate Anti-Discrimination Law," Daily Signal, February 9, 2015, http://dailysignal.com/2015/02/09/bakers-declined-service-sex-couple-found-violate-anti-discrimination-law/.

34.   Harkness, "State Says Bakers Should Pay $135,000 for Refusing to Bake Cake for Same-Sex Wedding," Daily Signal, April 24, 2015, http://dailysignal.com/2015/04/24/state-says-bakers-should-pay-135000-for-refusing-to-bake-cake-for-same-sex-wedding/.

35.   Ibid.

36.   Ibid.

37.   Harkness, "Emails Raise Questions of Bias in Case against Bakers Who Denied Service for Same-Sex Wedding," Daily Signal, June 1, 2015, http://dailysignal.com/2015/06/01/emails-raise-questions-of-bias-in-case-against-bakers-who-denied-service-for-same-sex-wedding/.

38.   Kevin Simpson, "Colorado Amendment 43: Gay Marriage Banned; Domestic Partnerships Also Defeated," *Denver Post*, November 9, 2006, http://www.denverpost.com/ci_4627249.

39.   Ford, "The Government Can Now Force You to Bake a Cake," Daily Signal, December 18, 2013, http://dailysignal.com/2013/12/18/colorado-baker-faces-fines-religious-beliefs/.

40.   Andersen, "Baker Says He'd Rather Go to Jail After Judge Orders Him to Bake Cakes for Gay Weddings," LifeSiteNews, December 11, 2013, http://www.lifesitenews.com/news/baker-says-hed-rather-go-to-jail-after-judge-orders-him-to-bake-cakes-for-g.

41.   "Revealed: Colo. Commissioner Compared Cake Artist to Nazi," press release, Alliance Defending Freedom, January 12, 2015, http://www.alliancedefendingfreedom.org/News/PRDetail/9479.

42.   Charlie Craig and David Mullins v. Masterpiece Cakeshop, State of Colorado Office of Administrative Courts, CR 2013-0008, December 6, 2013, available online at https://www.aclu.org/sites/default/files/assets/initial_decision_case_no._cr_2013-0008.pdf.

43.   Andersen, "Baker Says He'd Rather Go to Jail."

44. Harkness, "State Says 70-Year-Old Flower Shop Owner Discriminated against Gay Couple. Here's How She Responded," Daily Signal, February 20, 2015, http://dailysignal.com/2015/02/20/state-says-70-year-old-flower-shop-owner-discriminated-gay-couple-heres-responded/.

45. "Attorney General Wins on Key Issues in Case against Richland Florist," press release, Washington State Office of the Attorney General, January 7, 2015, http://www.atg.wa.gov/news/news-releases/attorney-general-wins-key-issues-case-against-richland-florist.

46. "Floral Artist Responds to Wash. Attorney General's Settlement Offer," press release, Alliance Defending Freedom, February 20, 2015, http://www.alliancedefendingfreedom.org/News/PRDetail/9524.

47. Ibid.

48. Harkness, "State Says 70-Year-Old Flower Shop Owner Discriminated against Gay Couple."

49. "Wash. Floral Artist's Home, Savings Still at Risk after Court Judgment," press release, Alliance Defending Freedom, March 27, 2015, www.adfmedia.org/News/PRDetail/8608.

50. Betty Ann Odgaard and Richard Odgaard v. Iowa Civil Rights Commission, Iowa District Court, Polk County (2013), available online at http://www.becketfund.org/wp-content/uploads/2013/10/Odgaard-Complaint.pdf.

51. Ibid., 14.

52. Harkness, "Fearing Another Lawsuit, Christian Business Owners Stopped Hosting All Weddings. Now Their Business Is Dead," Daily Signal, June 19, 2015, http://dailysignal.com/2015/06/19/fearing-another-lawsuit-christian-business-owners-stopped-hosting-all-weddings-now-their-business-is-dead/.

53. Betty Ann Odgaard and Richard Odgaard v. Iowa Civil Rights Commission.

54. "Iowa Agency Tries to Force Mennonite Couple to Host Controversial Religious Ceremony," press release, Becket Fund for Religious Liberty, October 8, 2013, http://www.becketfund.org/iowa-agency-tries-to-force-mennonite-couple-to-host-controversial-religious-ceremony/.

55. Grant Rodgers, "Grimes' Gortz Haus to Stop All Weddings in Wake of Discrimination Complaint," *Des Moines Register*, January 28, 2015,

www.desmoinesregister.com/story/news/investigations/2015/01/28/gortz-haus-owners-decide-stop-weddings/22492677/.

56. Harkness, "Fearing Another Lawsuit, Christian Business Owners Stopped Hosting All Weddings."

57. Ibid.

58. Ibid.

59. "Govt Tells Christian Ministers: Perform Same-Sex Weddings or Face Jail, Fines," press release, Alliance Defending Freedom, October 18, 2014, http://www.adfmedia.org/News/PRDetail/9364.

60. Donald Knapp; Evelyn Knapp; Hitching Post Weddings, LLC v. City of Coeur D'Alene, motion for temporary restraining order and/or preliminary injunction (2014), available online at http://www.adfmedia.org/files/KnappTROmotion.pdf.

61. Eugene Volokh, "Coeur d'Alene City Attorney Confirms: Conservative Christian Ministers' Wedding Chapel Business Must Provide Same-Sex Marriage Ceremonies," *Volokh Conspiracy* (blog), *Washington Post*, October 22, 2014, http://www.washingtonpost.com/news/volokh-conspiracy/wp/2014/10/22/couer-dalene-city-attorney-confirms-conservative-christian-ministers-wedding-chapel-business-must-provide-same-sex-marriage-ceremonies/.

62. Alliance Defending Freedom, "Setting the Record Straight: 4 Things You Need to Know about the Hitching Post Case," *Alliance Defending Freedom* (blog), October 25, 2014, http://blog.alliancedefendingfreedom.org/2014/10/25/setting-the-record-straight-4-things-you-need-to-know-about-the-hitching-post-case/.

63. Volokh, "Can Ministers Who Make a Living by Conducting Weddings Be Required to Conduct Same-Sex Weddings?," *Volokh Conspiracy* (blog), *Washington Post*, October 18, 2014, http://www.washingtonpost.com/news/volokh-conspiracy/wp/2014/10/18/can-ministers-who-make-a-living-by-conducting-weddings-be-required-to-conduct-same-sex-weddings/; and Volokh, "Coeur d'Alene City Attorney Confirms."

64. Melisa McCarthy and Jennifer McCarthy v. Liberty Ridge Farm, LLC, Cynthia Gifford, Robert Gifford, New York State Division of Human Rights, Recommended Findings of Fact, Opinion and Decision, and Order (2014), 7.

65. Abigail Bleck, "Liberty Ridge Denies Same-Sex Wedding," WYNT 13, October 17, 2012, http://wnyt.com/article/stories/S2802104.shtml?cat=300.

66. New York State Executive Law, Article 15, Human Rights Law, p. 14, http://www.dhr.ny.gov/sites/default/files/doc/hrl.pdf.

67. McCarthy and McCarthy v. Liberty Ridge Farm, LLC.

68. Ibid., 21.

69. Ibid., 19.

70. Ibid., 21.

71. Kelvin J. Cochran's biography can be found on this archived page of the City of Atlanta website: http://web.archive.org/web/20130829011804/http://www.atlantaga.gov/index.aspx?page=224.

72. Ibid.

73. Kelvin J. Cochran, *Who Told You That You Were Naked?* (3G Publishing: 2013).

74. Todd Starnes, "Atlanta Fire Chief: I Was Fired Because of My Christian Faith," Fox News, January 7, 2015, http://www.foxnews.com/opinion/2015/01/07/atlanta-fire-chief-was-fired-because-my-christian-faith/.

75. Dyana Bagby, "Atlanta Fire Chief Goes on Anti-Gay Crusade in Self-Published Book," Georgia Voice, November 24, 2014, http://thegavoice.com/atlanta-fire-chief-goes-anti-gay-crusade-self-published-book/.

76. Jim Redmond, "Atlanta Fire Chief Kelvin Cochran Suspended for Anti-Gay Religious Tract," Towleroad, November 25, 2014, http://www.towleroad.com/2014/11/atlanta-fire-chief-kelvin-cochran-suspended-for-anti-gay-religious-tract.html; Associate Editor, "Atlanta Fire Chief Given One-Month Suspension Over Religious, Anti-Gay Treatise," *LGBT Weekly*, November 28, 2014, http://lgbtweekly.com/2014/11/28/atlanta-fire-chief-given-one-month-suspension-over-religious-anti-gay-treatise/; Bagby, "Atlanta Fire Chief Goes on Anti-Gay Crusade"; and Jonathan Shapiro, "LGBT Group Calls for Immediate Dismissal of Atlanta Fire Chief," San Diego Gay and Lesbian News, November 26, 2014, http://sdgln.com/news/2014/11/26/lgbt-group-calls-immediate-dismissal-atlanta-georgia-fire-chief#sthash.4Lc6LVKG.P0biDd3Y.dpbs.

77. Kasim Reed's Facebook page, November 24, 2014, https://www.facebook.com/kasimreed/posts/10152925936289669.

78. Katie Leslie, "Reed: Atlanta Fire Chief Terminated Following Book Controversy," *Atlanta Journal-Constitution*, January 6, 2015, http://www.ajc.com/news/news/reed-to-speak-about-atlanta-fire-chief-book-contro/njg9W/.

79. Kasim Reed's *Facebook* page, November 24, 2014.

80. Leslie, "Reed: Atlanta Fire Chief Terminated Following Book Controversy."

81. Ibid.

82. Garcetti v. Ceballos, 547 U.S. 410 (2006), available online at http://caselaw.lp.findlaw.com/scripts/getcase.pl?court=US&vol=000&invol=04-473.

83. Ibid.

84. "Fire Chief Sues City of Atlanta over Unjust Termination," press release, Alliance Defending Freedom, February 18, 2015, http://www.alliancedefendingfreedom.org/News/PRDetail/9522.

85. Ibid.

Five: Religious Freedom: A Basic Human Right

1. George Washington, "Letter to the Hebrew Congregation of Newport, R.I.," August 21, 1790, available online at Teaching American History, http://teachingamericanhistory.org/library/document/letter-to-the-hebrew-congregation-at-newport/.

2. Kevin Seamus Hasson, *The Right to Be Wrong: Ending the Culture War over Religion in America* (New York: Encounter Books, 2005).

3. James Madison, "A Memorial and Remonstrance," letter to Honorable the General Assembly of the Commonwealth of Virginia, ca. June 20, 1785, available online at Founders Online, National Archives, http://founders.archives.gov/documents/Madison/01-08-02-0163.

4. Ibid.

5. Ibid.

6. Michael W. McConnell, "Why Protect Religious Freedom," review of *Why Tolerate Religion?* by Brian Leiter, *Yale Law Journal* 123, no. 3 (December 2013): 770–811, http://www.yalelawjournal.org/review/why-protect-religious-freedom.

7.   See Ryan T. Anderson "The Right to Be Wrong," Public Discourse (Witherspoon Institute), July 7, 2014, http://www.thepublicdiscourse. com/2014/07/13432/. For more on the natural-law case for religious liberty, see Anderson, "A Leiter Case for the Superfluousness of Religious Liberty," review of Brian Leiter's *Why Tolerate Religion?*, November 25, 2012, Library of Law and Liberty (Liberty Fund), www.libertylawsite.org/book-review/a-leiter-case-for-the-superfluousness-of-religious-liberty/.

8.   On state religious freedom restoration acts, see Christopher C. Lund, "Religious Liberty after *Gonzales*: A Look at State RFRAs," *South Dakota Law Review* 55 (2010): 466. Also published in the Wayne State University Law School Research Paper Series, no. 10-1, http://ssrn.com/abstract=1666268.

9.   Editorial Board, "A License to Discriminate," *New York Times*, February 25, 2014, http://www.nytimes.com/2014/02/25/opinion/a-license-to-discriminate. html?_r=0.

10. Amending Sections 41-1493 and 41-1493.01, Arizona Revised Statutes; Relating to the Free Exercise of Religion, SB 1062, 51st Legislature (2014), available online at http://www.azleg.gov/legtext/51leg/2r/bills/sb1062s.pdf.

11. Kirsten Powers, "Arizona Latest to Attack Gay Rights," *USA Today*, February 25, 2014, http://www.usatoday.com/story/opinion/2014/02/25/arizona-right-refuse-gay-religious-freedom-homosexuality-column/5817555/.

12. The professors' letter to Governor Brewer can be read online: http://www. azpolicy.org/media-uploads/pdfs/Letter_to_Gov_Brewer_re_Arizona_ RFRA.pdf. See also Awr Hawkins, "Exclusive—Bipartisan Law Profs Warn Jan Brewer: SB 1062 'Egregiously Misrepresented,'" Breitbart, February 25, 2014, http://www.breitbart.com/big-government/2014/02/25/law-profs-send-letter-to-gov-brewer-warn-sb1062-being-egregiously-misrepresented/.

13. Abby Ohlheiser, "Look at All of These Horrible Bullies Bullying Jan Brewer over Arizona's Anti-Gay Bill," The Wire, February 25, 2014, http://www.thewire.com/politics/2014/02/look-all-these-horrible-bullies-bullying-jan-brewer-over-anti-gay-bill/358524/.

14. "Get the Facts: Understanding Michigan RFRA," Michigan House Republicans, December 9, 2014, http://gophouse.org/understanding-mirfra/.

15. Ed Whelan, "Absurd Anti-RFRA Hysteria in Michigan," *Bench Memos* (blog), *National Review*, December 12, 2014, http://www.nationalreview. com/bench-memos/394566/absurd-anti-rfra-hysteria-michigan-ed-whelan.

16. Jason Miller, "Freedom of Religion Shouldn't Be Unconditional," *Time*, December 11, 2014, http://time.com/3629943/michigan-religious-freedom-restoration-act/.

17. This situation differs substantially from that of a pro-life pharmacist who has a conscientious objection to dispensing drugs that could kill an unborn child. It is unclear how such drugs would constitute a compelling state interest. Indeed, the religious liberty of such pharmacists has been upheld in the courts. For one example, see Dominique Ludvigson, "A Win for Religious Freedom in Illinois," Daily Signal, December 13, 2012, http:// dailysignal.com/2012/12/13/a-win-for-religious-freedom-in-illinois/.

18. David Bernstein and Doug Laycock, "What Arizona SB1062 Actually Said," *Volokh Conspiracy* (blog), *Washington Post*, February 27, 2014, http://www.washingtonpost.com/news/volokh-conspiracy/wp/2014/02/27/ guest-post-from-prof-doug-laycock-what-arizona-sb1062-actually-said/.

19. Marc Benioff's tweet can be seen here: https://twitter.com/Benioff/ status/581108959337136129.

20. Charles Riley, "Salesforce CEO: We're Helping Employees Move Out of Indiana," CNNMoney, April 2, 2015, http://money.cnn.com/2015/04/01/ news/salesforce-benioff-indiana-religious-freedom-law/.

21. Hillary Clinton's tweet can be seen here: https://twitter.com/HillaryClinton/ status/581267449523343360.

22. Chuck Schumer's tweet can be seen here: https://twitter.com/SenSchumer/ status/581225532005679105.

23. Dan Malloy's tweet can be seen here: https://twitter.com/GovMalloyOffice/ status/582554117324800000.

24. Greg Hinz, "Pence Camp on Emanuel Job Raid: Indiana Better for Biz 'by Just About Any Measure,'" *Crain's Chicago Business*, March 30, 2015, http://www.chicagobusiness.com/article/20150330/BLOGS02/150329784/ pence-camp-on-emanuel-job-raid-indiana-better-for-biz-by-just-about.

25. Tim Cook, "Pro-Discrimination 'Religious Freedom' Laws Are Dangerous," *Washington Post*, March 29, 2015, http://www.washingtonpost.com/

opinions/pro-discrimination-religious-freedom-laws-are-dangerous-to-america/2015/03/29/bdb4ce9e-d66d-11e4-ba28-f2a685dc7f89_story.html.

26.   "App Store Pulls Manhattan Declaration," *Christianity Today*, November 29, 2010, http://www.christianitytoday.com/gleanings/2010/november/app-store-pulls-manhattan-declaration.html?paging=off.

27.   Chuck Schumer's Facebook page, March 31, 2015, https://www.facebook.com/chuckschumer/posts/10153161618154407.

28.   Hans von Spakovsky and Andrew Kloster, "The Misplaced Outrage against Indiana," Daily Signal, April 2, 2015, http://dailysignal.com/2015/04/02/the-misplaced-outrage-against-indiana/.

29.   Ibid.

30.   Josh Blackman, "Is Indiana Protecting Discrimination?," *National Review*, March 30, 2015, http://www.nationalreview.com/article/416160/indiana-protecting-discrimination-josh-blackman.

31.   John McCormack, "UVA Law Prof Who Supports Gay Marriage Explains Why He Supports Indiana's Religious Freedom Law," *The Blog* (blog), *Weekly Standard*, March 29, 2015, www.weeklystandard.com/blogs/uva-law-prof-who-supports-gay-marriage-explains-why-he-supports-indianas-religious-freedom-law_902928.html.

32.   "Transcript: Robin Roberts ABC News Interview with President Obama," ABC News, May 9, 2012, http://abcnews.go.com/Politics/transcript-robin-roberts-abc-news-interview-president-obama/story?id=16316043&singlePage=true#.UdCMN4zD_cs.

33.   "Remarks by the First Lady at the African Methodist Episcopal Church Conference Gaylord Opryland Resort, Nashville, Tennessee," speech by Michelle Obama, June 28, 2012, transcript posted on the White House Press Office, http://www.whitehouse.gov/the-press-office/2012/06/28/remarks-first-lady-african-methodist-episcopal-church-conference.

34.   McKenzie Romero, "Salt Lake Police Officer Says He Was 'Uncomfortable' with Parade Assignment," *Deseret News*, June 9, 2014, http://www.deseretnews.com/article/865604835/Salt-Lake-police-officer-says-he-was-uncomfortable-with-parade-assignment.html. The officer "said he was 'uncomfortable' with the assignment to ride ahead of the Utah Pride parade." When he asked to be reassigned to a security or patrol position,

he was placed on paid administrative leave. According to a statement from his lawyer, "The officer simply felt that the level of participation required in the event could be perceived as endorsing or advocating in favor of the LGBTQ community, a position which made him uncomfortable given his personal and religious beliefs."

35. Robin F. Wilson, "The Calculus of Accommodation: Contraception, Abortion, Same-Sex Marriage, and Other Clashes between Religion and the State," *Boston College Law Review* 53, no. 4 (September 2012): 1417–1513, available online at http://scholarlycommons.law.wlu.edu/cgi/viewcontent.cgi?article=1130&context=wlufac.

36. Ibid., 1482.

37. Anderson, "ENDA Threatens Fundamental Civil Liberties," Heritage Foundation *Backgrounder* no. 2857, November 1, 2013, http://www.heritage.org/research/reports/2013/11/enda-threatens-fundamental-civil-liberties.

38. Tim Schultz, testimony on Kansas Religious Freedom Bill before the House Judiciary Committee of the Kansas State Legislature, February 18, 2013, available online at Nevada Families for Freedom, http://nevadafamilies.org/index.php?option=com_content&view=article&id=42:testimony-of-tim-schultz-on-kansas-religious-freedom-bill&catid=24&Itemid=139. See also Christopher C. Lund, "Religious Liberty after Gonzales: A Look at State RFRAs," *South Dakota Law Review* 55, no. 3 (2010): 466 (symposium).

39. Anderson and Roger Severino, "This Bill Would Stop Obama Administration from Punishing People Who Stand Up for Marriage," Daily Signal, June 17, 2015, http://dailysignal.com/2015/06/17/this-bill-would-stop-obama-administration-from-punishing-people-who-stand-up-for-marriage/.

40. Mark Oppenheimer, "Now's the Time to End Tax Exemptions for Religious Institutions," *Time*, June 28, 2015, http://time.com/3939143/nows-the-time-to-end-tax-exemptions-for-religious-institutions/.

Six: Antidiscrimination Law: Why Sexual Orientation Is Not like Race

1.   Dillon Thomas and Zuzanna Sitek, "Voters Repeal Fayetteville Civil Rights Ordinance," 5News (Fayetteville, AR), December 9, 2014, http://5newsonline.com/2014/12/09/voters-repeal-fayetteville-civil-rights-ordinance/.

2.   T. Rees Shapiro, "Fairfax School Board Approves Transgender Protections," *Washington Post*, May 7, 2015, http://www.washingtonpost.com/local/education/fairfax-board-approves-transgender-protections/2015/05/07/993d3b0e-f522-11e4-bcc4-e8141e5eb0c9_story.html.

3.   Dustin Siggins, "Feds Blackmail Virginia's Largest School District into Transgender Policy," Federalist, May 27, 2015, http://thefederalist.com/2015/05/27/feds-blackmail-virginias-largest-school-district-into-transgender-policy/.

4.   Ibid.

5.   Human Rights Campaign, *Beyond Marriage Equality: A Blueprint for Federal Non-Discrimination Protections* (Washington, DC: 2014), http://www.hrc.org/campaigns/beyond-marriage-equality-a-blueprint-for-federal-non-discrimination-protect.

6.   Ibid.

7.   Hans Bader, "Employment Non-Discrimination Act Makes as Little Sense as Chemotherapy for a Cold," *Open Market* (blog), Competitive Enterprise Institute, June 13, 2012, http://www.openmarket.org/2012/06/13/employment-non-discrimination-act-makes-as-little-sense-as-chemotherapy-for-a-cold/.

8.   Ibid.

9.   "LGBT Equality at the Fortune 500," Human Rights Campaign, accessed April 7, 2015, http://www.hrc.org/resources/entry/lgbt-equality-at-the-fortune-500.

10. "Median LGBT household income is $61,500 vs. $50,000 for the average American household. LGBT households supporting a child reported a median income of $71,100." "The LGBT Financial Experience," Prudential, accessed April 2015, http://www.prudential.com/lgbt.

11. This is not to deny that gays and lesbians have experienced unfair treatment. Such treatment should be condemned. Understanding marriage as the union of a man and a woman, however, is not an instance of such unjust treatment.

12. Luis Garicano, Claire LeLarge, and John Van Reenen, "Firm Size Distortions and the Productivity Distribution: Evidence from France," National Bureau of Economic Research Working Paper no. 18841, February 2013, http://ideas.repec.org/p/nbr/nberwo/18841.html.

13. Bader, "Employment Non-Discrimination Act Makes as Little Sense as Chemotherapy for a Cold."

14. Bader, "ENDA vs. Free Speech," *Open Market* (blog), Competitive Enterprise Institute, November 15, 2007, http://www.openmarket. org/2007/11/15/enda-vs-free-speech/.

15. Bader, "Employment Non-Discrimination Act Makes as Little Sense as Chemotherapy for a Cold."

16. These states are California, Colorado, Connecticut, Delaware, Hawaii, Illinois, Iowa, Maine, Maryland, Massachusetts, Minnesota, Nevada, New Hampshire, New Jersey, New Mexico, New York, Oregon, Rhode Island, Vermont, Washington, and Wisconsin, as well as the District of Columbia.

17. Good News Employee Association et al. v. Joyce M. Hicks, No. 05-15467 (9th Cir. 2007).

18. Walter Olson, *The Excuse Factory: How Employment Law Is Paralyzing America* (New York: Free Press, 1997), 250.

19. As a historical matter, Ramesh Ponnuru notes, "Religious exemptions from federal law have been part of the legal landscape for decades. The Supreme Court insisted on them as a matter of constitutional law from 1963 to 1990, and Congress made them part of statutory law with the Religious Freedom Restoration Act in 1993." Ramesh Ponnuru, "RFRA and Race," *The Corner* (blog), *National Review*, March 4, 2014, http:// www.nationalreview.com/corner/372537/rfra-and-race-ramesh-ponnuru.Yet during that time, only one lawsuit was brought to the Supreme Court claiming a religious liberty right to ban interracial dating

on campus. That claim was roundly rejected. Thus, there is little reason to worry that protecting religious liberty for beliefs about marriage as the union of a man and a woman will lead to claims made on behalf of racists arguing from religious grounds.

20.   Robin Fretwell Wilson, "Matters of Conscience: Lessons for Same-Sex Marriage from the Healthcare Context," in *Same-Sex Marriage and Religious Liberty: Emerging Conflicts*, eds. Douglas Laycock Jr., Anthony R. Picarello, and Robin Fretwell Wilson (Lanham, MD: Rowan and Littlefield, 2008), 77, 101.

21.   Adam J. MacLeod, "What's at Stake at the Bakery: How Property Rights Got Sexy," Public Discourse (Witherspoon Institute), March 4, 2014, http://www.thepublicdiscourse.com/2014/03/12391/.

22.   Ibid.

23.   Ibid.

24.   Ibid.

25.   John Finnis, *Human Rights and Common Good* (New York: Oxford University Press, 2011), 315–88.

26.   Ibid.; John Witte, *From Sacrament to Contract: Marriage, Religion, and Law in the Western Tradition* (Louisville, KY: Westminster John Knox Press, 1997); and Scott Yenor, *Family Politics: The Idea of Marriage in Modern Political Thought* (Waco, TX: Baylor University Press, 2011).

27.   Nancy F. Cott, *Public Vows: A History of Marriage and the Nation* (Cambridge, MA: Harvard University Press, 2000), Kindle edition, location 483.

28.   David R. Upham, "Interracial Marriage and the Original Understanding of the Privileges or Immunities Clause," working paper, p. 15, http://papers.ssrn.com/sol3/papers.cfm?abstract_id=2240046, citing Gordon A. Stewart, "Our Marriage and Divorce Laws," *Popular Science Monthly* 23 (1883): 224, 234, available online at http://en.wikisource.org/wiki/Popular_Science_Monthly/Volume_23/June_1883/Our_Marriage_and_Divorce_Laws_I.

29.   Irving G. Tragen, "Statutory Prohibitions against Interracial Marriage," *California Law Review* 32, no. 3 (September 1944): 269, http://scholarship.law.berkeley.edu/cgi/viewcontent.cgi?article=3614&context=californiala

wreview. See also Francis Beckwith, "Interracial Marriage and Same-Sex Marriage," Public Discourse (Witherspoon Institute), May 21, 2010, http://www.thepublicdiscourse.com/2010/05/1324/. The relation "of parent and child…is consequential to that of marriage, being it's [*sic*] principal end and design: and it is by virtue of this relation that infants are protected, maintained, and educated." William Blackstone, *The Commentaries of Sir William Blackstone, Knight, on the Laws and Constitution of England* (Washington, D.C.: American Bar Association, 2009), 49.

30. Beckwith, "Interracial Marriage and Same-Sex Marriage."

31. Cott, *Public Vows*, location 382.

32. Ibid., location 382.

33. Beckwith, "Interracial Marriage and Same-Sex Marriage."

34. Ibid.

35. Perez v. Sharpe, 32 Cal. 2d 711 (Cal. 1948).

36. Fay Botham, *Almighty God Created the Races: Christianity, Interracial Marriage, and American Law* (Chapel Hill: University of North Carolina Press, 2013), Kindle edition, location 310.

37. Ibid., location 313.

38. Perez v. Sharpe, 711, 715 (quoting Skinner v. Oklahoma, 316 U.S. 535, 536 [1942]).

39. See De Burgh v. De Burgh, 250 P.2d 598, 601 (Cal. 1952).

40. Loving v. Virginia, 388 U.S. 1, 7 (1967).

41. See ibid. at 11–12.

42. See Susan Dudley Gold, *"Loving v. Virginia": Lifting the Ban against Interracial Marriage* (New York: Cavendish Square Publishing, 2009), 71–72 (quotations in original).

43. T. B. Maston, *Interracial Marriage*, Christian Life Commission, Southern Baptist Convention, p. 9.

44. Ibid., 9. Of course, there were Christians who claimed the Bible supported their position, but Maston showed how they misinterpreted the Scriptures. Any Old Testament prohibitions about marriage "were primarily national and tribal and not racial. The main motive for the restrictions was religious.… The Prohibitions regarding intermarriage in the Old Testament might be used to argue against the marriage of a Christian and a non-Christian, and

even against the marriage of citizens of different nations, but they cannot properly be used to support arguments against racial intermarriage" (5). Maston went on to note that in the Old Testament, "there are a number of instances of intermarriages," and "many of the great characters of the Bible were of mixed blood" (5–6). Maston pointed out that a sound Christian view of marriage had nothing to say about race but everything to say about sexual complementarity of male and female: "The Christian view which is soundly based on the biblical revelation is that marriage, which was and is ordained of God is a voluntary union of one man and one woman as husband and wife for life" (7).

45. Paul McHugh and Gerard V. Bradley, "Sexual Orientation, Gender Identity, and Employment Law," Public Discourse (Witherspoon Institute), July 25, 2013, http://www.thepublicdiscourse.com/2013/07/10636/.

46. Ibid.

47. Ibid.

48. McHugh and Bradley, "Sexual Orientation, Gender Identity, and Employment Law."

49. The description of this "safe space" can be read at the Office of Residential Life's "Program Housing" page: www.wesleyan.edu/reslife/housing/program/open_house.htm (accessed April 7, 2015).

50. McHugh and Bradley, "Sexual Orientation, Gender Identity, and Employment Law."

51. John Finnis, "Law, Morality, and 'Sexual Orientation,'" in *Human Rights and Common Good: The Collected Essays of John Finnis: Volume III* (New York: Oxford University Press, 2011), 335–36.

52. Ibid., 336.

Seven: The Victims

1. Kristin Anderson Moore, Susan M. Jekielek, and Carol Emig, "Marriage from a Child's Perspective: How Does Family Structure Affect Children, and What Can We Do about It?," Child Trends Research Brief, June 2002, pp. 1–2, 6, http://www.childtrends.org/wp-content/uploads/2013/03/MarriageRB602.pdf.

2.   For the relevant studies, see Witherspoon Institute, *Marriage and the Public Good: Ten Principles*, (Princeton: NJ, August 2008), 9–19, http://www. winst.org/family_marriage_and_democracy/WI_Marriage.pdf. Signed by some seventy scholars, this document presents extensive evidence from the social sciences about the welfare of children and adults.

3.   Barbara Dafoe Whitehead, "Dan Quayle Was Right," *Atlantic* 271, no. 4 (April 1993), available online at http://www.theatlantic.com/magazine/archive/1993/04/dan-quayle-was-right/307015/.

4.   Ibid.

5.   Andrew J. Cherlin, *The Marriage-Go-Round: The State of Marriage and the Family in America Today* (Random House Digital, 2010), 6.

6.   Susan L. Brown, "Family Structure and Child Well-Being: The Significance of Parental Cohabitation," *Journal of Marriage and Family* 66, no. 2 (2004): 351–67, doi:10.1111/j.1741-3737.2004.00025.x; Jennifer E. Lansford et al., "Does Family Structure Matter? A Comparison of Adoptive, Two-Parent Biological, Single-Mother, Stepfather, and Stepmother Households," *Journal of Marriage and Family* 63, no. 3 (2001): 840–51; and Paula Fomby and Andrew J. Cherlin, "Family Instability and Child Well-Being," *American Sociological Review* 72, no. 2 (April 2007): 181–204.

7.   Elizabeth Marquardt, Norval Glenn, and Karen Clark, *My Daddy's Name Is Donor: A New Study of Young Adults Conceived through Sperm Donation* (New York: Institute for American Values, 2010).

8.   Matthew D. Bramlett, Laura F. Radel, and Stephen J. Blumberg, "The Health and Well-Being of Adopted Children," *Pediatrics* 119, no. supplement 1 (February 1, 2007): S54–60, doi:10.1542/peds.2006-2089I; and Brent C. Miller, Xitao Fan, Matthew Christensen, Harold Grotevant, Manfred van Dulmen, "Comparisons of Adopted and Nonadopted Adolescents in a Large, Nationally Representative Sample," *Child Development* 71, no. 5 (2000): 1458–73.

9.   Anthony F. Bogaert, "Age at Puberty and Father Absence in a National Probability Sample," *Journal of Adolescence* 28, no. 4 (August 2005): 541–46, doi:10.1016/j.adolescence.2004.10.008; and Jacqueline M. Tither and Bruce J. Ellis, "Impact of Fathers on Daughters' Age at Menarche: A

Genetically and Environmentally Controlled Sibling Study," *Developmental Psychology* 44, no. 5 (2008): 1409–20, doi:10.1037/a0013065.

10.   There's a significant literature in evolutionary psychology about the parental investment of fathers in their own (but not others') children. David F. Bjorklund, Jennifer L. Yunger, and Anthony D. Pellegrini, "The Evolution of Parenting and Evolutionary Approaches to Childrearing," *Handbook of Parenting* 2 (2002): 3–30; Sandra L. Hofferth and Kermyt G. Anderson, "Are All Dads Equal? Biology versus Marriage as a Basis for Paternal Investment," *Journal of Marriage and Family* 65, no. 1 (2003): 213–32. D. Paul Sullins, "Emotional Problems among Children with Same-Sex Parents: Difference by Definition," *British Journal of Education, Society and Behavioural Science* 7, no. 2 (February 18, 2015): 113.

11.   David Popenoe, *Life without Father: Compelling New Evidence That Fatherhood and Marriage Are Indispensable for the Good of Children and Society* (New York: The Free Press, 1996), 197. See also W. Bradford Wilcox, "Reconcilable Differences: What Social Sciences Show about the Complementarity of the Sexes and Parenting," *Touchstone* 18, no. 9 (November 2005), 36.

12.   Fomby and Cherlin, "Family Instability and Child Well-Being"; and Paul R. Amato, "The Impact of Family Formation Change on the Cognitive, Social, and Emotional Well-Being of the Next Generation," *Future of Children* 15, no. 2 (2005): 75–96, doi:10.1353/foc.2005.0012.

13.   See, for example, Elizabeth Marquardt, *Between Two Worlds: The Inner Lives of Children of Divorce* (New York: Three Rivers Press, 2005).

14.   Brief of Amicus Curiae American Sociological Association in Support of Petitioners, *Obergefell v. Hodges*; Brief of Amicus Curiae American Psychological Association in Support of Petitioners, *Obergefell v. Hodges*.

15.   Timothy J. Biblarz and Judith Stacey, "How Does the Gender of Parents Matter?," *Journal of Marriage and Family* 72, no. 1 (February 2010): 3–22; and Alicia L. Crowl, Soyeon Ahn, Jean Baker, "A Meta-Analysis of Developmental Outcomes for Children of Same-Sex and Heterosexual Parents," *Journal of GLBT Family Sciences* 4, no. 3 (2008): 385–407.

16.   For children growing up with two moms turning out even a bit better, see Biblarz and Stacey, "How Does the Gender of Parents Matter?"

17. Loren Marks, "Same-Sex Parenting and Children's Outcomes: A Closer Examination of the American Psychological Association's Brief on Lesbian and Gay Parenting," *Social Science Research* 41, no. 4 (July 2012).

18. Brief of Amicus Curiae American College of Pediatricians, Family Watch International, Loren D. Marks, Mark D. Regnerus and Donald Paul Sullins in Support of Respondents, *Obergefell v. Hodges*, 3, available online at http://www.supremecourt.gov/ObergefellHodges/AmicusBriefs/14-556_ American_College_of_Pediatricians.pdf. Hereafter called "ACP Brief" in endnotes.

19. James B. Londregan, "Same-Sex Parenting: Unpacking the Social Science," Public Discourse (Witherspoon Institute), February 24, 2015, http://www. thepublicdiscourse.com/2015/02/14465/.

20. Lofton v. Sec'y of the Dep't of Children and Family Servs., 358 F.3d 804, 825 (11th Cir. 2004).

21. See Regnerus, "How Different Are the Adult Children of Parents Who Have Same-Sex Relationships? Findings from the New Family Structures Study," *Social Science Research* 41, no. 4 (2012): 752; Douglas W. Allen, "High School Graduation Rates among Children of Same-Sex Households," *Review of Economics of the Household* 11, no. 4 (December 2013): 635; Sullins, "Emotional Problems among Children with Same-Sex Parents," 99; and Sullins, "Child Attention-Deficit Hyperactivity Disorder (ADHD) in Same-Sex Parent Families in the United States: Prevalence and Comorbidities," *British Journal of Medicine and Medical Research* 6, no. 10 (January 2015): 987. See also the Children from Different Families website, which "presents the latest social science data about how children who were raised in different family types compare, as adults, on a variety of outcomes and measures": http://www.familystructurestudies.com/.

22. Regnerus, "New Research on Same-Sex Households Reveals Kids Do Best with Mom and Dad," Public Discourse (Witherspoon Institute), February 10, 2015, http://www.thepublicdiscourse.com/2015/02/14417/.

23. Londregan, "Same-Sex Parenting."

24. Regnerus, "A Married Mom and Dad Really Do Matter: New Evidence from Canada," Public Discourse (Witherspoon Institute), October 8, 2013, http://www.thepublicdiscourse.com/2013/10/10996/.

25. ACP Brief, 4.
26. Regnerus, "New Research on Same-Sex Households."
27. ACP Brief, 29–30.
28. Ibid., 35, 42.
29. Ibid., 43–44.
30. The media circus surrounding the Regnerus study is well known. See Peter Wood, "The Campaign to Discredit Regnerus and the Assault on Peer Review," *Academic Questions* 26, no. 2 (2013): 171, 176; Matthew J. Franck, "Mark Regnerus and the Storm over the New Family Structures Study," Public Discourse (Witherspoon Institute), October 30, 2012, http://www.thepublicdiscourse.com/2012/10/6784/; and Franck, "The Vindication of Mark Regnerus," Public Discourse (Witherspoon Institute), October 31, 2012, http://www.thepublicdiscourse.com/2012/10/6786/. On the outrageous and fallacious attacks on the Sullins studies, see the defense articulated in the ACP Brief (25–29):

In addition, both the ASA and APA briefs speciously allege that the peer review for Sullins's articles was substandard. *See, e.g.,* APA Brief at 27–28, n.48. Just the opposite is true. Although Sullins has published in top sociological journals, in this case, aware that his findings challenged the stated political positions of the APA and ASA and the associated ideology of harm denial, and aware of the unprecedented pressure placed on the journal editor and the peer review process after Regnerus published similar findings, he elected to pursue publication of his studies, based on a large public health survey, in international hard-science medical journals, where the standards of evidence are generally rigorous, but the imposition of groupthink orthodoxy is much less, than in American social science journals.

The ASA brief complains (at 11 n.10) that the review by the British Journal of Medicine and Medical Research was too short and critiques too brief to have been rigorous, taking only 16 days to first acceptance. ASA apparently is unaware that the peer review process is much shorter, and critiques much less verbose, in hard-science medical journals than in family sociology journals. For example, the Journal of the American Medical Association (JAMA), the top American medical journal, reports that median time to first editorial decision is just 3 days, though subsequent peer review takes up to an additional 36 days, on average. JAMA NETWORK | JAMA | WHY PUBLISH IN JAMA, http://jama.jamanetwork.com/public/ WhyPublish.aspx (last visited Mar 12, 2015). The British Medical Journal, arguably the most rigorous medical journal in the world, advises authors: "We aim to reach a first decision on all manuscripts within two or three weeks of submission." PEER REVIEW PROCESS, http://www.bmj.com/about-bmj/resourcesauthors/peer-review-process (last visited Mar 12, 2015). By these standards, the time to acceptance of Sullins's article was not short. The ASA's complaint that proper peer review would take a full year is simply uninformed.

Similarly, the APA brief complains that "none of the journals in which Sullins's papers were published are indexed in major, reputable social science databases." APA Brief at 27, n.48. This is true but beside the point. As medical journals, the journals Sullins published in are indexed in medical indexes, such as Index Medicus and the National Library of Medicine database, not social science databases. This complaint also ignores the fact that the practice of abstracting, in which an information service gathers and organizes a body of research articles for scholars to search, has overtaken the older practice of indexing; and the journals in which Sullins published are abstracted by all the major scholarly services, including Ebscohost and Proquest, and thus are available to any academic research search process.

The APA brief next alleges that "a cursory examination of the reviews...reveals that they raised few substantive concerns at all." APA Brief at 28, n.48. Perhaps the APA should have given more than a cursory examination, because a closer look reveals the following regarding Sullins's central study on child emotional problems: Although the normal standard is for an editor to send an article to two reviewers, the journal, recognizing the complexity and significance of the study, sent the article out to four reviewers and appointed two independent editors to approve publication. See Sullins, *Emotional*, at 120 ("The peer review history for this paper can be accessed here: http://www.sciencedomain.org/reviewhistory. php?iid=823&id=21&aid=8172").

Thus, the article was subjected to twice the ordinary peer review. Moreover, though the usual practice is for one round of review and response before an editorial decision, in this case there were two rounds of review and response before both editors independently rendered a decision. *See id*. (directing the reader to a website where all the peer review information is contained). One reviewer, not satisfied merely with making comments about the article, presented Sullins with an extensively revised and commented draft using "track changes." See Peer Review Report 4, File 2, *available at* http://www. sciencedomain.org/reviewhistory.php?iid=823&id=21&aid=8172. This level of scrutiny is very rare in American social science journals.

The APA also fails to note that the publication of an article's peer review history for anyone to examine ("open peer review"), which enables them to express an opinion on the peer review of Sullins's articles, is itself a sign of peer review quality. Only a minority of the most rigorous journals in the world openly publish reviewer critiques and author defenses. No APA journal practices this level of transparency.

In a recent independent assessment of peer review at over three hundred scientific publishers by *Science*, the world's premiere scientific journal, involving the submission of a plausible but flawed study, the publisher of Sullins's studies attained the highest ranking possible for peer review rigor, a distinction earned by only the top 7% of journals worldwide. *See* John Bohannon, *Who's Afraid of Peer Review?*, 342 SCIENCE 60, 60–65 (2013) at 64; *see also* Supporting Data and Documents. The journals that published Sullins's studies have, in effect, passed peer review of their peer review with the highest mark.

The true objection of the APA and ASA to Sullins's articles has nothing to do with their scientific rigor, but with his findings, which do not conform to the ideology of harm denial. Despite mounting evidence to the contrary, the APA and ASA will doubtless continue to deny that any study has found evidence of harm to children with same-sex parents.

31. Londregan, "Same-Sex Parenting."

32. Lawrence A. Kurdek, "What Do We Know about Gay and Lesbian Couples?," *Current Directions in Psychological Science* 14, no. 5 (October 1, 2005): 251–54, doi:10.1111/j.0963-7214.2005.00375.x; and Gunnar Andersson et al., "The Demographics of Same-Sex Marriages in Norway and Sweden," *Demography* 43, no. 1 (2006): 79–98.

33. Margaret F. Brinig and Douglas W. Allen, "'These Boots Are Made for Walking': Why Most Divorce Filers Are Women," *American Law and Economics Review* 2, no. 1 (2000): 141.

34. Colleen C. Hoff and Sean C. Beougher, "Sexual Agreements among Gay Male Couples," *Archives of Sexual Behavior* 39 (2010): 774–87; Kara Joyner, Wendy Manning, and Ryan Bogle, "The Stability and Qualities of Same-Sex and Different-Sex Couples in Young Adulthood," working paper, Center for Family and Demographic Research (Bowling Green State University), 2013, https://www.bgsu.edu/content/dam/BGSU/college-of-arts-and-sciences/center-for-family-and-demographic-research/documents/working-papers/2013/CFDR-Working-Papers-2013-02-The-Stability-and-Qualities-of-Same-Sex-and-Different-Sex-Couples-in-Young-Adulthood.pdf; Joseph Harry, "The 'Marital' Liaisons of Gay Men," *Family Coordinator* 28, no. 4 (1979): 622–29; and "How Many People Have Americans Had Sex With?," in *Relationships in America Survey* (Austin: The Austin Institute for the Study of Family and Culture, 2014), http://relationshipsinamerica.com/relationships-and-sex/how-many-people-have-americans-had-sex-with.

35. Jeffrey T. Parsons et al., "Alternatives to Monogamy among Gay Male Couples in a Community Survey: Implications for Mental Health and Sexual Risk," *Archives of Sexual Behavior* 42, no. 2 (February 2013): 303–12, doi:10.1007/s10508-011-9885-3; and Regnerus, "Yes, Marriage

Will Change—and Here's How," Public Discourse (Witherspoon Institute), June 7, 2013, http://www.thepublicdiscourse.com/2013/06/10325/.

36.   Mark Regnerus notes: "We will also learn much more about the relationship stability distinctions that are common in the data between gay and straight parents. Unpublished research exploring the stability rates of same-sex and opposite-sex couples using data from yet more population-based surveys finds that claims about the comparability of same-sex and heterosexual couple stability (again, after a series of controls) are actually limited to couples *without* children. For couples with children, the dissolution rate for same-sex couples is more than double that of heterosexual couples. What remains unknown yet is whether this difference is an artifact that will disappear with legal marriage rights. I doubt it, given that same-sex relationships are distinctive in other ways, too. But it's an empirical question." Regnerus, "New Research on Same-Sex Households."

37.   Brief of Amici Curiae 100 Scholars of Marriage in Support of Respondents, *Obergefell v. Hodges*, 2, available online at http://www.supremecourt. gov/ObergefellHodges/AmicusBriefs/14-556_100_Scholars_of_Marriage. pdf. Hereafter called "Scholars' Brief" in endnotes.

38.   Ibid., 3.

39.   Ibid., 20–21.

40.   Ibid., 30.

41.   Ibid., 31.

42.   Ibid., 16a.

43.   Ibid., 14a.

44.   Gene Schaerr, "Redefining Marriage Would Put Kids of Heterosexuals at Risk," Public Discourse (Witherspoon Institute), April 15, 2015, http:// www.thepublicdiscourse.com/2015/04/14822/.

45.   Brief of Amici Curiae, Scholars of Fertility and Marriage in Support of Respondents and Affirmance, *Obergefell v. Hodges*, 28–29, available online at http://www.supremecourt.gov/ObergefellHodges/AmicusBriefs/14-556_ Scholars_of_Fertility_and_Marriage.pdf. Hereafter called "Fertility Brief" in endnotes.

46.   Ibid., 38–39.

47.   Scholars' Brief, 20a.

48. Ibid., 3.

49. Corbin Leonard Miller and Joseph Price, "The Number of Children Being Raised by Gay or Lesbian Parents," September 2014, available online at http://papers.ssrn.com/sol3/papers.cfm?abstract_id=2497095.

50. Robert Oscar Lopez, "Growing Up with Two Moms: The Untold Children's View," Public Discourse (Witherspoon Institute), August 2012, http://www.thepublicdiscourse.com/2012/08/6065/.

51. Ibid.

52. Brief of Amici Curiae, Robert Oscar Lopez and B. N. Klein in Support of Respondents, *Obergefell v. Hodges*, 7, available online at http://www.supremecourt.gov/ObergefellHodges/AmicusBriefs/14-556_Robert_Oscar_Lopez_and_BN_Klein.pdf. Hereafter called "Lopez and Klein Brief" in endnotes.

53. Ibid., 4.

54. Katy Faust, "Dear Justice Kennedy: An Open Letter from the Child of a Loving Gay Parent," Public Discourse (Witherspoon Institute), February 2, 2015, http://www.thepublicdiscourse.com/2015/02/14370/.

55. Heather Barwick, "Dear Gay Community: Your Kids Are Hurting," Federalist, March 17, 2015, http://thefederalist.com/2015/03/17/dear-gay-community-your-kids-are-hurting/.

56. "Lopez and Klein Brief," 19.

57. Ibid.

58. Ibid.

59. Ibid., 19–20.

60. Ibid., 20.

61. Ibid., 16.

62. Ibid., 20.

63. Doug Mainwaring, "I'm Gay and I Oppose Same-Sex Marriage," Public Discourse (Witherspoon Institute), March 8, 2013, http://www.thepublicdiscourse.com/2013/03/9432/.

64. Lopez, "Growing Up with Two Moms."

65. The Dolce and Gabbana interview is quoted in Mainwaring, "Nature vs. Synthetics: What's at Stake in the Dolce and Gabbana Controversy,"

Public Discourse (Witherspoon Institute), March 19, 2015, http://www. thepublicdiscourse.com/2015/03/14663/.

66. Ibid.

67. Mainwaring, "Hearts, Parts, and Minds: The Truth Comes Out," Public Discourse (Witherspoon Institute), March 9, 2015, http://www. thepublicdiscourse.com/2015/03/14510/.

68. Lopez, "Growing Up with Two Moms."

69. Lopez and Klein Brief, 17–18.

Eight: Building a Movement

1. See the website Humanum, founded following the colloquium: http:// humanum.it/en/.

2. You can see the videos online, on the Humanum YouTube channel: https:// www.youtube.com/channel/UCwmvD_-GE_rT2gNIc8h6jtA.

3. "Full Text: Pope Francis's Opening Address to Humanum Conference," speech by Pope Francis, November 17, 2014, transcript posted at *Catholic Herald*, http://www.catholicherald.co.uk/news/2014/11/17/full-text-pope-franciss-opening-address-to-humanum-conference/.

4. Ines San Martin, "Pope Confirms US Trip, Defends Traditional Family," Crux, November 17, 2014, http://www.cruxnow.com/church/2014/11/17/ pope-confirms-us-trip-defends-traditional-family/.

5. Jacqueline C. Rivers, "Marriage and the Black Family," Public Discourse (Witherspoon Institute), November 25, 2014, http://www.thepublic discourse.com/2014/11/14108/.

6. Russell Moore, "Man, Woman, and the Mystery of Christ: An Evangelical Protestant Perspective," The Gospel Coalition, November 18, 2014, http://www.thegospelcoalition.org/article/man-woman-and-the-mystery-of-christ-an-evangelical-protestant-perspective.

7. Carey Lodge, "Rick Warren on Gay Marriage: 'The Church Must Not Cave In,'" Christian Today, November 19, 2014, http://www.christiantoday. com/article/rick.warren.on.gay.marriage.the.church.must.not.cave. in/43247.htm.

8. "In Full: Lord Sacks Speech That Brought Vatican Conference to Its Feet," speech by Lord Jonathan Sacks to Humanum colloquium, November 17, 2014, transcript posted at Catholic Voices Comment, http://cvcomment. org/2014/11/18/in-full-the-lord-sacks-speech-that-brought-the-vatican-conference-to-its-feet/.

9. The Courage website is here: www.couragerc.org.

Nine: The Long View

1. Liz Crampton, "Abbott Signs 'Pastor Protection Act' into Law," *Star-Telegram* (TX), June 11, 2015, http://www.star-telegram.com/news/politics-government/state-politics/article23812777.html.

2. "Attorney General Paxton Applauds Pastor Protection Bill; Calls for Protection for All People of Faith in Texas," press release, Attorney General of Texas, Ken Paxton, June 11, 2015, https://www.texasattorneygeneral. gov/oagnews/release.php?id=5104.

3. Ryan T. Anderson, "N.C. Legislature Overrides Veto, Allows Government Employees to Not Do Gay Marriages," Daily Signal, June 11, 2015, http:// dailysignal.com/2015/06/11/n-c-legislature-overrides-veto-allows-government-employees-to-not-do-gay-marriages/.

4. Ibid.

5. Sarah Torre and Anderson, "Michigan Governor Signs Bills Protecting Freedom of Adoption Agencies," Daily Signal, June 11, 2015, http:// dailysignal.com/2015/06/11/michigan-governor-signs-bills-protecting-freedom-of-adoption-agencies/.

6. Ibid.

7. Editorial Board, "Anti-Gay Adoption Bill Another Shameful Moment for Michigan," *Detroit Free Press*, June 12, 2015, http://www.freep.com/story/opinion/editorials/2015/06/11/faith-based-adoption/71074414/.

8. Kelsey Harkness, "US Immigration Exam Replaces 'Freedom of Religion' with 'Freedom of Worship,'" Daily Signal, April 30, 2015, http:// dailysignal.com/2015/04/30/republican-senator-questions-why-immigration-exam-calls-freedom-of-religion-freedom-of-worship/.

9.   Quoted in George Weigel, "John Paul II and the Crisis of Humanism," *First Things*, December 1999, http://www.firstthings.com/article/1999/12/john-paul-ii-and-the-crisis-of-humanism.

10. Ibid.

11. Ibid.

12. "Indiana RFRA: 'Memories Pizza' First Michiana Business to Publicly Deny Same Sex Service," YouTube video of ABC57 News coverage, uploaded by YouLatestNews, April 1, 2015, https://youtu.be/94exLI-Y0z8.

13. Alyssa Marino, "RFRA: Michiana Business Wouldn't Cater a Gay Wedding," ABC57 News, updated April 1, 2015, http://www.abc57.com/story/28681598/rfra-first-business-to-publicly-deny-same-sex-service.

14. Kirsten Powers, "Gay Marriage Debate's Sore Winners," *USA Today*, April 7, 2015, http://www.usatoday.com/story/opinion/2015/04/07/indiana-gay-protection-memories-pizza-eich-column/25373045/.

15. Norvell Rose, "Here's How the Embattled Owners of Memories Pizza Plan to Share Their Newfound Fortune," Western Journalism, April 8, 2015, http://www.westernjournalism.com/heres-embattled-owners-memories-pizza-plan-share-newfound-fortune/#gueRG9DPyzOMUJtE.99.

16. Jason Howerton, "Gay Woman Who Donated $20 to Christian-Owned Indiana Pizzeria Reveals Why She Took Bold Stand," TheBlaze, April 6, 2015, http://www.theblaze.com/stories/2015/04/06/gay-woman-who-donated-20-to-christian-owned-indiana-pizzeria-reveals-why-she-took-bold-stand/.

INDEX

ABOUT THE AUTHOR

Ryan T. Anderson, Ph.D., is the William E. Simon Senior Research Fellow in American Principles and Public Policy at the Heritage Foundation, and the founder and editor of Public Discourse: Ethics, Law, and the Common Good, the online journal of the Witherspoon Institute in Princeton, NJ.

A Phi Beta Kappa and magna cum laude graduate of Princeton University, he earned his Ph.D. in political philosophy from the University of Notre Dame.

His writings have appeared in the *New York Times*, the *Washington Post*, the *Wall Street Journal*, *USA Today*, the *Harvard Journal of Law and Public Policy*, *First Things*, the *Weekly Standard*, *National Review*, the *New Atlantis*, and the *Claremont Review of Books*.

Anderson has appeared on ABC, CNN, CNBC, MSNBC, and the Fox News Channel. In addition to a memorable 2013 debate about marriage on CNN's *Piers Morgan Live*, his news interviews include appearances on ABC's *This Week* with George Stephanopoulos, CNN's *New Day* with Chris Cuomo, MSNBC's *The Ed Show* with Ed Schultz, and Fox News' *Hannity*.

Follow Ryan on Twitter @RyanTAnd and on Facebook at www. facebook.com/RyanTAndersonPhD.